ROMANCE ON THE HIGH SEAS

The Love Boats is the book that was single-handedly responsible for the boom in the cruise industry. Here in a new, expanded edition, Former cruise director, Jeraldine Saunders tells you again the true tales of love and hate, sex and silliness, greed and generosity, beauties and beasts, and Bali Hai and Shangri-La. Here is the real-life story of the creator of *The Love Boats* television series, whose name is synonymous with bringing romance to the high seas.

Come on along—enjoy the next wave...

About the Author

Jeraldine Saunders is a powerful, multi-faceted, bestselling author whose years of astrological practice, books, and lectures have made her a worldwide success. She is in the *World Who's Who of Women*. She has appeared on *Good Morning America, Merv Griffin*, and more than 350 other television and radio talk shows in the U.S., Canada, Europe, and the lands of the Pacific.

To earn a living while studying astrology, Saunders modeled for the finest couturiers. After she left the world of high fashion, astrology led her to a career in the cruise ship industry, where she lectured on Astrology, Motivation, and the Four Seasons Color Concept. She became the first female Cruise Director, and held this position for ten years. During this time she wrote the first edition of *The Love Boats*, and then created *The Love Boats* television series, now in syndication in over 115 countries.

To Write to the Author

If you wish to contact the author or would like more information about this book, please write to the author in care of Llewellyn Worldwide, and we will forward your request. Both the author and publisher appreciate hearing from you and learning of your enjoyment of this book and how it has helped you. Llewellyn Worldwide cannot guarantee that every letter written to the author can be answered, but all will be forwarded. Please write to:

Llewellyn Worldwide
P.O. Box 64383, Dept. K607–6
St. Paul, MN 55164-0383, U.S.A.

Please include a self-addressed, stamped envelope for reply, or $1.00 to cover costs. If outside the U.S.A., enclose international postal reply coupon.

THE REAL LIFE STORY OF THE CREATOR OF "THE LOVE BOAT"

Love Boats

ABOVE AND BELOW DECKS

WITH

Jeraldine Saunders

1998
Llewellyn Publications
St. Paul, Minnesota 55464–0383
U.S.A.

SECOND EDITION, Revised and Expanded
Formerly titled: *The Love Boats,* published by Pinnacle Books, 1974
Second Printing, 1998

Cover design by Anne Marie Garrison
Cover photo of ship by Allan Kayne/Index Stock
Editing by Connie Hill
Interior design by Christine Snow

Library of Congress Cataloging-in-Publication Data
Saunders, Jeraldine–
    Love boats : above and below decks with Jeraldine Saunders / by Jeraldine Saunders
        p.   cm. --
        Includes index.
        ISBN 1–56718–607–6 (trade paper)
        1. Ocean travel—Anecdotes.   I. Title.
0550.S273   1998
910.4'5—dc21   98-35514
                                                                    CIP

Llewellyn Publications
A Division of Llewellyn Worldwide, Ltd.
St. Paul, Minnesota 55164-0383, U.S.A.

Printed in the U.S.A.

*Life is a banquet—but most landlubbers
are starving to death!*

Other Books by Jeraldine Saunders

The Love Boats (Pinnacle Books)

Cruise Diary (Houghton-Mifflin)

Complete Guide to a Successful Cruise (Contemporary Books)

Frisco Lady (Pinnacle Books)

Frisco Fortune (Pinnacle Books)

Legacy of Love (Medallion Books)

Spanish Serenade (Harper & Row)

Hypoglycemia: The Disease Your Doctor Won't Treat (Kensington)

Journey with Jeraldine (Travel Column)

Love Signs (Revised and expanded, formerly titled *Signs of Love,*
Llewellyn Publications)

Acknowledgments

Thanks to Carl and Sandra Weschcke for their faith in publishing this book, and a big thank you to Senior Editor Connie Hill and all the staff at Llewellyn.

Table of Contents

# FOREWORD

IF, AS MY AUNT LADY BIRD JOHNSON ALWAYS SAYS, "IT'S THE journey, not the destination that matters," then Jeraldine Saunders has had the ride of fifteen lives.

I've known Jeraldine since 1961. Her daughter Gail was my roommate and best friend at George Washington University. Back then Jeraldine was modeling her daughter's way through college. Then, during the 1964 World's Fair in New York, she managed the Hollywood Pavilion and I got to see a lot more of her. One of the things I remember most is that she was more fun than a barrel of monkeys.

The point is that I've known Jeraldine for quite a long time, through many career incarnations, and never met anyone quite like her. She is the epitome of the can-do person; if a mountain is in her way, she'll go around it, above it, through it, underneath it. Like the ancient warrior Hannibal, who scaled the Alps with elephants, if she cannot find a way, she'll make a way.

She's been called the "female Rocky." She could also be characterized as the Energizer Bunny, because it is, after all, her energy and zest for life that set her apart.

She has been a mother, a wife, a model, an actress, a cruise director, a lecturer, a nutritionist, an astrologer, a writer (who can't spell), and through it all she's kept her sense of humor intact. While never taking herself too seriously, she's taken each and every project very seriously.

When her daughter Gail died, she said that if she could survive that she could survive anything. Survive she has, and moreover, she has prevailed. On a personal level, I can't help but speculate what a mother-daughter team they would have made if Gail had lived.

F. Scott Fitzgerald said there are no second acts in American life. With Jeraldine there have been not only second, but third, fourth and fifth acts. Who would have believed that my college roommate's mother would become the world's first female cruise director, a bestselling author, creator of one of the longest-running TV shows in history, and a lecturer of renown? I vividly recall the guffaws that met Jeraldine's announcement that she was going to write about her adventures at sea as a cruise director (remember I said she couldn't spell?). The rest is Hollywood history.

To this day Jeraldine's closest advisors are her husband Arthur and her brother Jack (each a prince among men). And I'm still around, pleased as punch that Jeraldine has kept up our friendship. Both mother and daughter have enriched my life.

I recently saw Jeraldine. She was updating this book, reading palms and autographing copies of her book at a celebrity fair, and working on a new Love Boat movie. It is mind-boggling to contemplate that the journeys of Jeraldine continue. Read on and fasten your seatbelts. It will be a marvelous ride!

— Susan Grey Taylor
January 4, 1998

NTRODUCTION

SHE HAS RED HAIR...HER PRINCIPLES ARE FIERY...YET SHE IS A gentle blend of sensuality and intellectuality. Some people claim she knows her own mind. She knows it enough to ignore the naysayers and skeptics who say they know everything. They know the price but the value of nothing.

Single-handedly she revived the cruise industry with her first book *The Love Boats*, a term that became a part of the language around the world.

She is a fountain of knowledge, a true renaissance person. Her interests range from "A" in astrology to "Z" in Zowie.

With all of this, she remains full of tenderness when little people need help and although she is affluent now, she has never forgotten those days when a little girl asked how her dog Jiggs spelled his name.

In this volume, a revised and expanded edition of the original book, Jeraldine Saunders lets us in on not only what's happening on the top decks but on the decks below which are filled with a variety of real life characters, young Lotharios to smooth-talking salesmen, to would-be Valentinos, and the lady passengers, young and old, who come to her to have their palms read. Though they possess an intelligent curiosity, they are vulnerable, just like all of us, when it comes to LOVE. This is almost always the quest, as it has been since the beginning of time, but especially so on *The Love Boats.*

—Sydney Omarr
Santa Monica, CA

When the Los Angeles Times Syndicate honored Sydney Omarr on the 25th anniversary of his astrology column, Jeraldine was there to congratulate him. Front: actress Julie Newmar, Sydney Omarr, Jeraldine Saunders, and actress Susan Strasberg. Back: Syndicate executives Lou Schwartz and Willard Colston.

$\mathcal{U}$P ANCHOR— HERE WE GO!

chapter one

FATE HAS CAST ME UPON THE SEAS OF THE WORLD AND upon the sea of life. I have actually ridden the waves and determined the destinies of cruise ship passengers for more than a decade.

My term, "Love Boat," is now known all over the world because my creation, *The Love Boat* television series, is now being seen in 115 countries where it has become a happy television habit. With new episodes and reruns, *The Love Boat* will probably be showing somewhere every minute for the rest of my life, and I intend that to be for a good, long time.

The witty *Los Angeles Times* writer Paul Dean wrote, "Jeraldine Saunders now has an annuity in perpetuity." He's referring to the royalties from the television series but then he goes on to say, "Saunders is a woman of Beverly Hills presence, Fifth Avenue style, and a Main Street sense of what titillates." Well, I blush. But I have to tell you, that titillates me.

And I had an even greater thrill recently when that legendary entrepreneur, Peter Uberroth, presented me with an award on behalf of the cruise industry. He called me the "patron saint" of cruising, and said I had increased business 3,000%! Well, I blush again, but there's a story behind that.

When I first started working on shipboard the cruise industry was almost dead and about to be buried at sea. Famous old ocean liners and cruise ships were being chopped up for scrap.

But *The Love Boat* changed all that. The life on board that people viewed on TV was a life they wanted to live, so they did! Now, old ships come out of mothballs, are refurbished, sometimes cut in half and lengthened, and become floating palaces rivaled only by the incredible new super-liners which are glamorous, glittering, moveable cities.

When a cruise ship sails out beyond twelve miles from shore, the laws of the land no longer apply. Maritime law takes over...but something else takes over the passengers. A sense of adventure? I think it's even more than that. People refer to the ship as being "far out" but they don't realize that they become "far out" too! When those giant turbines and propellers start to move through the ocean the rhythm of life revs up as well. And that's my subject.

I have a vivid imagination but I don't have to use it in relating this true story—except for coming up with fictitious names to preserve the crew and passengers' privacy. When I was a cruise director I led a heartbreaking and hilarious life myself, and I observed the best and worst of human nature in the microcosm of those ships. You name it, I've seen it: love and hate, sex and silliness, greed and generosity, beauties and beasts, and Bali Hai and Shangri-La and a lot of flotsam and jetsam along the way. Now I'm writing about it, and what I'm writing about is just the stuff of life.

Jiggs and Us

To step back in time for just a moment.

When I was a little girl we had a dog name Jiggs. One time I asked my mother, "How does Jiggs spell his name?" and everyone laughed so I never had the nerve to ask again. He was a red, short-haired terrier and who knows what else. He guarded us kids. My father always drove a new Cadillac and my mother would drive the model T Ford with us kids in it. Jiggs didn't give a hoot about the Cadillac but no one could come near the Ford, even if it was empty. He would growl if anyone pretended to slap it. You could kick, slap, or do anything to the Caddy—he didn't care. He was our protector and no one had better come near the kids' chariot.

After my dear father had been sick for over a year the doctors suggested a certain hospital that was far from our home. He had been there for several months, and Mother and we kids missed him so very much.

Then one night Jiggs did something he had never done before. It was so very strange....

The only way I can describe it was that he *howled.* We had never heard him howl before or utter such a screeching sound. He kept it up most of the night. It was so ecrie! We didn't know what to make of it. If I tried I could not imitate it. We tried to calm him but he just raised his nose straight up to the sky and shrieked his heart out. To this very day I can remember this strange cry.

The next morning we received a telegram that was a terrible shock. My dear father had died during the night. We have always wondered how Jiggs knew what happened before we did. There is so much we don't understand!

Albert Einstein said, "The most beautiful things we can experience are the mysterious."

After my father's death Mother kept reminding us, "Busy hands are happy hands." Mother was raised in a large, comfortable home in Pennsylvania. She came from a rather cloistered, rarefied world of graciousness. She and her family kept busy endlessly, it seemed, washing their sixty-four windows every week. The girls learned to sew their own clothes and do needlework. Then there was the baking and cooking and all the things that keep a well-organized home spotless and lovely. Her brothers fixed things and did the outside work on the acreage around the house. In their spare time, all the brothers and sisters took music lessons and helped out at church functions. They were gentle people and she would tell us of her serene childhood.

I admire the way Mother adapted to the situation and kept us together after becoming a widow.

My father's illness and death was during this country's worst depression. There wasn't any such thing as Social Security in those days. You either worked or starved. I remember an evening when we all sat around our kitchen table for our bedtime snack.

Mother had placed glasses of milk and a bowl of graham crackers in the center of the table. My baby brother reached out and filled his hungry little hands with about half of the crackers. When the precious tyke saw the rest of us looking at him, quickly he calculated that he was taking more than his share. Now what to do—in response to our stares he said, "This is for all of us," and then passed some of his much-desired handful around to each of us.

Sometimes, after dinner, we kids would say, in our childlike way of joking, "Mother, do you know what this dinner tastes like?"

Obligingly, she would say, "No, dears, what does it taste like?"

In unison, we would all say, "It tastes like more." She would always laugh with us, but how it must have hurt her because she knew there wasn't "any more."

She had such dignity. We never were made to feel poor. It was just referred to as a temporary situation, that certainly we would survive and find a way out.

Mother didn't ever look for a job outside of the home, not that there was one, anyway. Being there for her children was more important than working to buy things we probably didn't need in the first place; we did need some income, that was a certainty, but from where?

Prevail. That's the word. It means to be victorious, to master a problem, to triumph over it, and that's what our mother taught us. I had two brothers and two sisters and Mother very firmly convinced us that "where there's a will, there's a way." Oh, I know it's a cliche now, but back in those days we had to find the will and then we had to find the way because my father passed on at the tender age of forty-two, leaving my mother with five children and no skills except *petit point* and no income except a small insurance policy. But she knew how to prevail. She would say, "The harder we work the luckier we will be."

She devised a unique housing program that managed to feed us, clothe us, shelter us, and even educate us. Realtors now call this "house-switching," but I think my mother was one of the pioneers. She would make a small down payment on a shabby but promising piece of property, and all six of us would pitch in to paint the inside and outside, peel off old wallpaper, put putty around windows, retile, reroof, replumb, and generally refurbish it, do a little landscaping, put a fence around it, and put it up for sale, and net a profit (there was no capital gains tax in those days). Then we would repeat the whole routine. Sometimes we moved twice a year, but always in Glendale, California, which was and still is my home.

Glendale is between Hollywood and Pasadena. Geographically we may be close to Hollywood, but in lifestyle we are a vast distance away. Glendalians shun glitz and glitter. Most are conservative—no one tries to impress others with flashy cars or other extravagances. Most people have an understated approach to living. There is a lot of wealth but you would never be aware of it. A lot of my school chums still live here; we do charity work for the Glendale Adventist Medical Center, one of the biggest and most advanced hospitals in the world, and we are active in the Glendale Symphony Orchestra Association. Our city is growing, but it is still full of good old-fashioned values. We are surrounded by beautiful mountains and we have a wonderful city ordinance that doesn't allow anyone to destroy them. My family were the nomads of Glendale—I really think the city should give my mother some kind of beautification award because we certainly beautified a lot of houses here. We survived and thrived, and laughed a lot; we had everything but money.

However, there was a downside; it wasn't very romantic. Boys who wanted to date my sisters or me were warned by their friends that they'd end up as van and storage workers, helping us to move in or move out of a house. It is not a joke when I say that my teenage years were a moving experience. And we prevailed!

I am a Virgo, Sagittarius rising, with Moon in Gemini. I wonder if the stars may have had something to do with my being the only woman cruise director on those "anything goes" ships, the Love Boats. Did those twinkling stars have something to do with my being plucked from a sedate life in Glendale and introducing me to an adventurous life of love, laughter, and reward?. Did those revolving planets give me the nerve, with no experience, to start a modeling career with a world-famous couturier?

You see, I've had some experience with stars. I recall standing on the deck by the railing, late at night, all alone, looking at an ink-black sea all around and listening to the splashing, surging sound of the waves. That's when I would stare up at a billion stars and thank the Universal Intelligence for my life at sea, letting me see and feel these dramatic oceans and visit these colorful ports, listen to and dance to beautiful music, and meet and have fun with so many remarkable people. I don't pretend to have all the answers.

What I do know is that I am here, that I am what I am, and that I am going to tell you my story. To do that, however, I will need to reveal myself, my hopes and my hang-ups, my victories and my defeats. I have created an abundant and happy life. I had no "pull" or other support and you readers will come away with hope, feeling that you too can make it "a real "Love Boat" ending that reveals life's limitless opportunities for everyone. Amen.

Speaking of hang-ups, maybe this is the time to reveal one of mine: I don't spell very well. Growing up, I was ashamed of this problem because people think that if you can't spell you're just plain dumb. But I wasn't dumb—I just couldn't get all those letters to fit into the puzzle of a word. If you share this problem with me, and a lot of people do, you know that it's a real challenge and for me it was an opportunity to prevail. Today I can spell "dyslexia," the fancy new word for this condition, and today we know that it's just a genetic quirk like nearsightedness or flat feet (neither of which I have).

Early on here I should also reveal that I have learned to conquer my fears. I had to find a fair bit of courage to live through all the adventures you'll read here. No matter what happened I had to constantly remind myself that I volunteered for this—I asked for it.

Just out of school—I sure wish I could spell and type.

But I had my moments. There was the icy sting of fear when I tried to retrieve the keys from a warm corpse as the stunned and silent widow looked on. And there was that time I walked into a cabin to find a strange nest of glistening black hair in the middle of the floor. This time I was stunned to remember the beautiful Asian girl whose hair was her crowning glory, and a chilling instinct told me I would never see her again...alive.

These were rare instances, of course; much more often my job gave me the opportunity to help others change their attitudes. I feel selecting a proper attitude is the key to happiness. By helping passengers to choose a joyful attitude, it seems to bring them a new lease on life and certainly adds to the meaning of mine.

On Christmas cruises a number of the passengers are family rejects, the troublemakers who have been sent on the voyage so they wouldn't disrupt the holiday around hearth and home. Most of the time I found these folks to be lost souls who really responded to the gaiety and opulence on board. They may have had a better time than those who stayed home.

Is that the sign of Virgo again? Virgos like to mother people and be helpful, but I think any good cruise director helps the voyagers forget their troubles and find joy. I like to think there's a big bin right beside the gangway where you walk up onto the ship from the pier. The bin should have a big sign saying "STORE ALL INHIBITIONS HERE." Maybe in smaller print it should say "These inhibitions can be reattached upon disembarking."

So who are all these people who are now my flock, my congregation, my responsibility?

Well, they are probably not who you think they are. They do not come on board solely in twos like the animals on Noah's ark. They do not look like the pictures you've seen. They are not all wealthy elderly couples in side-by-side deck chairs, reading Agatha Christie mysteries.

They are usually successful because it does take money to take a cruise. There is a difference though between luxury cruises and mass market cruises. The latter really doesn't take much money. The passengers are of all ages, of all nationalities, and from amazingly different lifestyles, which makes them interesting to be with, and they are usually endlessly curious about everything around them because life on shipboard is totally different. It's a whole new world!

Most of all, cruise passengers are adventurous. They have to be. They have entrusted their lives to a huge steel hull with a monster engine that's going to slice through a bottomless ocean for a week or two. That takes a certain amount of courage, and people with courage are usually fun to be with.

Wait a minute! Here comes one of the passengers now. An attractive, well-dressed lady. Good luggage. Good intentions. She has promised to write a detailed letter home each day. She will forget that promise at the top of the gangway. She gives a big smile to the second officer, the one with reddish hair, the one who looks over the passengers as they board. She decides to let her hair down on this trip. He notes that she is traveling alone.

See the large, buxom woman and the heavy, gray-haired man behind her? She'll let him do the boarding formalities while she gets down to the stateroom to take off that oppressive bra and get into something comfortable. He smiles at the welcoming orchestra. You couldn't get him on a dance floor at gunpoint back home, but here he's beginning to tap his foot.

Here comes a group of university students—won't they have fun in the disco? The young people gravitate to one another immediately and they have a great time together.

Virgos are the great "note-takers" of this world and I take notes. Don't laugh. I think it's one of the reasons I got this glamorous job, and when I arrived back home and got all my notes out, they made this book!

Now, there's a steady stream of passengers boarding, some smiling and expectant, some serious and worried. I've always been fascinated by those two masks that depict the theater: one, the big grin of laughter, the other, the downward mouth of despair—Comedy and Tragedy.

We're going to see it come to life here because traveling at sea really is theatrical.

It's going to be earthy and funny, and there will be some smiles and some tears. It might even be angelic. Or lurid. Or both at the same time! One thing is certain: twelve miles out, anything goes, and it's up to the cruise director to make sure it does "go."

Remember our Inhibition Bin next to the gangway? Look at it now! It's overflowing! And that booming blast of the horn is going to make everyone jump. So get ready, ma'am, get ready, mister. Pull up anchor! Here we go!

Chapter Two

GENESIS

THE PAST SIX MONTHS SEEMED LIKE ETERNITY. WE HAD been sailing from Tahiti to Fiji to Tonga and back to Tahiti on eleven-day cruises, with never an overnight stop. Even the wonderful paradise of the South Pacific began to frazzle and come apart at the seams because I didn't have time to get enough sleep and never had a single day or even a night off from my cruise director job. A pretty passenger with an eagerness to become a cruise director asked me, as we were leaving the pool games, "Jeraldine, what do you do with your weekends?" Flabbergasted, I replied, "Weekends? I don't have weekends or any days off. I work eleven months a year. In fact, I never even have a night off. I work from eight to eighteen hours every day." At that pace, maintaining a happy, cheerful manner for the ever-new groups of excited, gleeful, expectant passengers was not easy. The facade of joy, adventure, and pleasant surprises must be kept up, however, no matter what the work load. The show must go on! It was easier to bear because I knew instinctively that change is the only constant in life and that each passing day meant that the cruise season would shift eventually from the beautiful South Pacific to lovely, beauteous Alaska. That meant when we reached Los Angeles I had something really big planned—Are you ready for this?— THREE DAYS OFF! Then I was to fly to Victoria, Canada for the beginning of the Alaska Cruise Season.

After six months in the South Seas, the long voyage to Los Angeles was a terrible hassle. Being the cruise director on this voyage back to the United States was doubly hectic. I was not only the entertainer, I was in complete charge to make sure that the passengers continued to have interesting and full activities both day and night, but I had to find the time, also, to plan and prepare daily programs for the Alaska cruise season. I had to pack my South Seas gowns, costumes, and shore-going clothes and then plan my wardrobe and costumes for the new cruise season, which commenced (immediately) when we off-loaded the current on-board passengers. These items had to be selected, purchased, and packed during my coveted three days at home. My dwindling inventory of supplies for passenger activities, shipboard parties, arts and crafts, and varying festivities had to be planned for and replenished for the coming season.

The last night out, after entertaining until 1:00 A.M., I gathered my costumes, props, and other cruise-director equipment and rushed to my cabin. Tomorrow we would arrive in Los Angeles and tonight was my last chance to complete packing. With arms loaded, I made my way through empty, deserted, quiet but creaky, swaying alleyways and in almost a complete state of exhaustion, I entered my cabin and just dropped everything on my extra bunk. Wearily, I turned to secure the latch on my cabin door—staring at me like blank eyes were the holes in the door frame where I'd had "Chippy," our ship's carpenter, install an extra safety chain lock for me when I first boarded the ship.

Realizing the chain lock was gone, I automatically froze, dreading, but certain that someone must be in my cabin! If you saw *Psycho*, that shower scene was far less terrifying than the sight that horrified me when I turned and saw a man hiding in my shower with a screwdriver in one uplifted hand and my safety lock dangling from the fingers of the other. I screamed but no one could hear me because my isolated cabin was aft by the noisy, rotating propeller shafts.

The ensuing struggle was as if I had six octopi attacking me at once. I guess no woman except me had ever said "no" to this handsome chief officer. He had managed to seduce every good-looking woman he desired that came on board. This being our last night of the cruise, I guess his absurd ego would not permit him to accept another rejection from me. Here he was, trying one more time, but he was beyond mere seduction. I frequently had Tom, our hair stylist, guard my door because this officer was always lurking around the corner, waiting for an opportunity to try to get into my cabin. I managed to fight myself free and fled down the alleyway, praying that the night steward would be at his station to help me.

To make a terrifying story short, I arrived safely in the Port of Los Angeles the next day. As usual, it was a hectic departure. I had packed all of my year's supply of clothes, costumes, and cruise director paraphernalia. At the very last minute, the captain forbade me to leave. I had been given permission by the head office on land to disembark when we reached Los Angeles and to have three days off, but the captain, at the thought of having my assistant entertain and juggle the passengers, their problems, and their complaints, whims, and fancies, reversed himself and ordered me to remain on board until the ship reached Vancouver.

There we would immediately launch into our summer season of Alaskan cruises. That meant not one day or night off for another whole season. It would be a whole year of exhausting work without a day off. The captain pounded the table. "Dammit, Jeraldine, you don't like to take orders, but you are going to obey my orders! Even captains take orders—from God!"

Nevertheless, I told him that I had to take the time off. He fumed! I was sorry that he might have to work with the passengers.

On the dock, surrounded by all my gear, waiting for the customs inspection, I telephoned my agent. I was determined to devote every minute of these precious three free days to finding a way off what seemed to me a floating "Devil's Island" of a ship, and hoping to get assigned to a better one.

My agent, Dorris Halsey, had sent my *Love Boat* manuscript to Pinnacle Books, a New York publisher. When she answered my dockside telephone call, she informed me that the publisher, David Zentner, and executive editor, Andrew Ettinger, were in town for a book convention. She had told them that my ship was due in this evening, and they had asked that I call them as soon as I arrived. She gave me the information necessary to reach them. I thought, I can't call them now from the dock because of all the hurly burly— happily shouting passengers, scurrying porters, impatient long-shoremen, horns, whistles, screaming relatives outside the restricted customs area with their "Here we are! Here we are!" to the milling passengers trying to secure their luggage, provision trucks and buses arriving, and taxis fighting for space. If I do call, they won't hear me, I won't hear them. All the confusion and tension just added to my already weary state. My primary motivation was to get my gear through customs, find a cab, crawl into my little apartment, hide from the world, catch up on my much-needed sleep and try to gather in my wilting aura. But—being a Type AA personality—I finally decided to call the publisher, anyway.

"Hello, this is Jeraldine Saunders, the cruise director. My agent, Dorris Halsey, told you about me."

"Well, hi there," the deep-throated voice of Andrew Ettinger greeted me from the other end of the wire.

I said, "Pardon the noise. My ship just arrived and I'm calling you from the dock. It's been a rather hectic, long season."

When he asked if I could meet them for dinner that evening, I replied, "I can't because I have to gather all my gear and go all the way to Glendale. I'm about to collapse from six months of working day and night without one day off."

"Oh," he said, "that's OK, we can see you tomorrow."

I answered, "Great, where shall I meet you?"

He thought a moment. "Well, first give us a call tomorrow to make sure that we are still here. We may have to leave for New York, but we will be back in a month or two."

I could hear my mother saying, "Opportunity knocks only once."

Lordy, I thought, in a month or two I'll be dodging icebergs and that demented first officer in Alaska. The adrenaline surged and quickly I replied, "Oh, I'll meet you tonight then. What time and where?"

I dragged my body into a cab and headed for Glendale. I soon realized the limping vehicle was even wearier than I. I prayed that it wouldn't breath its last sigh on the freeway. Somehow, we made it. The cabbie dumped my gear on my living room floor and that's where I left it.

Frantically, I searched for what I hoped would be just the right outfit that would package me as I thought an author should dress. Rush, rush, rush. Is there no time to have the luxury to waste a moment? I hope the battery is up and my car will start. The car started and on the way to the Beverly Wilshire's elegant dining room, I prayed and imagined the meeting a success. Well, it certainly was! I sold my manuscript! The manuscript that I sold that night opened another chapter in my life, otherwise I probably would still be slaving away at sea.

After my autobiography, *The Love Boat,* was published, I felt that it would be perfect material for a TV Movie of the Week, and perhaps even a television series. I inquired and found that to protect this concept all I had to do was to write a "treatment" of how I felt the movie or series should be done and register it with the Writers Guild of America. I could do this even if I was not a WGA member. I took my precious treatment in for registration when I had a few hours off in port on April 5, 1974. That accomplished, I had scads of copies reproduced and sent them to every studio and producer in Hollywood. I really didn't have much time to do this because I was still slaving away on the cruise ships. By now, I had graduated to a lovely new ship, the *Royal Viking Star*. I boarded her on her maiden voyage. The planet of good fortune, Jupiter, was direct.

I had sent my manuscript of *The Love Boats* to Jerry Hulse, the travel editor of the *Los Angeles Times* to read. He wrote, "*The Love Boats* is more fun than a trip around the world on a sea of sun, sex, and booze." Well, we liked that nifty recommendation so much we decided to put it on the cover of the book.

My agent, Dorris Halsey, called me shore-to-ship and, breathlessly excited, informed me that one of Hollywood's top producers, Douglas S. Cramer, "wants to make *The Love Boats* into a Movie of the Week!" In all my entire life, I can't remember having been so deliriously excited. Think of it! Finally I can get off this maritime merry-go-round!

Cruising is never dull and most of it is really great, especially if you are a passenger. But when you have dessert three times a day, you crave the entree. To live on land, to be able to look out of a window and see a tree, make a peanut butter sandwich, read a daily newspaper less than a month old—simple, ordinary things become luxuries.

Now, with the passing of time and fantastic success in all areas of my life, I look forward eagerly to my occasional assignments as a cruise ship celebrity lecturer where I can impart knowledge on my favorite subjects. How pleasantly different the ships and ports look when I arrive fully rested. No wonder passengers return over and over again to these fabulous playpens at sea.

I'm telling my story for a purpose. Your life can become like a Love Boat cruise—for success, love, and prosperity need not be a stranger to you—life's limitless opportunities are waiting to come into your life, too.

My whole life now is like a beautiful Love Boat cruise, but it wasn't always like this, was it, Gail?

chapter three

How to Start at the Top

My daughter's name was Gail and at this point in my story she was a precious seven-year-old. I was what they call a "single mother." Actually, that term hadn't been invented yet but I was certainly single (divorced) and I was a conscientious, twenty-seven-year-old mother who knew how to cook and keep a clean house. I wasn't prepared to earn a living. Since I had always had trouble with spelling I hadn't bothered to learn how to type, so office work was out of the question.

Reading a newspaper, one morning, I saw photographs of some models. I thought, "Well, gee, I am tall, maybe if I could learn to put my makeup on correctly, I could be a model. You probably don't have to know how to do anything." Wrong!

I had never seen a fashion show but one was advertised for the coming week. A modeling job would be perfect, I thought, because I could pick and choose my hours so that I could be at home each day when my daughter, Gail, returned from school. I looked in *Vogue* and *Harper's Bazaar* and compared the models to the reflection in my three-way mirror. I was and remain five feet seven inches tall, 120 pounds, with green eyes and reddish hair. I seemed to match pretty well except for a couple of things. My neck is not long and swan-like and high fashion models are small-busted, but I'm not. I have a narrow rib cage, so by using a smaller cupped bra, I was able to effect a redistribution of my figure that was uncomfortable but in no way damaging. I called the designer's office and the following day went downtown for an interview. As I entered the couturier's salon, I saw all these lovely girls in the waiting room with their photo portfolios and hat boxes. In those days a model's hat box was a big round leather case with a carrying handle. I was to learn that it was for carrying extra pairs of shoes, gloves, costume jewelry, and all kinds of bras and merry widows. I didn't realize one doesn't do one's very first show with Howard Greer, the famous top couturier; one is supposed to start at the bottom.

Howard Greer's outfits and dresses were utterly beautiful! He was doing the interviews personally. When I was called into his office, he met me with his distinguished manner and looked at me with his soft brown eyes. Quickly I said, "I have just returned from modeling in New York and my luggage hasn't arrived yet, that's why I don't have my things with me." I didn't know what they called those boxes the models were carrying.

I had never seen a hat box or portfolio before, much less a fashion show. I had never been in New York. The only time I had been out of California was a visit to Tijuana. Mr. Greer said, "Well, please go in and try on one of the samples." I didn't know what a sample was, but he pointed to a door and I went into that room. There I found a rack of dresses and guessed that I was to wear one. They had been cut on the famous model, Jerry Cameron. Thank goodness, the dress fit perfectly. I walked out to let him see and luckily he didn't ask me to model it. After all, I was supposed to be a big-time model from New York. He looked approvingly and said, "Are you booked for May 18?" I told him I was free that day. What I didn't tell him was that all my days were free. He said, "Good, I want you to do the Beverly Hills Hadassah Chapter Show at the Coconut Grove."

I arrived there with knees trembling. As I opened the door I heard music, then I saw the twenty-piece orchestra. The huge, beautifully decorated room was filled with elegantly dressed women. My heart jumped right into my mouth as I found my way backstage to the models' room. Eight slinky models were seated in front of their mirrors applying their theatrical makeup. As I entered, they looked at me with curiosity because they had probably done hundreds of shows together and had never seen me. I took a seat at a mirror and pretended to put on my makeup but actually I was sneaking glances at them so I could learn how they were doing it.

Suddenly the orchestra burst out with a loud drum roll and the overture, our cue. We were on! The butterflies in my stomach were having a fist fight! It was too late to turn back now, I was committed!

Howard Greer made his entrance, stepping up to the microphone to deliver his commentary regarding his fashions. There was a folding screen between the dance floor and the models. We all lined up as we waited our turn on the dance floor under the critical gaze of the audience. I took the opportunity to peep between the cracks in the screen so that I could see what I was to do when I got out on the floor. One move the models made really worried me. Mr. Greer was showing a new group of designs that were fashioned to perform a dual role—what appeared to be a pretty suit worn during the day could be converted into a lovely lace-top cocktail dinner dress simply by removing the jacket. The jackets all had buttons, little thin belts, and the models wore hats and gloves. It was customary in those days to wear costume jewelry over the gloves. The models who preceded me showed the afternoon outfit and then did some magic things to gracefully remove the jewelry, gloves, and jacket, showing the beautiful cocktail dress with gloves, jewelry, belt and jacket all under control on one arm. I was terrified, for I had visions of throwing gloves, jewelry, belt, and jacket all over the dance floor. I needed to learn a lot.

I was fifth in line. The girl in front did this very quick, pretty step till she reached the corner of the dance floor. Then, she brought her fingers up to the brim of her large hat and did a very slow turn. Again, quickly to the next corner, then the slow, graceful turn. Wow! I thought, that looks very professional. So that's what I tried to copy when I went out. To make a long story a bit shorter, in the beginning when I first started modeling I got fired a lot.

Undaunted after that Hadassah Show, I tried to get registered with a modeling agency that also ran a modeling school. The owner, a very sophisticated, chic lady, found that I didn't have the $1,000 tuition fee for her school. She said to me in a very confidential, motherly tone, and I think she was sincere, "Jeraldine, let me save you some heartbreak. You will never make it as a model because your neck is too short, your bust is too large, and, besides, you just don't have the look of a model." But, you see, she didn't understand that in my mind, I had no other choice.

I had to be a model, whether my neck was too short or not. With unfailing determination to support my daughter and myself, I found shows to do, and I was fired a lot, but I learned enough each time that I was able to model my daughter's way through college by working in the high fashion and photography fields and even in a few TV commercials. So my being unable to spell turned out to be an advantage. My mother always said, "Where there's a will, there's a way."

I had chances to remarry but I knew intuitively that marrying someone just for money and security wouldn't bring happiness.

After my precious daughter Gail got married, I felt that I could take jobs away from home. Big fashion shows were not as popular as they once had been, I was getting older and I needed to find a different career. I was getting a little panicky about my future by the time I was called to do a show on board a cruise ship—an astrological fashion show. One dress for each sign of the zodiac would be featured. What a great idea!

While on this three-day cruise, I noticed the cruise hostess. What an easy job she must have, I thought. She gets paid to enjoy this like a passenger! I didn't realize she was slaving away with a million duties. I thought to myself, Bet she doesn't need to know how to type or to spell; she just wears pretty clothes and walks around smiling. I was qualified for this job!

Once back home, I started bugging the main office of the cruise line for a job as a hostess. I continued this for about a year. Every time I got publicity for doing a fashion show or TV commercial, I would send them clippings and remind them that I was eager to be their hostess. Finally, I guess because my mail outweighed anyone else's, they gave me a call and asked that I come in for an interview.

I rushed to the cruise line's office in Los Angeles, and was escorted down a long hall decorated beautifully with ships' models, and paintings and photos of ships. My heart jumped, and with fistfighting butterflies in my stomach, I entertained the idea of living at sea. When we got to the interviewer's office I was greeted and asked to "Please sit down," by a handsome young Italian man who introduced himself to me as Mr. Sandello. I tried to appear relaxed and confident but I was so eager, and in need of a job, that my stomach butterflies seemed to be expanding in population and vigor.

"Now," said Mr. Sandello, "tell me about your qualifications."

I told him I was free to travel now that I had raised my daughter, she was married and settled. I was a very dependable, hard worker.

"This would not be for just a few weeks," he said, "but for seven days a week, eleven months a year!!" I drooled at the prospect. What an escape from modeling, which was really beginning to bore me. "Do you speak any foreign languages?" he asked.

With a gulp, I asked, "Which do I need to know?"

His reply was, "Since all the crew is Italian, you will need to know Italian, and since all our ports of call are in Mexico, you will need to know Spanish."

Bravely, I said "Good! Those are the two languages that I know." I knew what *mañana* meant in Spanish, but I didn't know a single, solitary word of Italian. I figured that I could go to Berlitz for about six weeks and learn enough to fake those two languages.

He asked, "Do you know how to run a bingo game?"

I replied, "Certainly." I thought, I can always go to church to learn that.

Then, he asked, "Well, how about running a bridge tournament?"

Unfortunately, I had never played cards and didn't know one from another. As a matter of fact, I didn't know any games. I was always too busy working, keeping house, going to PTA meetings and my garden club. But I sat up straighter to help me with yet another white lie and said, "That would be a cinch." I felt the pressure building, now I would have to find someone to teach me to play bridge. Let's see (I was mentally organizing my schedule): about two nights a week for language lessons, one night for bingo and now another night for learning bridge. I guess I could be ready to fake all of it in about six weeks.

"That's fine, Miss Saunders; tell me, can you run a horse race?"

I thought maybe I'd better tell him that there was something I didn't know, since I was running out of nights for study, so I replied, "Mr. Sandello, that is one thing I know nothing about."

He replied, "That's all right, we'll teach you. You have the job, Jeraldine. Our hostess got sick and has left us. We will need you aboard to report for work tomorrow morning. Please be at the ship at 9:00 A.M.

"You can meet our cruise director, Steve Potter, and get your gear settled in your cabin. We sail at 8:00 P.M. sharp. Oh, and bring a long formal dress with you."

So, there I sat with all my fibs. I had no choice but to report aboard. I needed the job and maybe they wouldn't fire me at sea. Mother did say, "Where there's a will, there's a way." I would soon find out.

I drove home trying not to panic. Quickly, I had to buy a long dress and pack, but what? Sandello had mentioned the formal, but what else did I need? At least my daughter and her nice husband could move into my apartment and that would save them rent. Thoughts kept swirling through my brain. My mother and brother already lived next door to me. Now they and Gail could look after each other. It was good that Gail and her husband, Nelson, loved Uncle Bud and Grandma. Luckily, these thoughts took over and kept me from thinking about how I was going to perform all the duties required of me.

On that nervous and exciting morning I kissed my loved ones goodbye. As I drove down to the pier, I hoped that I wouldn't have trouble finding the ship. The long drive gave me time to push my fears into my consciousness. How to pry them out? I had recently taken a self-improvement course called PACE. The focus was on the power of positive mental imaging. In a nutshell our subconscious has no reasoning power; it believes anything we program into it by our thinking. We all talk to ourselves, whether we realize it or not. Like a reflection in a mirror our lives show our attitudes and are the picture of what we have been saying to ourselves. In computer terms, "Garbage in, garbage out," or "fear in, fear out; love in, love out." Our subconscious is like a scale: one side is fear and the other is faith and abundance—which side we focus or dwell on tips the scale. When we have fear thoughts, we are fearful, but when we consciously make ourselves remember that we are in charge of our computer mind (our personal computer), by selecting the correct attitude we can control the scale and bring into focus positive images of hopes and wishes and success.

I tried to erase my fearful thoughts with images of how I would like things to be that morning. In this case I used a sentence I have enjoyed sharing ever since because it is so powerful and fundamental. On this nervous morning, it made all the difference. Please write this down and place it on your refrigerator, for it is a sure-fire way of getting what you want. Here it is: "You tend to move towards that upon which you dwell." So, *dwell well!* Sure enough, whatever you dwell upon comes about. That morning I was dwelling on travel and imaging my working on a cruise ship, and boy!—did it ever work and work and work and work

So there I was. I'd conned myself into a job I knew nothing about, needing languages I was completely unfamiliar with, and requiring me to supervise games I'd never played, for a highly critical group of participants, nor would I have the chance to watch through a crack in the folding screen to see how the real pros did it before going up to bat.

Arriving at the dock, I was directed to the correct pier. There before me was a thrilling sight! This beautiful white ship was waiting to take me into her loving, cradling arms. The ship was registered in Italy and many of the Italian crew members were by the gangway. On stepping aboard, I introduced myself. "Jeraldine" seemed difficult for the Italian tongue, so I said, "Please call me Jerry."

"*Buon giorno*, Miss Jerry, *buon giorno*, Miss Jerry," they repeated gladly and I thought, Oh, good, I know two words in Italian, already.

After I had unpacked, I met good-looking Steve Potter, the cruise director. He began explaining my multitude of duties. My brain was spinning, trying to remember all that I had been told. The instructions seemed to end only because we were running out of time. I was told to go to the gangway—it was nearly five o'clock and the passengers were to be greeted upon boarding. I stood there all evening, confident in my just-acquired knowledge of the Italian language. I smiled at each passenger and in warm tones said, "*Bon giorno.*" These American passengers all think I'm Italian, I thought to myself. I relaxed, feeling certain that I was a natural for this job.

Then, a kind Italian crew member came over to me and said, "Miss Jerry, you say 'good morning' to everybody, that is what mean '*bon journo.*' You should say '*buona serra,*' that is how you say 'good evening.'"

I must have given him a strange look—I thought I was saying, "Welcome aboard!"

chapter four

THE SEA OF FANTASY

STEVE POTTER WAS AN EXCELLENT CRUISE DIRECTOR, A super organizer, always sober, great personality and gifted with a beautiful voice. Most important, he had just gone through hell with a hostess who was not dependable even before she got sick. He was eager to put this red-headed, green-eyed fashion model (me) to work to find out if she could hack it. If not, he would have to get rid of her right away because he simply had to have dependable, hard working help with all of his duties.

The cruise director is responsible for all of the daily passenger activities, starting at 6:00 A.M. and lasting all through the day until 1:30 to 2:00 A.M. the following morning. Also in his charge are two big orchestras and he arranges when and where they play aboard ship. In port he determines which is the duty orchestra and which is free to go ashore. He also supervises the entertainers who come aboard for one cruise or several, depending on their contracts. He must watch the rehearsals to be certain the material is appropriate to present to the passengers, both in format and content.

On this ship the orchestras were really great, but there was a bit of a problem. One was made up of Mexicans who spoke no English, the other group was Italian and spoke only that language. A further complication was that while the great Mexican musicians read music and were very well behaved, the Italians created really beautiful music but could not read a note, and as for their behavior, they had a certain lack of control where beautiful women were concerned. You can imagine the chagrin of the entertainers when they learned during rehearsal that the Italian Lotharios couldn't read their personalized arrangements and that neither orchestra could communicate verbally. Some of the entertainers reacted like prima donnas and threw fits. Others just took it in stride.

In addition to those temper-straining, nerve-wracking duties, passenger morale is the responsibility of the cruise director. He must see that there is a choice of activities in the public rooms throughout the day and evening. This calls for split-second scheduling. Each new activity must start on time and "just another five minutes" of any ongoing activity cannot be permitted. This takes very strong discipline.

The passenger activities include show time, bingo, horse racing with wooden horses, embarkation information (who's who on the ship, what to wear, where to find the public rooms, etc.), information about the next port, the history of the port, what to see and do, what not to do, what to buy and where, the money in use and the exchange rate, whether you can drink the water, and any other information necessary to make a port visit a happy one. God help the cruise director if there is a Godzilla or two on board!

The term "Godzilla" was adopted by the cruise staff to designate the complainers. These passengers blame the cruise director if it

The very first day of my new career at sea…seeking my fortune.

rains, if the shops in the port are closed because of a local or national holiday, if the air conditioning is too cold or not cold enough, if their toilets don't flush, if the stewards haven't made up their room, if...if...if....It is up to the cruise director to change the Godzilla syndrome in these passengers before they can pass on their unhappy attitude to the rest of the passengers. Unfortunately, there are those whose happiness lies in criticism and complaint.

Usually, the officers on the ship are seen only at night when they come out to enjoy the social life. Most of the hotel staff is seen only during meal times. The cruise staff is composed of the cruise director, his assistants, the hostess, the sports director, and sometimes more staff, depending upon the vessel you are on, and these are the cruise staff members with whom the passengers interact throughout the cruise. We are the walking complaint department, the "spot psychologists," the folks who see to whatever you need (within reason, of course!).

Thankfully, most passengers are not Godzillas; the majority of them are eager to have a good time, even if it kills them, and sometimes it does just that (but that's another story). We find that most passengers experience a kind of universal love while on a cruise. A beautiful magic comes over them. Protective walls come tumbling down and they feel very loving toward one another. They relax and become playful for they know they are on a sea of fantasy. From the decks they watch nature's display—the vast sea, the moon, and the stars that seem so close one could reach up and touch them! The beauty of it all can be overwhelming! This is when the human soul is touched by the Divine.

chapter five

FEAR IS A FOUR-LETTER WORD

PERHAPS IT'S THE MOTION OF THE SHIP. PASSENGERS SEEM to lose their equilibrium and become more childlike. I don't mean childish; I mean many adults learn how to play again. Working as a cruise hostess was eye opening for me. I was used to the way we gals behaved at our Oak Ridge Estates Garden Club or the PTA. The lovely fashion models I had worked with were also models of decorum, so I was shocked when I actually saw how "sex rears its ugly head" as a ship passes the twelve-mile limit from shore. I would notice ladies come on board wearing Adolfo suits and pearls, looking so sweet and innocent. Because I was the only female working on board I would eat with the officers. They got so accustomed to my being there, they would go ahead with their usual conversation, which was almost always about women. I was beginning to understand the Italian language by now. For the first time I got a good peek into the psyche of men. All they seemed to talk about was women. I found out what was going on with these sweet little Adolfo-suited ladies, and I couldn't believe it! Some of these women were having a steward in the morning, a passenger in the afternoon, and an officer in the evening.

A bollard is nice to lean on for picture taking. In landlubber terms, a bollard is one of the huge wooden posts that hold up a wharf.

I'm introducing the passengers to the captain on my very first ship. I bought this long dress the day before we sailed.

That is when I felt I had to tell the world what happens when passengers board cruise ships. I would somehow find time to write home to my family in Glendale, California. These letters usually started out, "Dear Family, you will never believe what happened today," and then I would go into detail of what I had witnessed—perhaps something hilarious, something sad, or something dramatic. Sometimes I wouldn't have time to write a letter before I fell exhausted on my bunk at night.

Working as a cruise hostess was incredibly complex because of the long hours, multitude of duties, and the unbelievably harried schedule. At first I wrote notes to myself to help me remember all the supplies I needed to gather for each activity. When we decorated the public rooms with the theme for an event, we had to herd the cruise staff together so they would all help. It was like a cat and mouse game. I didn't find out for months where the assistant cruise director hid after lunch. He had placed a pad behind the electrical panel in a small space behind the stage. I later learned this pad was a busy place. Any crew member with an urgent desire to satisfy his lust with a passenger who couldn't use her cabin for this, either because of a roommate, spouse, parent, etc., would sometimes, I learned, be desperate enough to resort to this crude spot on the ship. I suppose it seemed romantic enough in the heat of passion when the Italians made use of their inborn talent for seduction. They were smooth as Alfredo Fettucini!

Besides all her regular duties, the hostess is responsible to the cruise director for any assistance he may need. The long hours and the pressure was terrible—really slave labor—but I loved my job. Thank goodness I eventually made it pay off because I worked incredibly hard. Sometimes in a free second I'd just grab the daily program and jot down an incident that had happened so it would trigger my mind when I wrote home about it. At the end of my letters home, I would usually write, "Dear Mother, please save this letter. I may try to write a book some day."

So my dear mother saved all of them for me. I never felt I could write well because my English teachers had combined the English studies with spelling tests. I was good at comprehension and diagramming sentences, but my spelling was so very poor that I always got red Fs.

Perhaps it was the tension of a new job and my wanting to be good at it so I could keep it, and having to hide my fear of being on my own, all by myself at sea. When I returned from the first couple of eleven-day cruises, I would get into my car to drive home for a few hours, but before I could start the engine, I had to sit and cry for a few minutes. I had always had the emotional support of my family and I had never lived alone. Slowly though, as I became more confident in my job, I got over my fears, and those few minutes of crying seem very funny to me now. FEAR is definitely a four-letter word.

chapter six

With Only Myself to Blame

I PAID DEARLY FOR MY NERVE IN CLAIMING QUALIFICATIONS I did not have when I talked my way into my first job on a cruise ship. When one is naughty, one gets punished and I was punished later, but I couldn't complain about my chastisement without revealing that I was sailing under false colors.

My first ship was one under Panamanian registry, crewed by Italians, who took pride in their work. We were sailing off the West Coast of Mexico, visiting Mexican ports. I ate with the officers, but at first their talk was all Greek to me. Well, actually it was Italian.

I had done little more than smile knowingly when asked if I could serve as mistress of ceremonies during evening galas. Though I'd appeared before thousands of people as a model, I'd never faced a microphone. This, however, is only a small part of the responsibilities of a hostess, which, in turn, are somewhat minor compared to those of the cruise director. You are up when the first passengers awake, and you go to bed after the last passengers do. Occasionally, you may be propositioned to go to bed *with* the last.

During these sixteen to eighteen hours there are changes from daytime apparel to poolside wear, and then into an evening gown. On a rare occasion there might be time for a ten-minute nap, or less. If you do try to sneak one in, you have to lie on your bunk on your back with your arms crossed like you're in a coffin; otherwise your face may get a sleeping crease or your makeup be disturbed, and you haven't time to fix it.

The cruise staff also runs a very big supply depot, and the hostess is largely responsible for making certain that we never run short in any category. Like a good Virgo, I will now make another list.

A typical requisition for a short cruising season, simplified enormously, would go something like this: twenty dozen felt-tipped pens, colored red and black; six dozen large rolls of transparent adhesive tape with dispensers; 300 of the latest hard-cover and paperback books for the library; jump ropes, crayons, and coloring books for the occasional small fry; a gross of scoring pads, six gross of pencils, and 100 new decks of bridge cards; at least ten dozen new Ping-Pong balls, and occasionally a replacement for one of the tables; a couple of thousand dollars' worth of prizes; thousands of straight pins and safety pins, horse race tickets, bingo cards, and door prize tickets; hundreds of garlands and thousands of variously shaped balloons and leis and noisemakers, along with funny paper hats for gala nights and costume parties and parades; and other items too numerous to mention. If something ran short, there was no trotting down to the neighborhood store to rectify the situation. After months and months of marking up my supply order I learned that I had been misspelling crepe paper; I was ordering "crap paper." How embarassing.

I'm still pleased with the way I handled the bridge problem. It was certain to be the most serious. Bridge players can be like lynch mobs if they feel toyed with or that they are being made light of.

Knowing this could be my *bete noire*, on my first cruise I posted a notice and also had printed in the daily bulletin that those who cared to play bridge should meet in the cardroom. Before lunch on the first day out about thirty players appeared. I told them that I loved the game of bridge, but suspected that they were wiser about it than I. They liked that. Then I proposed that, since this group would be playing together in this tournament for the next ten days, they themselves should decide on the rules they wanted to follow. They were informed that when they came up with their full instruction sheet, I would have it printed, and that would be the final voice in any dispute.

They went to work immediately and came up with a code of conduct so good that I held on to it for dear life for the rest of my sailing career. I was always sweet to the passengers but with bridge players, if there was even the smallest quibble, I would say, admonishingly, "You haven't read the rules, have you?" then I would smile and the problem would be settled at once. I suppose the only real complaint I have against bridge players is that they're all so darned smart!

The print shop was what gave me the real willies in those first days at sea. The printer was Italian and knew no English, but could follow copy. He also knew some Spanish, which I was supposed to know a *lot* of. My responsibility was to get the cruise director's daily activity program made into a printed agenda each day.

Fortunately, all natives of foreign lands are terribly keen to improve their English, and the less they know, it seems to me, the more eager they are. After I'd confided my own interest in extending my knowledge of Italian (from zero, if you insist) the printer and I were able to work out a means of communication with words and sign language that got the job done.

The experience was an exhausting, nerve-wracking one. In order to keep any track at all of what my duties were and whether I had fulfilled them, I stuck small sheets of paper to my cabin bulkheads and the backs of the doors. They bore notes of what had to be done and what supplies to take to each activity. There was seldom an inch of space in the cabin that did not contain a fluttering reminder of some projects I needed to learn. They fluttered because of the air conditioning. They mocked me, they waved at me all night when the lights were out and I was trying to sleep.

At first the passengers were really getting to me. For a while I had a recurring nightmare that would awaken me in a cold sweat. A substance much like putty would come seeping under the cabin door until it threatened to inundate the cabin. Then it would begin to swirl and bubble and assume the form of passengers who would lean over my bunk and look down at me accusingly. That's when I would wake up, turn on the light, and stare at all those moving pieces of paper. Tomorrow I would take care of every last one of them! It was six months before it was no longer necessary to use this method of keeping myself on the ball.

A different kind of nightmare was an Italian officer named Mario who worked for the company operating our ship. He was the nephew of the owner, but he was not actively on duty. Mario was making this Mexican cruise because there was a possibility that he might be shifted from his ship, which cruised the Mediterranean, and given a more responsible position on ours. He was a big, extremely handsome man with a rock of a jaw. He had a fair complexion and curly, light brown hair, as do many men from the north of Italy.

He initiated his campaign pleasantly enough. He was attentive and courteous in the extreme. In Italian, interspersed with broken English, he said something about me and Portofino. Having Sagittarius rising, I thrill at the opportunity of seeing new sights and my face lit up as I said, "Oh, I would love to see Portofino." I was thinking that perhaps one day I might visit there. He excused himself and said he would join me in the bar after the evening floor show. Oh, Mario was intriguing and I wondered if he was married. He came into the main salon around midnight, when the crowd was beginning to thin out to those groups of night-owls who would stay up, putting away the booze, as long as the bartenders would serve them, which was all night, if need be.

Mario had several drinks with some of the merry-makers he was particularly friendly with, while I ran activities and occasionally joined them, but my visits were brief, because I never drink at all, and I did have work to do.

When the floor show in the nightclub was over, I immediately went below, locked my cabin door, and went to bed. I always do this. I never say good night to anyone in the bars of the ships, because we're in the saloon business and I don't want to put a damper on the parties and the sales of the booze.

In about twenty minutes, my phone rang. It was Mario.

"What are you doing?" he asked accusingly. I guess Women's Lib might have a point.

I really was imagining how it would be to have those nice, strong arms around me. I was new to ship life, I was used to being protected with my family around me, so I was a little frightened, living out at sea alone with no one to lean on or tell my troubles to.

But I said, "I'm trying to sleep. I have to get up early in the morning." Oh, I did so need to feel some touch, some reassuring arm around me that night, but I would have to use my head.

I didn't know this guy from Adam. He said, "I thought we were going spend evening together."

"The evening's long over," I said. "I have work to do early in the morning." End of conversation.

A few minutes later, he was banging on my cabin door. "Jeraldina, open!" In a gruff, angry voice he spouted something in Italian, I don't think it was very nice.

"Let me in. I want talk you," he yelled.

"No!" I yelled back. "Be a nice man. Go away!"

He began pounding at the door and kicking at it, alternating one with the other. It was a good thing I didn't allow this mad man in. I turned on the lights and watched my notes flutter. I wasn't going to be able to sleep with all that racket, which was probably what he was counting on. Then, I had a terrible thought. Mario knew our ship intimately. He need only go to the night steward, (also a nut) and ask for the passkeys. The steward would hardly refuse an officer.

Mario screamed something, "Portofino, you promised—*mia cabina, Portofino.*"

Good Heavens! Then I remembered. One of our posh cabins was called the Portofino Suite. He was inviting me to his cabin, not the resort near Genoa. No wonder he thought he had hit pay dirt, and that explained his reaction now. Who thought an officer would be staying in the Portofino Suite?

I phoned the assistant purser, a nice young man name Guido.

"What's all that noise?" he asked.

"Mario—he's trying to get into my cabin. You've got to do something. I think he must be a little angry."

"That big son-of-a-bitch would kill me, Jeraldine," he complained.

"No, Guido. Don't try to talk to Mario. Just find the night steward and tell him not to give the pass keys to anyone under any circumstances. He'll get fired if he does."

"Well." He sounded doubtful.

"Please, Guido," I begged. "Everything will be all right if you do just that."

Mario kept thumping away at the door like a wild man for some time, but then he went away. I kept waiting fearfully for the sound of a key in my lock. I waited but it didn't come.

Finally, I fell into a fitful sleep. What a scary world it seemed— to be on one's own, at sea, in the middle of nowhere.

chapter seven

ℬE SHAMELESSLY PAMPERED

EVEN THE MOST JADED OF SOPHISTICATES USUALLY FIND themselves joining in the fun on cruise ships. Something beautiful happens that doesn't happen in a resort, a hotel, or on an airplane. Maybe it's the fact that there are no freeways to fight, no business to conduct, no aggravating phone calls (people think twice before calling someone on a ship), or maybe it's the shameless pampering and the great activities and shows all day and most of the night that are planned by the cruise staff. This might be an overstatement, but in some ways I feel that if everyone could experience the loving feeling that happens on a cruise, there wouldn't be any wars.

There are various levels of "poshness" and pampering, depending on which ship you choose. There are mass-market cruise ships and there are ultra-luxury-level ships. In fact, there is a dazzling galaxy of choices these days; all of them are architecturally spectacular and beautifully decorated, no matter how little you pay. The only difference is in the degree of service. The expensive cruises have more crew members per passenger—therefore more pampering. You can have breakfast in bed on Pratesi sheets, lovely quilts, video and video cassettes, fluffy terry cloth robes, personalized stationery, hair dryers, walk-in closets, private verandas, a complimentary in-cabin bar, and caviar on demand, served on Limogé china. One suite I know of has a grand piano and a private, tuxedo-clad butler.

The music on all the ships is great to listen to and even greater for dancing. Do you have a partner? I used to write to the home office when I first started cruising and ask if they would please give a half-dozen retired gentlemen a free cruise if they would dance with the single ladies each evening. I'm afraid the company was shocked at my suggestion. Now it is almost standard on all good cruise ships to have a dozen such gentlemen aboard for this purpose. It's romantic for the women to be asked to dance and they want to express themselves to the rhythm of the music. Sometimes they just want to be able to show off their pretty evening gowns. Most men think that they have to be good dancers before they can ask for a dance. Believe me, nothing could be further from the truth. How many men have lost out on a chance for romance because they were afraid they weren't good enough dancers?

The gentlemen who receive a free cruise for dancing are called "cruise hosts" or sometimes "social staff." This program has turned out to be a big attraction for women who travel without a man. The rules are strict. The host must not ask the same woman for a dance twice in a row. If he wants to dance with her again, he must ask another lady first, and then go back to the first. The hosts are sometimes given other duties such as helping the cruise staff load the tour buses and going along on the tours to make certain everyone gets back on the bus after the stops or filling out a report on how well the tour conductor performed. The cruise lines have to keep finding new hosts because they often find a soul mate aboard and get married.

chapter eight

FINDING YOUR BLISS

WHEN I WAS TOLD WE WERE GOING TO INAUGURATE THREE months of continuous three- and four-day cruises I couldn't imagine why anyone would want to go to all the trouble of packing and unpacking for such a short cruise. No one had done this before so I was amazed at all the fun, food, and frolic passengers could absorb in such a short period.

We sailed from Los Angeles (whenever I say Los Angeles, I mean the nearby Port of San Pedro) to Ensenada, Mexico. These mini-trips were called "Party Cruises" and they were very successful. Other cruise lines have these "Parties" from all the major ports. The passengers are mostly younger people who are not retired. They can't get away from their business or jobs for a longer cruise, so they make up for it by squeezing their bliss into just a few days. The party cruisers get smog-free days and carefree nights, fine cuisine and an endless program of entertainment—usually for less than it would cost them to stay in a medium-priced hotel room ashore.

By their nature these brief holidays get kind of nutty. Our itinerary was a quick visit to Ensenada, Mexico, the next day a couple of hours off Guadalupe Island, then the return to Los Angeles.

We anchored off Guadalupe where I would stand at the top of the gangway with clicker counter in hand as we loaded forty passengers to each tender. The tenders would then take the passengers alongside the island to have a close look at the elephant seals. In their adult stage these great animals are as large as a walrus and have a long nose that resembles an elephant's trunk.

Passengers found the colonies fascinating to watch, and when the captain let loose a blast of the ship's whistle, the seals would galumph around on the rocky shingle at a hurried pace.

Despite the fact that the island is a sanctuary, some clowns from the crew decided to capture one of the baby seals that ventured too close to the tender. They put a rope around the seal's neck and another around the flippers on the rear, and although it must have weighed more than a hundred pounds, they managed to get it alongside the tender so that it could be towed back to the ship. They thought it would be great to put the baby seal in one of the swimming pools on the ship and bring it to Los Angeles as a sort of mascot.

Well, if there is anything—repeat anything—that will unite a group of citizens of the United States of America, it is the mistreatment of an animal. The passengers on our ship were threatening mutiny, demanding that calls be made to the State Department. Some of the men passengers were ready to beat up the crew members. The captain had to get on the public address system to assure everyone that the little animal was unharmed and would be released safely to return to its family on the rocks.

On the same trip, at four in the morning, a man was discovered in one of the public rooms. He was blissfully removing a stunning mosaic of large tiles, at least ten by six feet. He had grown very attached to this particular work of art and planned to sneak it ashore. The thing must have weighed a ton. He would have needed a moving van and I wondered how he thought he would get by customs with it.

The most popular cruises are those of an intermediate length—from eight to twenty days. The passengers will be of mixed ages, younger as well as older, and people of average means as well as the wealthier. A great many career men and women, young and unmarried, want to completely forget their work and their usual surroundings. They are usually a playful but sophisticated lot who have no intention of letting this brief cruise intrude on their business life and they seem to shed the experiences of the cruise as readily as they have thrown off the yoke of work.

The longer cruises—those over a month long, and extending to three months, even a year—are the best, of course. Some of the passengers are older, but you can forget the accepted picture of a bunch of ancients bundled in blankets, reading Agatha Christie's mystery novels. These people are lively and they've been around. Boy! Have they been around!

The long cruise is a favorite pastime of wealthy widows and widowers, high school and college teachers, novelists and playwrights, executives and people with a lot of time and money who love the sea and love to travel. The most fascinating people I have met on cruises were on these longer voyages.

On very long cruises the ship owners add more crew per passenger and more expensive entertainment. Some women with lots of money take two cabins. The extra one is just for their ball gowns.

People who have never been on a cruise usually want to know what to do if you just hate it once you are aboard. I don't think you'll have any problem. Give the cruise ship a little time to work her magic—one day at the most. This is why most cruise lines have over fifty percent repeat passengers and on one cruise, on the *Vistafjord,* we had over ninety percent repeat passengers.

On the day passengers board, after the long trip from home, perhaps getting up at 4 A.M. and having missed a meal en route, they board with grumpy complaints. I blame this all on their low blood sugar. I've had many people complain to me at the very tops of their voices about some small detail. Halfway through the tirade, there will be a call on the public address system saying that I am urgently needed in the print shop. This is an arrangement the cruise staff has with one another when a situation looks pretty rough. However, these beefs die down by the end of the first day and are gone the next. The really big complainers usually announce at the end of the cruise that they had a great time and will be back. I sometimes end up with them as my best friends.

The next question most often asked by folks who have not been on a cruise ship is, "What yardstick can I use to get an idea whether a particular cruise will be an enjoyable one?"

I will assume that you know where you want to go, what time you have available, and how much you have budgeted for the adventure. There are deals called "Play Now, Pay Later," but I call them "Play Now, Pray Later." You'll have a much more enjoyable time if the loot is in your hands, free and clear, rather than on someone else's books. I also assume that you have made inquiries, studied brochures, and argued the merits of one cruise against the others. By all means, talk to travel agents (you don't pay them, the carriers do).

But now you ask yourself, "What if I end up on the *Bounty*, with a slobbering martinet of a captain and a crew of cockroaches manning a bucket of rust that will sink to the bottom with the first heavy sea?"

I have some rules of thumb for those whose first look at a cruise ship could be as they move across the dock to the gangway to board it.

You can be almost dead certain that the crew will make sure that you enjoy impeccable service from people who are proud of their jobs and do them well. The food on most ships is superb—there is a general agreement on this matter among gourmets. Just remember there is a difference between luxury cruises and mass-market cruises.

I would be extremely careful about booking myself on the maiden voyage of any new ship. You might be very excited about being aboard a vessel during her very first cruise, but all brand-new ships have a breaking-in period. This was true of the majestic Queens, *Mary, Elizabeth* and *Elizabeth 2,* as well as the trim little 3,000 ton coasters that ply offshore waters. This is when the "bugs" occur, sometimes with passenger discomfort. However, if you are an adventurer, the most memorable cruises are experienced when something unexpected happens. It all depends on your attitude.

If you would like to sail with people of similar tastes to yours, there are specialty cruises. Everything from wine-tasting, golf, astrology, numerology, and music ranging from country to jazz to symphony, opera, barbershop quartets—all kinds of options are afloat.

Jeraldine lectures on Numerology, one of several topics that cruise passengers enjoyed learning about.

If you are active, inquisitive, and interested in learning, specialty cruises have a lot to teach you. Savvy cruise lines have theme cruises on everything from computer lessons to foreign languages to photography to the fundamentals of tai chi. Whether you are an avid gardener, novice golfer, or aspiring Rembrandt, there is a cruise for you. Try to match the ship to your lifestyle. Each ship has a unique personality of its own. Comparing ships is sort of like trying to compare New York to Hawaii. They are both great, but in completely different ways. To help you narrow your choices when choosing your ship, read *Cruise Diary* (POSH Publishing, P.O. Box 12303, Long Beach, CA 90809, Tel: 562/498-3211).

Big Band cruises play tunes from the 40s and 50s and some lines put on extra social hosts (dance partners) for these cruises. On St. Valentine's Day all Princess Cruises ships hold a renewal of wedding vows for their passengers, and on their new *Grand Princess* they have a wedding chapel. How romantic! The Silversea's Cordon Bleu Cruise is hosted by chefs who have trained at that famed school. Cunard Line has the answer to keeping fit: they have a Golden Door Spa on board. Holland America Line has all of the above with the exception of the Golden Door; additionally they have Magic Cruises, Life Style Improvement Cruises, Finance Cruises, Cruises on How to Retire Well, Comedy, and Super Bowl Cruises. Crystal Cruises has a Computer University at Sea Program, PC Basics On How to Create Your Own Home Page and twenty-two state-of-the-art computer work stations and laptop computers available. They are noted for their "Wine & Food Festival."

These are the highlights of some of the activities that cruise lines offer. Space restricts my trying to list all of the ships and their activities, but I assure you that you will find a ship tailor-made for you.

chapter nine

THE GOOD AND THE BAD

AFTER WORKING ON MY FIRST SHIP, WHEN IT WAS TIME TO go to drydock the company had the ship almost deadhead to England. Except for about two dozen passengers, there were just the crew, officers, and cruise staff. On that beautiful small ship, which held only 475 passengers, the cruise staff consisted of Cruise Director Steve Potter, and his wife Cathleen, who was our talented singer. She was an opera star but usually on ships she did songs from Broadway musicals and Steve had a voice very much like John Charles Thomas or De Luca, a typical Irish lyrical baritone. I was the cruise hostess. We also had a dance team on our cruise staff. Even though we had merely a handful of passengers we had to keep up our regular daily and nightly activities for them and at the same time, in between, we had to pack all the prizes, costumes, and equipment to be stored in the hold of the ship while it was drydocked in Rotterdam. The company sent Steve a small amount of money for us to live on while we waited in Europe for the new ship they were adding to their cruise line. This ship was being completely refurbished in Genoa, Italy, for some staggering amount of money. We were to stay in touch with the company office until the new ship would be ready, which they estimated would be about one week, at most. We could go anywhere we wanted to in the meantime, at our own expense, of course.

Before I left on this crossing, I was a little hesitant at the thought of being in Europe alone, so I asked my ex-husband if he would like to meet me in Rotterdam when our ship arrived. He agreed, otherwise I wouldn't have had the courage to go. It had been a very rough crossing and when we arrived in Rotterdam our ship's stack was loose and her bow was caved in. Small ships get a lot of movement when there is a storm and this storm had really been a wild one.

When we disembarked in Rotterdam, it was good to be on land. My ex-husband got sick and couldn't join me, so there I was tagging along with Steve and Cathleen. Steve is a Pied Piper with a lot of planets in Sagittarius; we girls followed him as he showed us nearby Amsterdam, the Dutch capital. We were amazed at Holland's homes with their clean, sparkling windows trimmed in Dutch lace curtains, each of different design. We were using Steve's copy of Arthur Frommer's *Guide to Europe on Five Dollars A Day*. We took the book's advice and stayed at the Embasssde. It was formerly a seventeenth-century sea captain's home. It was tall and skinny and had points at the top. It was so clean and the inexpensive rooms also included breakfast that, much to our delight, consisted of meats, cheeses, eggs, all kinds of bread and muffins, jam, and any kind of beverage, and the owner was so very hospitable.

We found in our *Five Dollars A Day* guide a restaurant called something that sounds like "Mudder's Cooken." If we got there before 5:30 P.M. we could eat upstairs for half price. One evening as we enjoyed this delicious repast the very first snowflakes of the season began to softly accumulate on the wooden-framed, multi-paned windows. Being a native Californian it seemed like something out of a fairyland to me.

The next day we went to London where our Pied Piper showed us museums, subway, the Tower of London, and other interesting sights. We couldn't plan anything too far in advance because we never knew when we would have to leave.

Steve got himself a nice gig while there. He went to see Lew Grade at the Talk Of The Town and substituted one night for Englebert Humperdinck.

The weeks went by and we loved London. Just about the time we were beginning to get settled in for a long stay, the company called and informed us that our former little ship was finished with drydock and would be leaving that same night, so if we wanted to get our things off that were stored in her hold, we had to be there before she sailed at 8:00 P.M. that very night. Good Heavens! We needed those supplies for the new ship, which we were going to board in Genoa as soon as she was ready. Our own personal things were also stored in the hold of the old ship.

In a mad rush we left London after packing so fast our heads were swimming. We dashed to catch a plane for Rotterdam which wasn't a very long flight. Cathleen and Steve found seats together and I found a vacant seat across the aisle from them. My blood sugar had dropped by this time and as usual I had food in my bag for just such emergencies. Usually I keep nuts because they are easy to pack, however we were so rushed all I had available were a couple of bananas. I hated the thought of peeling one, they are so aromatic, while sitting so close to this stranger in the seat next to me. I waited a while and thought it over. Yes, I had to have something quickly so I decided the best thing to do was to just eat the smelly thing. As I pulled the banana from my bag I decided to get both out and I said to this distinguished looking man next to me, "Would you care for a banana?"

Much to my surprise, he said, "Yes, I would, thank you." As we munched the fruit, we introduced ourselves. He said, "I am the Baron Lodi van Bonninghausen."

"Where do you live?" I asked.

"I live in Terheyden, Holland." Later he told me he was the Burgemeester there.

I guess I didn't react with an appropriate response, so he asked "You know what is a Burgemeester?"

For some strange reason I had seen a movie or a play and somehow gotten the impression of people in costume, drinking beer and celebrating. So I said, "Yes, isn't that the person in each village who can drink the most beer?"

He was shocked at my reply! He sat up straight to show his dignity and said, "No, a Burgemeester is, I think, you call a Mayor."

Oh, I was so embarrassed. He was a tall, thin, elegant gentleman. I should have realized he didn't look like a beer drinker or he would have had a big tummy. As the flight went on he told me of his town in Holland and I explained how my boss Steve and his wife Cathleen and I were hurrying to try to get to our former ship before she sailed.

"What are you going to do when you have retrieved your things?" he asked.

I thought a while and since this was so sudden, I didn't know if we were going back to London while we waited for our new ship, or what Steve wanted to do. I was afraid to leave them and be alone. So I said, "We haven't any plans, yet."

He said, "Well, why don't you come home with me and be my guest for a week? I have the Burgemeester's mansion and lots of servants to care for you."

Of course, I wouldn't go alone so I said, "Oh, how sweet of you, but I am traveling with my boss and his wife."

He had the answer to that. "Oh, of course, I meant for all of you to come. I have lots of bedrooms. I would love it if all three of you would stay with me for a week in my lovely town of Terheyden."

I asked, "What is your birthday?" I now forget what it was, but then I asked if I could see his palm. After some quick calculations on his birthdate and studying his palm, I felt safe in telling the Potters of our invitation. Steve and Cathleen agreed to come along. He gave us his card and we told him we would join him tomorrow.

By the time we landed at the Rotterdam Airport we were really worried—if we didn't hurry we would certainly miss the ship. Steve and I got through customs OK, but I looked across the aisle and Cathleen was pulling all of her clothes out of her bags. Gads, now what? We were sure to miss the ship if we didn't get to the dock. Steve and I ran over to her—she was crying.

"I can't find my passport!"

Steve explained to her if we didn't leave that minute we would be too late to retrieve our needed things in storage. I would have to identify some of the boxes I had packed, so I had to be there with Steve. Steve comforted her and wrote down the name of the hotel where we would all spend the night. She should meet us at the hotel or call us there for help if she couldn't get by customs.

We got to the ship just as they were pulling in the gangway. We went down to the hold and pointed out to the crew which boxes were ours. I had bound them with 3M tapes—the see-through kind that has threads in it. Boy! does that stuff hold up well. They off loaded our things and we sent them to Genoa to our company representative. He had just arrived there and would be staying while the refurbishing of our new ship was completed. As we entered our hotel in Rotterdam, we heard a happy voice call to us. There was Cathleen, waving her passport.

"Was I in luck," she said. "The man at the American Embassy was from my hometown and gave me a temporary passport!"

The weather had turned very cold; it was the first of November. I couldn't sleep much that night because my feet wouldn't get warm enough. We were glad to leave that cold hotel for the unknown stay in Terheyden.

Talk about a dream week! We were given spacious, luxurious rooms with a view of the lovely town and the maids served us breakfast in bed. The rooms were so nice and warm. All the furniture was original Beidemier and the rest was all beautiful priceless museum-quality 200- to 300-hundred-year-old pieces. My bed was carved in the shape of a swan and we all had linens trimmed in handmade Dutch lace. The lamps throughout the lovely place were Meissen or Dresden. We loved all this beauty, especially Steve, who later became a famous set and art director for the TV and motion picture industry. The rooms were light and cheery and the cooks couldn't have been better.

Every night Lodi, our host, would invite interesting international guests for candlelight dinners in his dining room. The walls of this room were covered with paintings by the old masters, as were the other rooms in this charming old mansion, and on the floors leaning against the walls were dozens more priceless paintings.

Steve and Cathleen helped to entertain Lodi's interesting guests each night by singing and I read a few palms. During the day our host drove us to all the sights and we had our picture taken near a huge windmill for the local papers. Our generous host was a true intellectual and kept us fascinated with his views on metaphysics and life in general.

It was time to leave after this delightful week. Our company notified us that our new ship would be ready to sail in a week. I felt that Steve and Cathleen needed some privacy from me for a while. After all, once our ship sailed we would be living in our side-by-side cabins for a full year. They wanted to go to France on their way to Genoa. I looked at a map. It must have been drawn by the Spanish Tourist Bureau because it showed Spain as a stop practically on the way to Genoa, so, I said, "I have never been to Spain. I think you dears should take the French route and I'll go to Spain on my way to meet you in Genoa on November 27, our sailing day."

We left what were for us generous tips for all the servants, thanked Lodi for his hospitality, and told him how much we enjoyed our heavenly stay. He had his driver take us to the airport in Belgium where we parted company, temporarily, on our way to our final destination in Genoa, the Potters to France and I to Madrid. On the flight there I read the newspaper and was shocked to learn that the English pound had just been drastically devalued! While in England, I'd had to cash a bond that my brother had sent me and hadn't realized that it of course was paid off in pounds, not dollars. I had no other money except these English traveler's checks and a couple of dollars.

On top of that I pulled out the map that was in the seat back in front of me. Wait a minute! Spain isn't on the way to Genoa; it's way out of my way. By going to Madrid I traveled three times as far as necessary. How scary. I felt like "Wrong-way Corrigan"!

I checked into a hotel someone had recommended. I think it was called the Curzon. When I entered my room I really felt guilty. It was huge, with two king-sized beds, and everything was decorated tastefully. The bathroom, equally large, had beautiful marble from floor to ceiling. I asked myself, "How can you stay here when you don't have any money?"

I spent a most exciting week there and charged all my meals to my room. The street car stopped right at our corner and I would hop on every day (it only cost a nickel each way) and visit the Prado Museum. I called my ex-husband and asked him to send me some money. I explained about the English pound, etc. and my plight. I had never asked him for money before, even when we got divorced, but this was an emergency. I asked him to send it to me in care of American Express, which he said he would do. Every day I would take the street car to American Express, hoping to receive the money, which never came, and then I would go to the Prado. Finally it was time for me to fly to Genoa and still there wasn't any mail for me. Well, now what do I do? I know, I'll just walk into a travel office and order my flight ticket and then hand them my traveler's checks in English pounds; maybe they won't remember about the crisis in England. So that is what I did. They not only gave me my flight ticket but they gave me change in, would you believe it, Spanish *dineros*. Was I relieved to be able to pay my hotel bill and cab fare to the airport. I hated to leave Madrid. I love that city and the polite people there.

Our sojourn in Europe was far from over. The Potters and I arrived in Genoa the same day, where the company had rooms for us at a precious little hotel, a former palace called the Elysees Palace. Our hotel had hand-painted murals on the walls and all the rooms had mini-Sistine Chapel-like ceilings. I could lie in bed and pretend I was in heaven.

Our company rep was staying there, too. He had it in for poor Steve—this rep always hated the cruise directors. Later we were to refer to him as "Johnson, the Flood." Our beautiful new ship was way overdue for delivery to our company in Los Angeles, who was leasing it along with all the Italian officers and crew. The owners had a thousand workers living on board and working around the clock to deliver the ship on time to our company or our company wouldn't lease it. Every day they said they would sail the next day.

After a few very cold but fun December days, seeing Genoa and attending movies that were naturally all in Italian, the rep told us to move onto the ship as it was about to be finished and we needed to be there when they sailed for the U.S.A. "for certain the next day."

When we boarded her and walked forward to the forecastle and then turned around and looked aft, the ship was so long we couldn't see her fantail. She was gorgeous and she was BIG! The thought of our small cruise staff handling such a huge ship was intimidating.

We found our cabins, unpacked, and then realized the pressure for the plumbing had not been turned on, so our toilets and showers didn't work. The cabins were cold because the heating wasn't working yet. We went down to the main dining room for dinner. We were to eat at the captain's table, with all the 1,000 workers. We were all served the same food: one pitcher of red wine per person, a flat, salty white bread and tiny fleshless fishes fried with their tails and eyeballs still on, to be eaten bones and all in one mouthful. The crew and the officers were enjoying the food. Perhaps the captain just pretended he did. I know I pretended to eat by pushing things around a bit. A sweet dessert followed with strong espresso coffee. This Virgo, with my hypoglycemia, can't drink liquor or anything with caffeine in it. I don't eat white bread, by choice, and I can't have anything with sugar in it. So you can understand my situation when I learned this was the menu for breakfast, lunch, and dinner until we reached the U.S.A. By the second day we were getting pretty raunchy, not having a shower, and we had to find an unlocked cabin when we wanted an empty toilet. Steve told the rep we were going to go to town to rent a room with our own money, have dinner, take a shower, and sleep in warm rooms.

The rep flipped as he threateningly told us, "The ship is leaving for a trial run and I don't know what time it will return but when we get back, if all is OK, we will sail immediately. So you can't go!"

Steve thought about that for a while, then he looked at Cathleen and me. We were so cold, shivery, hungry, and in need of a shower—we must have looked pitiful. He said, "We are going and that's that!" Not really diplomatic.

The rep's face became blood red with anger. "OK, if you miss the ship I'll see to it that you're all fired!"

We found a taxi at the dock and treated ourselves to two rooms in the nicest hotel, the Columbus. To save money we got one room without a shower and one with, which we could share. Our rooms were adjoining. We enjoyed the warm water, the warm room, and when we got into our clean clothes we all went down to treat ourselves to a delicious Italian dinner, and it was divine! Now for some warm slumber in a warm room with toilets that flushed.

There would have to be a way to know when, and if, the ship would return. Steve and I took turns. He set his alarm so it would ring in two hours. I was to set my alarm for four hours of sleep. When the alarm went off each, in turn, had to dress, find a taxi, and head for the dock where the ship was to return. Every two hours one of us would check to see if our ship came in. My first shift at

3:00 A.M. was so weird. I wore my long brown mink coat with matching hood attached and my high-heeled boots. It was so dark, eery and cold. I handed the taxi driver the address of the place the ship was to return. This was my first year with Italian ships, so my Italian language skills were still very limited. The driver said something to me and I finally realized he was trying to explain that the place where I wanted him to take me was deserted and there weren't any ships there. I tried to explain my situation and he couldn't understand a thing I was saying. Finally, I just said, "*Avanti, per favore.*"

He shook his head and shoulders reluctantly and took me to that dark, desolate spot. When we got there, I said, "*Attendere per favore.*"

He waited in amazement and much suspicion as I walked out on the beach a bit. It was so cold and windy. I looked out to sea as far as I could, looking in the distance for the lights from our beautiful ship. By this time, I think the driver must have been wondering if I was a Mata Hari doing some kind of spy signaling. When I got back into the taxi and asked to be returned to the Columbus Hotel, I think what he said to me in Italian was something that probably meant "See, I told you there isn't anything at that address."

Back to bed. Steve took the next shift. My next turn was at 7:00 A.M. Same thing, not a ship in sight. When I returned the Potters were awake and we ate a hot breakfast in the cozy dining room. We shopped in the bakery for good bread, cheese, and lots of sardines to take back to the ship to keep us from having to eat the salt bread and fish bones on board.

We headed for the spot where the ship was to return. Of course, it wasn't there. We waited in a watchman's shack until the late afternoon when the ship finally did return, and we sailed for the U.S.A. within a few hours. Later, after sailing past Barcelona, it was after dinner and everything was working just fine on board. Steve and Cathleen said good night to me before going to their cabin. I closed my cabin door and everything looked so much better now that the heat was on and the bathrooms worked. I was going to enjoy this very beautiful big ship, but while I was undressing I heard the public address system. An excited Italian voice that probably was the captain was frantically hollering something in Italian—giving some kind of orders—and I opened my cabin door to see terrified faces of the sailors and workmen as they ran down the alleyways. Steve and Cathleen came out—he had understood the Italian announcement and said to me, "Jerry, quick, get your coat and a big hat, the ship's on fire!" He and Cathleen were already dressed to board a lifeboat. (One thing I always knew I would need if adrift in a lifeboat is a big hat because of my redheaded skin; the sun would get me before Davey Jones' locker did.)

Since the ship wasn't finished, life jackets hadn't been distributed to the cabins yet. The three of us ran to the purser's office. He spoke some English, and we asked him, "Where are the life jackets located? There weren't any in our cabins!"

He was very calm when he replied, "I'll get you some life jackets, but why are you so excited? Is something wrong?"

We couldn't believe it. All these Italians running like crazy and the captain announcing something about a fire, and this fellow is trying to tell us that nothing is wrong! Then we figured it out. Everyone on the ship but the three of us were working for the ship's owners, who were under the gun to deliver this ship on time to fulfill the leasing contract. They couldn't let our company know that there was anything wrong or that everything wasn't just perfect. The purser assured us all was fine. We could go to bed and enjoy a good night's sleep. The Potters and I walked around the ship a bit. How could we sleep when they wouldn't tell us what kind of trouble we were in? I was especially nervous because if an emergency was announced on the public address system, at least Steve could understand it—I would be in my cabin alone and maybe catch only a word or two of it.

We went out on the open decks and watched the moon and worried about our safety. Some sailors went by and we heard something about Barcelona. We went back to the purser's desk and asked him, "Are we going back to Barcelona?"

He asked, "Where did you hear that nonsense? We are on our way to the U.S.A."

We must have misunderstood the sailors. Then as we walked along the deck, in the distance we could see lights. Lights in the middle of the ocean? More sailors came by, they were smiling and happy, and mentioning Barcelona. Steve understood from them that we were going back to Barcelona because we had had a big fire in the engine room and needed new parts.

Immediately we realized that the owners didn't want us, or our rep, to call our company and tell them what was happening.

In a few hours, when we arrived in Barcelona, we were told we could go ashore for one hour and then we were to sail again. The three of us tried to see as much as we could by having a taxi drive us around a bit and then back to our ship.

We sailed again at 1:00 A.M. and we were very unhappy about this whole situation. We went to bed and a few hours later I almost fell out of my bunk. Yes, we were listing! Now what? I quickly dressed, as did the Potters. No one would tell us why the ship seemed to be hanging sideways, no doubt for fear we would call our company. A couple of hours later we saw lights in the distance; sure enough, yes, it was again, Barcelona!

We packed a few things, left almost everything else on the ship, and when we pulled into port, we announced to the rep that we were flying home. Steve had to bypass the rep. He called the main office and demanded they fly us home. We would board ship when and if it made it to California. Something good comes out of everything, and that year I got to be home with my daughter, Gail, and the rest of my family for Christmas!

chapter ten

ꭔew Year's Eve

THE SHIPBUILDERS WERE LATE IN DELIVERING THE SHIP TO our company, which made everything else late all the way down the line. The ship was staffed completely by Europeans except for us, the cruise staff. Since it was not delivered on time our company had to fly 750 passengers, plus the cruise staff, to Acapulco to board the vessel after she had been brought through the Panama Canal.

It would have been very simple to just scrub the whole cruise and make the second sailing her maiden voyage. However, there was a special reason the passengers wanted to get aboard so badly. It was the last day of the year and New Year's Eve would be spent in a great, swinging party, sailing off the Mexican coast in the star-studded night. She was a beautiful ship, exquisitely appointed, with the most

59

sophisticated navigational gear on her bridge and all kinds of electronic doodads for the comfort of the passengers. As the eager passengers came aboard and their luggage was stowed, they could do nothing but gasp with delight over the prospect of what lay ahead. However, remember what I said about maiden voyages, and this ship was a maiden. Everyone still had to learn about her little idiosyncrasies.

We were out of the harbor of Acapulco and on our way to Puerto Vallarta when there were the first whispers of what could be a minor disaster. Acapulco is a hot, dusty place, even on December 31. There was an enormous party this evening. Indeed it was the reason for all the bustle of changing plans, jet flights, and hurrying by bus from airport to dock.

So where was the soap?

Well, the soap—hundreds upon hundreds of bars of a hard-milled castile preferred by the cruise company to the harsher stuff that would have been sent along from Europe—was in the holds of the jet planes that had brought us all from Los Angeles. The soap now was more than halfway to Miami!

Very few of the 750 passengers had the foresight or good luck to stick a few bars of soap in their luggage before leaving home. When the full facts of the situation were disclosed, there began one of the greatest soap-sharing and bathing parties in history! It was a splendid way to get to know your new neighbors.

First, there were parties all over the ship while everyone drank to soap-swapping. The main salon of the ship, where the gala was to be held, was very posh and we had open sittings for dinner rather than the assigned places of a first and second sitting. Following that came the anticipated New Year's Eve show in the night club.

The nightclub was even more Port Over-Starboard Home (the origin of the word "posh," referring to the ideal cabin location for a voyage from England to India and back). The dance floor was of large, square fitted panels of thick, frosted glass through which lights glowed in an ever-changing pattern of colors. It was a romantic scene with low-hung paper lanterns and the beautifully dressed men and women in their tuxes and long gowns and funny hats, whirling their noisemakers and getting in the way of the waiters who staggered under trays loaded with champagne.

The entertainers on this ship included a very professional Mexican dance team who were adept in all phases of their art, as well as being excellent teachers.

Ramon, the very handsome male dancer, was scheduled at the very top of the New Year's Eve show to get things off to a properly lively start, although he wanted the star's spot at the end of the program and I could see he was going to be temperamental. The

Rehearsal time with Los Lobos, the great Mexican orchestra. That's actor Coby Denton on Jeraldine's right, and singer Cindy Hunter Leach on her left.

orchestra played the introduction as Ramon whirled onto the dance floor, brilliant in a Spanish costume. However, as he smashed his heels down in the very first move of a violent flamenco, the glass panel on which he stood shattered completely. In fact, Ramon very nearly went through into the maze of wiring and lights below. For the next hour and a half, our New Year's entertainment was provided by a precision team of sweating repairmen replacing the panel in our beautifully lighted dance floor.

A hundred unforeseen things can go awry with a brand-new ship. Even though none is of any great moment, they can be annoying. By the second sailing of the same ship most of the time these things will have made themselves known and been corrected. It's something to keep in mind when planning a cruise.

You should also be a bit leery about a ship which, though not brand-new, has come under completely different ownership. The minor difficulties here will not arise so much from the vessel herself, but from the staff and the crew. They will be new to the ship and very often new to one another. The thing that enabled us to make a possible disaster into an enjoyable adventure was that the cruise staff was already a team, and the crew knew each other. So we were able to switch what could have been the occasion for all-out bitching into positive, memorable fun. And the Italian food on the ship was the greatest. I never gained weight though because I never ate dessert. Oh, I learned to love that ship and I loved working with the Italians; I loved the Italian food. I lived on the ship for two years, but the first New Year's Eve I'll never forget!

chapter eleven

I Hope You Won't Take This Personally— But No, Thanks

My greatest surprise on going to work on cruise ships was the promptness and blithe good spirits with which the majority of the passengers who are traveling alone (particularly the women) and the crew members set off on their search for romance.

There's really no delay at all in starting this enterprise. When the passengers board, the chief members of the crew are lined up in the gangway lobby in a combination welcome and assessment ceremony. At the same time, the passengers are making their own inspections and considerations. The females are checking out the male passengers and the crew and the male passengers are looking for ladies who seem possessed of a roving eye.

Jeraldine introducing passengers to the captain at the Welcome Aboard Party (above).

Having fun playing "Get Acquainted" games with the passengers (left).

Jeraldine taking a break on deck—dance class starts in the Forward Lounge in five minutes (right).

This mutual weighing of possibilities continues during the first informal evening meal, when the waiters, barmen, and busboys first come into view. Liaisons are quickly made, and they are sometimes quite numerous. There's a fantasy I've sometimes indulged in that may help you get the picture.

In the Army, there was a precaution taken by company commanders when a sizable group of marching men approach a long bridge. When the company reached the span, the soldiers would be ordered to break step so that the rhythmic pounding of their feet would not set up vibrations that might cause the structure to collapse.

Similarly, I suspect there is an unwritten law that takes effect at sea, particularly on a cruise ship knifing through the phosphorescent water late at night, under a languid full moon in a star-spangled sky. There must be a subconscious "break cadence" order for the occupants of the cabins. Otherwise, to a passing liner, the cruise ship would be bounding along like a playful porpoise, even in a dead, flat calm.

Newlyweds and happily married couples rarely play the looking-for-a-new-partner game, but the game is by no means limited to the young crowd.

On one of my first cruises I was stunned when a sweet-looking elderly lady summoned me into private consultation on the deck when we were no more than a day at sea. "Jeraldine," she said in a soft voice, "I would like help in securing a supply of marijuana at the first port in Mexico and would you please find some sturdy young crewman and inform him of my availability and send him to my cabin?" She said she was willing to pay handsomely for both services if I could tell her where to find them. At that time, I didn't think either was available, but boy, did I find out differently as the months went on!

The instances in which the apparently unencumbered woman or man was not panting on the trail of romance is so rare it looms large in my memory. Often a passenger's intentions of remaining above all that came to naught. Obviously I remember much more vividly the very few times when a passenger manages to stay true to his or her convictions.

One passenger I remember quite well was a really gorgeous girl who would book herself alone for a ten-day Mexican cruise twice a year. She'd been doing so before I joined the cruise staff of this ship and I presume continued to do so after I left.

She didn't seem to suffer from any particular emotional hangups, took spirited part in the activities each day, drank her proper share but no more, and enjoyed the small social gatherings late in the evening, especially if they grew a bit ribald. Her name was Natalie, and she was the dark, exotic type; but she drew the line at any hanky-panky with anyone—passengers or crew. Nor was she demure about turning down romantic advances; she'd be coolly aloof, then downright furious if some character persisted in his attempts.

A bachelor passenger once complained to me about it. "I know she's no dyke," he said stubbornly. "What in the hell's wrong with her?" I had to confess that I didn't know—except that what he had in mind was obviously not Natalie's cup of tea.

Natalie was on two cruises where I served as hostess, then after a year the ship went into drydock for refitting and an engine over-haul. I had a much-needed month at home and one night I was invited to a gala ball to benefit a favorite children's charity. It was held at the Ambassador Hotel, the scene of my first appearance as a fashion model. I was having a marvelous time and during the evening I saw Natalie. She was with an English actor, famed for his ability, both as comedian and a tragedian, as well as an unshakable conviction that his private life was something important only to himself.

A man at our table saw me watching her. "Good-looking broad, isn't she?" he said. They moved on through the crowd and were lost to sight. "What does she do?" I asked.

"Who?"

"The girl with Sir Whosis."

"Joannie?"

"I think I've met her as Natalie."

He shrugged. "She's the most expensive and exclusive call girl in Los Angeles."

Well, I had to hand it to Natalie; when she took a vacation, she really took a vacation.

Oddly enough, the other two people not actively on the prowl that I remember best were male members of the crew, rather than passengers.

Captain Eugene Grayley was in command of a ship sailing the Caribbean. He was one of the most able of the captains I worked under (I use the phrase figuratively rather than geographically), and he had a great deal of style.

Captain Grayley was a handsome man, with such quiet authority that he had no need to go out of his way to impose it. He was wonderfully courteous and charming to the lady passengers, and the men too looked forward to a few moments of his time. He had a store of absorbing stories about life at sea and about his homeland in Europe.

He was devoted to his relatively new wife, whom he had met aboard a command he'd had in the Mediterranean four years before. It was a first marriage, rather later than most, and he seemed to be celibate except during those times when he returned home.

Of course, the female passengers drooled at the very thought of him. But he was so adept at putting them off that they couldn't get angry; they only frothed at the mouth a little less openly.

Except for one, whose name was Maryanne. She was very pretty, with the mating instincts of a mink, and a nice supply of ladylike cool. She was also very rich. This was a long cruise, and because my job is to make everyone comfortable as quickly as possible, we met early and became friendly.

We were talking one day, only a few days out of our originating port. Suddenly she asked, "What about Captain Grayley? What's with him?"

I told her something about his career and about his lovely wife, who had accompanied him on one cruise a few months before. I also told her he didn't play around. She smiled and didn't say anything more, but she went to work. A real challenge, she must have thought to herself.

This must be credited to Maryanne. Every available stud, as well as some not so available, was hot on her trail. She was seldom without a wake of clowns behind her. However, she brushed them off and, by laying a little loot on the proper palms, became a frequent guest at the captain's table. This is a privilege not easily achieved and I had to admire her technique. She neither fawned on her prey nor did she quite ignore him. She was frequently the center of laughter, in which the captain joined heartily. It was beautiful to see him enjoying himself.

This continued for several weeks—and several weeks were all Maryanne had, for she was leaving the ship at La Guiara, Venezuela. We were to arrive early in the evening and stay overnight so that the passengers could take a tour to Caracas, farther inland. As we disembarked, it appeared that Maryanne had spent a lot of money for preferred seating and had received nothing in return other than special attention from the maitre d'.

The cruise staff had been invited to dine that evening at an exclusive restaurant on the outskirts of Caracas. Our hosts were passengers, a most knowledgeable elderly couple who assured us the food was great and the orchestra even better.

They were right on both counts. And it turned out that the captain also knew of this remote spot and went there to be out of sight of passenger and crew. There they were—Maryanne and Captain Grayley—moving soulfully as they danced across the glossy floor. He forced a pleasant nod when he spotted us at our table, but he looked as if he wanted to fall through the floor. The two finished dinner and left.

Evidently, the captain sneaked the lady back to his quarters in the sacrosanct area behind the bridge on the ship. I know because the officers standing watch were most considerate. The captain didn't know that they had posted discreet little signs on his quarters door reading, "Quiet—humping going on," and "Sex fiend at work."

In the morning, the captain arranged privately with the chief steward for a large breakfast to be served in his quarters shortly before noon. Still later, he slipped his paramour out to the dock, confident no one would be the wiser except for a trusted few.

However, he reckoned without Maryanne. Back ashore, she started collaring the passengers as they returned from the tour bus, announcing, "I've spent the night balling the captain in his very own private cabin." Was she uninhibited?

When the passengers, never very reticent, saw the captain, there were naturally some comments. "A bit pale this morning, Captain." "Something you ate" and "Was she anywhere near as raunchy as she looked, Cap?" Most of the women became very cool toward their idol with feet of clay. Poor guy.

Then there was our third engineer, Arthur, who wasn't married. He was all man, but he had his sights set on a career as a marine engineer, and that was just about all that entered his mind. He was extremely cordial in his relationships with the passengers, but he spent most of his time hitting the books in his cabin or rapping with the chief engineer.

Maybe this self-imposed and restricting lifestyle shaped the events that almost cost Arthur his job. Whatever the case, the incident was set in motion because something was wrong with the turbines of the ship.

Ship's engineers are a strange breed. They can worry more than any living person. They all do the same thing when the ship is underway. They walk around, canted over to one side, listening to some sound no one else can hear, even though they may be talking to you at the time. They listen and they fret. Sometimes they straighten up suddenly, as if their worst fears had been confirmed, excuse themselves, and rush below decks. Maybe they're just going to the bathroom, but there are times when they don't reappear for days. However, the ship usually keeps plowing along, slicing its momentary furrow through the water.

Arthur's adventure began with an engine room problem which had been bugging the captain and chief engineer for a whole day. Finally, the decision was made to put in at a port where we customarily stayed only briefly, lay over until four in the morning, and by that time the chief engineer felt he could have the malfunction repaired.

Everyone applauded the idea. It would certainly remove any possibility of a really serious breakdown during the long leg to the next port. We were in a tiny harbor city, a very beautiful one, built at various levels on the steep mountain slopes that virtually surrounded it. And it meant an unexpected night off for the cruise staff.

As it turned out, an even better prospect lay before us. The important people of the town—the wealthy residents, officials, and the more prominent merchants—were delighted by our emergency. It gave them the opportunity to do some public relations and entertain the cruise staff and officers, so we were invited to one of the large estates in the mountains behind the port, there to drink, dance, and eat an elaborate buffet dinner.

Arthur, being a third and very junior officer, was not considered versed in the art of making a mountain out of a molehill, so instead of staying behind to help with the repairs, he was sent along to enjoy the festivities. He didn't like the fact then; he hated it later.

He wandered around our host's grand mansion, wondering aloud about the progress on the ship. Then, since no one else cared about the problem, he began to talk about walking up to one of the higher levels behind the mansion so that he could get a full view of the port.

I noticed that a very lovely, extremely quiet young woman had started to drift around after him. She was married to a much older, flamboyantly dressed rich man who commanded attention wherever he went, but she was not a forward person at all. She was content to remain on the fringe of the action, though usually with a drink in her hand. Arthur was also drinking heavily.

At this point our gracious hosts were getting into the actual purpose of the party. They felt it would be a fine idea if our good ship "Anything Goes" were to make this a regular overnight stop.

Their shops, restaurants, and nightclubs were splendid ones; they would do everything to make sure the passengers had a night to remember (even if it was only when counting their money the next day).

About this time, Arthur again proclaimed his intention of taking a walk, and the quiet young lady had a sudden attack of the vapors.

She asked Arthur if he would mind taking her home, since he was going for a walk anyway. Arthur said it might be too much for her if she didn't feel well. She explained that she had her own car. He could drive it; then, if he liked, he could use it to drive even higher in the mountains, which would afford him a far better view. He could leave the car at the dock when he returned to the ship and it would be picked up in the morning. So off they went.

A little before 3:30, the appointed time for boarding, the officers and cruise staff got to the dock, where we took tenders to the ship anchored in the harbor. The difficulty had been repaired. We could see steam pluming from her stacks in the brilliant moonlight that flooded the scene.

However, no Arthur. And no car.

For a crew member to miss his ship is a crime unsurpassed even by being prone to *mal de mer*. Either is just cause for instant dismissal without hope of recourse, but at least in the case of seasickness, others feel a little twinge of pity.

Everyone was sore at Arthur, but they were also a bit fearful. He was alone late at night in a waterfront city. Ugly things have happened under such circumstances.

Sailing time had passed, and we were just about to cast off when a small Mercedes whipped into the dock area, screeched to a halt, and disgorged Arthur. He was alone, disheveled, and still slightly bombed.

Nothing was said to him on the way to the ship. However, once aboard, he was immediately called to account by both the captain and his chief.

The next morning at breakfast I twisted Arthur's arm until he told me why he had almost missed the ship. The fellows on board all confide in me like a sister, and I was eager to know what had happened. After much pleading on my part he finally said, "Jeraldine, I'll never forget last night as long as I live."

"I drove this woman to her fancy house in the mountains. When we got there, she said that if she had a drink, she might feel better. They must have a lot of servants, but there weren't any around, so she poured two stiff drinks and we sat in this huge living room talking for a while. I finished my drink, and she refreshed it.

"When I had almost finished that, she had another attack and asked if I would help her to her room. I did. This room you wouldn't believe.

"It had huge, recessed windows overlooking the sea and in the moonlight that came through them, I could see the fancy headboard of a tremendous bed. What a setup!

"She literally ripped her clothes off and flung herself on the bed with her head back. Her hair came undone and went streaming out over the pillow.

"I took my own clothes off and climbed onto the bed beside her. I was pretty drunk, but not so much that I didn't realize she was angled the wrong way. I wrestled her around so she was parallel to the sides of the bed, and she didn't resist a bit."

"Arthur! What a night you had—tell me more," I begged.

"I hadn't missed sex much, but it had been a long time, and the animal in me took over. When we finished, I just fell over beside her. She was making sounds in her throat. Then all of a sudden she gave out a yelp. She had tried to sit up, but we had bounded around so much that her head had gone completely through one of the openings in the headboard! Lord, Jerry, what a spot to be in. By that time I was so weak and befuddled with booze that all I wanted was to lie on my back for a while. But she was stuck in the space behind the headboard. Her head was at an uncomfortable angle, and her ears hurt terribly. When her head had been jammed through the slit, if you'll pardon the expression, her ears could have been sliced right off and she wouldn't have noticed it but now they were killing her.

"I tried to figure out what to do. The biggest problem was that the headboard was made of cast iron, so there was no give at all. I tried pulling her up by the shoulders to find a wider opening, but even the widest wasn't good enough, since her ears were so tender. I found some cream in the bathroom and spread that all over her face and neck and on the headboard, too. I might have been able to wriggle her head out then, but at that point even the slightest touch on her ears was unbearably painful."

"Go on, tell me the rest," I said, tears running down my face. By this time I was holding my sides and screeching with laughter, and my ribs and jaws were aching from trying to control my hysteria.

"An anesthetic would have worked," Arthur went on, apparently undaunted by my laughter, "but there wasn't any around. I thought about knocking her out, but her chin was out of reach. Beside, by that time it was getting really late. I finally had to leave her there, Jeraldine, and she was sobbing. But I jumped into my clothes and raced back to the dock. I felt like a heel, but I didn't want to miss the ship."

Arthur wasn't fired, but we still tease him about that night. I've often wondered exactly how the young lady explained her predicament to her husband. Maybe when he finally got home, he was too smashed to notice. Anyway, I hope she didn't end up with a bad case of cauliflower ears.

chapter twelve

Mexico: the Land of the Conquistadors and Montezuma's Revenge

I HAVE AT LEAST 1,000,317 LITTLE TAG ENDS OF MEMORA-bilia from cruises in Alaska, the Caribbean, the South Sea Islands, the Mediterranean, and Scandinavia. My notes are stored in three very large packing boxes that virtually fill a big storage bin.

For instance, I have the daily dinner menus during an entire season in the Caribbean because their covers have extremely attractive reproductions of the old masters. How-ever, the one darn thing I cannot find would have made a good send-off for this chapter. It was a parody of the daily activities bulletin which is printed and placed under the cabin doors each night. This bulletin outlines what will be going on the next day, from early morning until late at night and makes a handy checklist for activities you may want to attend.

The witty man who made up the parody was a passenger. I cannot recall his name, but I do remember a few of the items he included in his timetable of make-believe events. For example, he noted that the "Drunk Walking Contest" would resume immediately after the "Start Your Heart" session in the main bar at 6:30 A.M. The photographer was going to be in the main reception area all day with photos of the activities of the previous night. Prints would be a dollar each but some negatives a great deal higher. The cruise director was going to conduct an advance seminar in bar check forgery, teaching people to sign their neighbors' names. There was going to be an afternoon dance, but the men were warned to bring their own partners, since the crew refused to go in drag before sundown. There was going to be an "After Dark Fun and Games" period during which a crew member would be thrown overboard; the ship would turn around and try to find him but a ten-minute time limit was imposed. It was suggested that everyone make an effort to occupy his or her own cabin that night; those uncertain of its location, check with the purser's office. The fellow who made up the list ended by saying that if you looked like your passport picture, you needed a vacation.

The Mexican cruises that originate in Los Angeles at the port of San Pedro are delightful ways of taking a holiday. The west coast of Mexico is recognized as the Riviera of the Americas and a cruise is not very hard on your purse.

The cruise ships that originate in Los Angeles don't usually stop at Ensenada or La Paz, the two major ports in Baja California. That area is bursting with activity and new vacation resorts. Most ships make directly for Mazatlan, Puerto Vallarta, and Acapulco. Those three stops in two weeks offer enough to satisfy anyone. Most passengers wish it were longer.

The Mexican sun is hot. If you are not used to it, take it in small doses, just as you would an infrared or UV lamp; if you don't, you may end up in the hospital. Take sunscreen, a hat, a long-sleeved shirt, and covering for your legs, particularly if you intend to do any fishing. This is a hard rule to follow; extra clothing is a nuisance and the Mexican climate can be so lulling you think you will never need long sleeves. But take time to study the Mexicans themselves. They never run around half-nude, and it's not modesty but common sense.

The Mexican *siesta* does not mean that Mexicans are lazy. The siesta means Mexicans are smart. When you see someone dozing in the shade, *serape*-wrapped and wide straw sombrero pulled down, remember he's been working since the crack of dawn, and after this respite during the worst heat of the day he'll return to work until dark.

Montezuma's Revenge is cruel, but amoebic dysentery isn't a wholly owned subsidiary of Mexico. It plagues people throughout the world, particularly in the tropics. The culprit is usually untreated water or unwashed fruits and vegetables. Eat them only if they are cooked.

The ship's doctor can provide quick-acting relief. If you're ashore and there isn't time to get back to the ship (there never is), Mexican pharmacies sell Entera Viaforma as a preventive; or if you already have it—and you'll know when you have, because you will be walking funny—get Lomotil. It works like liquid cement.

However, prevention is the best cure—don't drink the water. I always order the *agua minerale* (mineral water) and they say bottled Mexican beer is excellent. But remember, ice cubes are made of water too!

It would be a waste to visit Mexico on a cruise and not return with some of the things they make so well. These articles are more expensive than they used to be a few years ago, but they can still be marvelous bargains.

Allow me to digress a bit. Mexico is the world's largest producer of silver, and no one does lovelier work in it than Mexicans. The government is a very diligent supervisor of all traffic in silver. Every item fashioned of silver will be plainly marked with either "sterling" or ".925," and sometimes both, along with the silversmith's hallmark; ".925" means that for each 1,000 grams of weight, the metal contains 925 grams of pure silver. This is just about as pure as silver can possibly be worked.

Of course, your own taste will have to govern your selection from the enormously varied silver artifacts that are available. Personally, I am a bit critical of pieces inset with stones. Mexico is not noted as a producer of precious gems, and silver requires a great deal of care— silver polish can be detrimental to semiprecious stones.

Mexican basket work boggles the mind; it's so intricate and varied, and Mexican cottons are great. Mexicans make wonderful-looking clothes for women. Their designs never seem to wear out or go out of style, and the embroidery is beyond compare.

Men's serapes are available everywhere. They're very colorful, made of both cotton and wool. The equivalent for women, the *reboza* (scarf or stole) is a useful garment. Mexican women employ it to carry their enchanting brown-eyed babies, or to protect themselves from a sudden shower, or to lug packages. The reboza comes in a variety of styles, material, and weights, and you can find a hundred uses for them at home. I tie mine around my head as a turban after swimming.

For men, the *guayabera* jacket is a must have. It is a light shirt-jacket worn outside the trousers, and an acceptable substitute for a sports jacket and shirt. Well tailored, very cool and comfortable, the guayabera is made in many intricate designs and several of them should be among your first purchases. You won't regret owning them because they are great to wear on board ship, too.

The Mexicans are excellent leather workers and their thonged sandals and huaraches never seem to wear out. I bought a pair and wore them for years until I lost them when a wave knocked me over. I was rescuing passengers on a live reef in Bora Bora during a tour—we scrubbed that tour from our agenda immediately.

Bypassing the whole of Baja, California, the first part of the Mexican cruise, is comparatively long and akin to ocean voyaging. You will find yourself out of sight of land most of the time, but there is plenty to do aboard ship and the passengers seem eager to know one another as we head for the first port, Mazatlan. The cruise staff goes all out these first few days of the cruise, providing activities to help everyone get acquainted.

The first morning at sea when the passengers come to the "Welcome Aboard" talk we also had a "Get Acquainted" game. Each passenger is given a bingo-type card with blank spaces to be filled in by other passengers. We pick out names from a basket that holds the names of all the passengers. Everyone has fun going around the ballroom, asking complete strangers to sign their card. This is always a great icebreaker.

On one cruise we wondered why we didn't have any names called that were on the cards. I whispered to the assistant cruise director, "Good heavens, Toby, what on earth is going wrong here? This game has been going on for so long and we haven't had one winner yet." The mystery was solved when we realized we had cut up the passenger list from the previous cruise!

When we would reach Mazatlan, I often wished I didn't like swimming so much. The water is like crystal and the North Beach rivals the one at Waikiki. The waters teem with fish and it is one of the best deep-sea fishing areas anywhere. But where there are fish to eat, there are sharks to eat them. I am poo-poohed, tut-tutted, and openly derided for being chicken but I just cannot work up any kindly feelings about a shark. I didn't usually swim at Mazatlan, but everyone else did.

Mazatlan's El Indio is a fine place for silver and gold and lovely gifts. I love to shop there and sometimes I just ogle the beautiful things.

"Fiesta Nights at the Hotel Playa" in Mazatlan was a night tour offered by one of the best cruise ships on which I worked. We really had to do some selling for this dinner tour because passengers could eat on the ship free. The Playa Hotel was a sumptuous place with a vast dining room at its top, affording a view of the whole city and harbor. They served copious tequila drinks and excellent food. I remember little tamales, green chilis done in a light cream sauce, and frijoles with beef prepared over open braziers. The orchestra played infectious music and everybody got stoned and really had a ball. Wild, really! The Playa Hotel knows how to put on the best Mexican show in all of Mexico.

Occasionally, a small group of passengers would complain that they never liked Mexican food and insist they be escorted back to the ship. I would make the smiling suggestion that they have a dipperful of a special refreshing lemon drink. I told them it would get the dust down and maybe settle the problem. I didn't say the "refreshment" was a Margarita served in a goblet the size of a horse trough. When they found out, they didn't care any longer.

Our assistant cruise director, Paul Lorenz, a great guy, had just joined our ship and this was his first Fiesta Night.

"You probably won't need me tonight, will you?" he said. "I'm not much of a dancer and maybe I should stay on board and work, Jeraldine."

"Oh," I assured him, "you're a big, strong fellow and there will be plenty for you to do."

Paul downed a couple of giant Margaritas, sampled some of the great food, and decided he was Fred Astaire. He asked all the single women to dance and kept hollering "Viva Mexico!" (He eventually became a very good cruise director.)

When it was time to round up the passengers and load them in the waiting taxis, I would have to make sure we had all of them because the ship sailed at 1:00 A.M. I checked the restroom and I found one woman. I called to Paul, "Come help this lady, she has passed out on the floor of the restroom."

Dutifully, he carried her down the stairs and put her in a taxi. "Jeraldine," he said, "I like this job, but I wonder if my back will hold up?"

At this fiesta, sometimes passengers would go skinny dipping and they had to be rounded up too. One lady found that the most fun she'd ever had in her life was swinging on the great woven-reed *piñata*. When we returned to Los Angeles, she was on the dock waiting. She'd missed the ship, and because she was without a passport or any other identification, had been thrown in the Mazatlan jail.

Getting back to our fiesta night, the taxi brought the woman who had passed out back to the ship, but we couldn't get her to tell us her cabin number. It was late, we all had to get up early for work the next morning and we were becoming very impatient. One last time we screamed at her, "What is your cabin number?"

She was starting to come to and sober up a bit. Slurringly she said, "Cabin number? I don't have a cabin number. I'm staying at the La Playa Hotel!"

Puerto Vallarta is three hundred miles, more or less, south of Mazatlan but much more tropical in feel and appearance. When I visit Puerto Vallarta, I wish I had time to paint. There's a picture at every turn, winding dirt roads with bougainvillea spilling over ancient brick and stone walls, tiny burrows moving steadily along under mountainous loads of seining nets, wood, reeds for baskets, and board-stiff steer hides intended for the saddlemakers and the huarachi cobblers.

Puerto Vallarta is, I guess, my favorite place in Mexico. It's charming and still a small town. Few people knew about it until they filmed *Night of the Iguana* there starring Elizabeth Taylor and Richard Burton back in the 60s. Actually, the movie was shot in Mismaloya, seven miles south of town. Now there is a lovely hotel there called the La Jolla Mismaloya, a corner of paradise.

I was escorting a tour of our ship's passengers across Puerto Vallarta's bridge. We stopped to look at the local Mexicans as they washed their clothes by pounding them on the rocks in the riverbed below. One passenger remarked, "Jeraldine, look, they have hired extras to put on this show for us!"

I replied, "Those aren't actors, those are the locals and that's the way they really wash their clothes." Can you imagine, she thought it was posed!

The town of Puerto Vallarta is in a bay called Bahia de los Banderos, which sounds like it is named for bandits. To give you an idea of how the folks around there once regarded life in general, the most beautiful beach used to be called Playa de los Muertos, or "Dead Men's Beach." Since the coming of the tourists, it has been changed to Las Delicias.

Both the jungle and the town tumble down steep hillsides to the beach. The streets are narrow and cobblestoned, and the sidewalks are steps carved into the rock or fashioned of stones. Along the winding streets the villas are old and secretive, presenting an impersonal facade to the passerby. There is hardly any motorized traffic, but saddle horses are both reliable and available, so take a morning's ride into the mountainous back country. I have a friend who has one of the most beautiful and unusual homes I've ever seen anywhere in Puerto Vallarta. It's called "Casa Guillermo."

The cruise staff usually gets together one night in Puerto Vallarta and splurges on a Mexican dinner at one of the romantic outdoor restaurants with only jacaranda trees and stars for a roof. We eat wonderful fish dishes, and wonder about the ghosts of the dead men for whom the beach was originally named. Some will feel like they are going to join the dead the next day if they slip up and drink the water.

Acapulco is, well, it's Acapulco! I've been a lot of places. I keep wondering why I ever go anyplace else. I would guess Acapulco is the western terminus of the International Set because it absorbs famous people so effortlessly.

It lies deep in the tropics, of course, and the wide strands of white sand stretch endlessly in both directions from Acapulco Bay, broken only occasionally by cliffs that rise abruptly from a divinely colored sea. The harbor, seen at night from our ship, must be the most spectacular in all the world (except maybe Rio). It's either the Mod City or the Mad City—I'm not sure which—and maybe both!

You won't find a better place to learn to water ski because the experts who teach you work in pairs. The training skis are of a special very buoyant construction, so if you fall—and you will—you just float, hanging on to a ski, until the boat swings around, hauls you back to shallow water, and you start all over again. I've known rank beginners who were giving a good account of themselves within fifteen minutes and after an hour lesson you'll have it made!

Members of the cruise staff with some rare time to themselves like to go by taxi to Puerto Marguez Beach, south of the main section of the city on the road to the airport. A tiny sailboat called a *bolero* can be rented, along with a young boatman to navigate it, and it is heavenly to go skimming along with the gentle swells of the bay. It's not very chic, so most passengers don't go there, and since we don't have to be charming, we can relax. One day we couldn't get a taxi to the ship, so we rode back on a Mexican bus and laughed when we all ended up with live chickens on our laps and rain pouring in on us from broken windows.

Far to the other side of Acapulco, at the base of the crooked peninsula that forms the northern rampart of the large bay, is the Hotel El Mirador. It is here that the brave diving boys hurl themselves from the Quebrada cliffs in a beautiful arcing dive toward the boiling sea more than a hundred feet below. This is a must see.

I'm not going to carry on about hotels in Acapulco because your ship is your hotel. There are many hotels, all beautiful, but none more beautiful than Las Brisas, and you should make a point of seeing it. Or maybe you shouldn't because you might try to hold up a Brink's armored truck so you could live there forever. It lies above the scenic drive on Puerto Marquez, all bungalows of pink and white, each with a private pool. Attentive waiters tool around in tiny pink Jeeps and carts, steering with one hand while they hold aloft cartwheel-sized trays loaded with linen-covered goodies. As if this weren't enough, there's a splendid beach club. And, adjacent to Las Brisas, my friends, Sara and Ben Manasenn, built some unique and fabulous homes. Believe it or not, only the bedrooms have walls and the spectacular ocean view is the backdrop for all the other rooms. The Princess Hotel is probably the ultimate in hotels, and another must see. It is really spectacular! Here is another swimming pool where you can sit at the bar while still in the pool and wet your whistle at both ends.

There's so much to do and see in Acapulco that cruise ships always lay over at least two days.

The wildest place was the Paradiso Restaurant at La Condesa Beach, only a little way from the Acapulco Hilton. The Paradiso opened around noon, and the fuzz insisted that it be closed by or immediately after sundown. They couldn't very well allow the things that go on there in the daytime to continue after dark.

The Paradise Club, as it's also known, is directly on the beach, with a thatched roof covering the large dance floor, a bar that produces strange potions, and an orchestra that plays tropical music hotter than the sun. Everyone who goes there is dressed for swimming, which means that they have virtually nothing on. The Mexicans are modest, but not the tourists who frequent this place. Beautiful girls seem drawn here because they really receive a most unusual welcome.

The cooks, dishwashers, swampers, waiters, busboys, musicians, and management of the Paradise Club all have a deep appreciation of the female form, particularly when it's mostly all hanging out. Therefore, when a gal wearing a wisp of a bikini enters, the waiters all drop their great tin trays to the floor with a crash, the musicians beat the tar out of drums and tom-toms, the busboys slam utensils around and whistle, and all hell breaks loose. This pandemonium of appreciation of her pulchritude is might heavy stuff for a gal to handle. There have been those who have tried to earn an even greater response by taking everything off. How different from the U.S.A. where a look or a whistle could be considered harassment.

Anyway, the couples dance, down their drinks, form themselves into conga lines, dash down to the surf for a cooling dip, and return to repeat the process. The barbecued shrimp and the red snapper are out of this world. They serve a whole fish to one person— eyeballs and all. We tell the passengers not to miss this fun place.

Jeraldine conducting the Acapulco tour. The passengers enjoyed the Mariachi music, especially well-known film actor Coby Denton (center).

There were also a couple of great discotheques in town that never seemed to close. Boccaccio's was my favorite. They gave everyone a tambourine and at midnight they turned off the lights and gave everyone on the dance floor a dish with a burning candle in it. You should try the candle dance sometime. It was a beautiful sight.

Emi Fors is the Perle Mesta of Acapulco, a lady who knows everyone and gives parties at her home high in the mountains overlooking the harbor. Everyone she wants to invite goes to Emi's. She has a way of knowing who is in town and, if they are celebrities, they end up at her parties. She has invited me on several occasions to attend her galas, but I've never been able to accept because night tours and the early morning Taxco tour required my attention.

However, on the day before Christmas several years ago, she invited me and several of the cruise staff to attend a Christmas Eve party. The ship was scheduled to sail on a proper tide at two that morning in order to keep its schedule. On board we had a Christmas Eve show, and we did our best to hurry it along so it would be over in time to make some part of Emi's party before the ship sailed. When the show was over it seemed ages while we waited for the launch to take us ashore.

When we got ashore we found that Acapulco cab drivers had their own idea of Christmas. It did not include driving a cab bursting with passengers to the top of the mountain and waiting around to bring them back to the dock. We were desperate but we finally backed one driver into a corner, and after crossing his palm with *mucho dinero*, talked him into taking us, and more importantly to wait for us—but then again, he was half gassed.

It was a lovely looking party, with all of Acapulco gleaming far below through wide windows opened on the soft night breeze. Emi had just announced the dramatic moment of the evening. She had put on this party to raise money for some Mexican orphans, and she had the lights turned off as they came out of hiding upstairs and sang Christmas carols as they walked down the stairs carrying lighted candles.

There was going to be dancing, lovely music, and beautiful people—but we could stay only five minutes before we had to turn around and go back, or miss the ship and get fired from our jobs.

I did manage to see some of the celebs, but when we ran out to get back in our cab it was gone. Gads! We would all miss the ship and be fired for sure this time! Desperate, we ran back to the party and pressured some poor man into squeezing us all into his tiny sports car and taking us back. Whee! Bless him, whoever he was.

I was never able to work up a love affair for the Taxco tours, even though I conducted them every eleven days for more than two years. I always had to handle the nightclub tour the evening before, made up of the spirited element who like to contribute to the overall merriment and profit of Acapulco night life. Those who opt for the Taxco tour are a much hardier breed, up at five in the morning, bright-eyed and bushy-tailed, and ready to tackle the buses that will grind their way over the mountains. My job was to explain that the air-conditioning system doesn't always break down and, if one suffers from vertigo, one shouldn't stare down the cliff sides. It was not my favorite assignment but the Taxco tours are a profitable item for the cruise company, and the cruise director made me chaperone them, so I had little choice except to go along and keep up the morale.

One time we all had to get off one of the older buses so the driver could back and turn in order to get around a hairpin curve. One of the lady passengers stood beside me, watching.

"Jeraldine," she said, "do you make these trips often?"

"Once every eleven days," I told her, as a couple of small boulders hurtled down the five-hundred-foot cliff.

"Well, you certainly don't value your life very much," she snapped.

Taxco is a quaint, picturesque, and intriguing town four hours inland from Acapulco over that tortuous road. It is a return to life as it was lived a century ago in most of Mexico, with cobbled or dirt streets narrow as alleyways. There's just about room for one person on either side of a burro and another on top of the tiny beast. Taxis must take over the hauling of our guests from the bus, and then they make their forays on the shops afoot.

The work of the silversmiths here is incredibly beautiful. The native artists create simple lines, but they produce works in the English and Swedish manner that rival the work from those countries. Remember, there are four more hours to be spent on the return drive to the ship. This time we hope the brakes hold instead of hoping that the motor doesn't fail. I often wonder what Taxco looks like when one doesn't have over 200 passengers complaining to them and one has had more than three or four hours sleep the night before.

chapter thirteen

THE BAND LEADER AND THE QUARTER-TON LADY

THE CRAZIEST, FUNNIEST, AND MOST HEART-WARMING EXPE-
rience I have had in all my years of sailing occurred on a
Mexican cruise and it took one whole season for the slap-
stick romance to play itself out.

The cruise ship was crewed by Italians, and the cruise
staff was mostly Americans. There were two orchestras as
part of the entertainment, along with dancers, singers,
comedians, etc.

Like the passenger list, we were quite an international
group. One of the orchestras was Mexican; the other, Italian. Both were talented and capable of fine musicianship.
The only difference was that the Italians were temperamental and wild. They didn't drink any more wine than the
others and I don't think they were on pills or pot or anything like that; they were just natural-born madmen.

The leader of the band, the head nut, was a stumpy, good-looking horn player whom I shall just call Red. He had a love-hate relationship with his sidemen and they all had love-hate relationships with one another. They were virtuosos who had been beaten into a single unit, and they seethed under the restraint. There was usually no conflict while they were playing; they played as one and they made really great music, but when they put their instruments to one side at the end of a set it was "Katie-bar-the-door."

Red wasn't very big, but he had an explosive temper and he was really strong. I remember some cock-eyed decision regarding the music came down to us from our land-based home office. Since it directly affected Red and it didn't make much sense, we expected him to blow his stack, but he took it calmly, which was more surprising than if he'd ripped off the afterdeck and tossed it into the wake.

Each night following dinner, there was music for dancing and a floor show in the grand ballroom. After the first dinner sitting, passengers would move into the ballroom and enjoy the music while the dining room served the second sitting. Then, the show would begin. On this particular evening, about halfway through the second sitting, someone came up to me in the dining room.

"Jerry," he said, "there's no music in the ballroom so no one can dance."

"Well, tell the musicians to play something," I suggested.

"Oh, they're playing. But you can't hear anything," he explained.

I went in to check. Except for Red, the musicians were on the stand, apparently playing, but they sounded like a transistor radio when the battery has had it.

The intricate arrangements played by Red's orchestra depended on amplification. This was supplied by several carefully positioned microphones that fed to two speakers standing on seven-foot wrought-iron pedestals. This equipment was used for the entire show, but it was owned and specially designed by Red—and it was not there. Evidently he had disassembled the whole intricate system, carried it to his cabin four decks below and locked himself in. Do I need to tell you that the changes in procedure from the home office were never carried through?

Usually, Red's reactions were much quicker and more direct. There were two dining rooms on the ship, the smaller one used for luncheons, midnight buffets, and the evening meal of the cruise staff and entertainers. The food was elegant. We could sit over our shrimp scampi or beef au jus or oysters Rockefeller and compare notes about the days' experiences with the passengers, who were eating in the main dining room.

One night, the assistant cruise director was getting off some pretty good jokes when, with no warning at all, a large plate flew through the air, struck the velvet paneling on the wall, and left bits of salads dripping down on the dance team seated below. Then we heard screaming and shouting in Italian, and Red was jumping up and down beside his orchestra's table. We figured it was pretty serious this time. It seems dinner had included generous servings of escargot—our Italian chef could prepare snails better than just about anyone in the whole world. Red had asked for a second serving and had been refused and that was the whole problem! Pow! Bam! Crash! Just like in a cartoon strip.

The orchestra members used to have fights below decks after the night's work was over. A couple of them would show up the next evening with Covermark disguising black eyes. Oddly though, the horn players never came up with bruised lips or the guitarist with busted fingers as a result of these melees. Living so closely and being together twenty-four hours a day it is almost like living on a submarine. Talk about propinquity!

Only once did the orchestra interrupt a show by exploding into action. That happened after midnight toward the end of the season, when everyone's nerves were on edge. They'd been playing beautifully, the couples swaying, dreamy-eyed, to the dulcet rhythms of a Jerome Kern medley and a few lovers remaining at the tables, toying with drinks and whispering to one another.

Suddenly there was a tremendous crash of cymbals and bass drum, and all seven of the musicians were fighting. They were hitting one another with their instruments, but the guitarist and the piano player were using their fists, so it was serious. They fell off the platform, climbed up again, and got knocked back off. They yelled Italian obscenities, which sound terrible even if you don't understand them.

Then the fight erupted onto the dance floor. No one tried to stop it—they just got out of the way of flying objects. The musicians rolled around and out through the big open doors that led to the swimming pool and fought some more there. Then it stopped. I've no idea why, nor was the reason for the battle royal ever explained. One minute they were trying to kill one another, and the next they were sitting around the pool gasping for breath. One by one, they got to their feet and resumed their beautiful music. They really were very talented and very Italian.

The next day after lunch, the athletic director did tell the battered Red that if he'd wanted to stop the dancing, he could have just as easily had the boys play "Good Night, Ladies" or "Auld Lang Syne." Red accepted the remark in good grace, but he didn't volunteer any information, either.

Maybe they fought over the fat lady. It's possible.

Her name was Felicia. She first boarded our ship on the initial cruise of the season, a woman so grossly huge that she supported herself with a cane and one of those three-legged aluminum affairs used by the very old or disabled. Her girth took up the entire width of the gangway and she inched herself along grimly until she was on deck.

It was impossible to tell how old she was. Her features were lost in rolls of flesh. Her hair was very black and carefully coiffed. She had engaged one stateroom for herself alone and there had been some advance preparations made for her.

When I appeared in one of the lounges to give a lecture on charm and grooming, she was settled on a settee at one side of the room.

Years as a busy fashion model have left me with a lot of lore about the beauty game. I love sharing what I know and fitting it to special needs. I talk generally about clothes, makeup, diet, and health habits; I also give tips on how to carry oneself whether walking or dancing or doing such a simple thing as sitting down or going up and down stairs. Every one of these moves has its secrets, and they can be very helpful.

Felicia was a most attentive listener, but she did not join in the general discussion that always follows one of these sessions. However, the next morning she was overflowing a steamer chair on the promenade deck and called me to her side when she saw me.

She had a perfectly lovely voice with no trace of an accent, and she also spoke liquid Spanish and fluent Italian and French. She was a real Californian whose family had come to the Los Angeles area from Mexico long before the United States was even coveting the California territory.

She said she had found my talk most interesting and asked for further details on the special diet I had mentioned. I told her it was one I had designed myself in keeping with unorthodox, advanced medical theories. I explained that people who tend to gain weight are biochemically challenged. They can't utilize refined carbohydrates correctly. There aren't any illnesses caused by a lack of carbohydrates, but the lack of protein can cause harm. The purpose of avoiding refined carbohydrates is to keep the blood sugar on an even keel. It's also a great way to keep your energy up at all times.

Felicia looked at me doubtfully.

"I spoke to my waiter about you," she said. "He says you eat like a horse."

"You tell your waiter I eat like two horses. He's probably seen me at breakfast, lunch, and dinner. I also eat between meals, from morning to night, and I never miss the midnight buffet. It isn't how much you eat, it's what you eat that matters."

She didn't believe me, of course, but she asked if she might have a copy of my diet. I arranged for one to be sent to her cabin.

Felicia attended my lectures regularly and she also struck up a firm friendship with Red and the members of his orchestra. She loved music and they played beautifully. When we went to Mazatlan and Puerto Vallarta, they gathered at her table in the nightclub and sat talking with her in Italian. At Acapulco, she took them to a grand luncheon at one of the most exclusive restaurants in the whole city, the Rivoli. She also bought them all exquisite Mexican shirts, which they wore that night for the show. Back in Los Angeles, the orchestra was invited to Felicia's home for luncheon when we had a few hours in our home port

Two cruises later, Felicia booked passage again. She was not noticeably lighter in weight, but she was depending only on the three-legged crutch this time. Her face was beginning to come alive and it had promise. She told me she was adhering very closely to my diet and feeling a great deal better.

The battling Italians were overjoyed to see her, but she had greater freedom of movement so she spent more time with some of the passengers, who learned that she had a great store of knowledge and a ready, kindly wit. I enjoyed talking with her when I had the time, and she was curious about my astrology and palmistry lectures.

This time, in each of the ports Felicia took the orchestra to lunch or dinner. She bought them things and, not to be outdone, they banded together and bought her things. She seemed to have no interest at all in tourism.

For the rest of the season, Felicia cruised with us at least once a month. Each time, she was lighter in weight. First, the three-legged "helper" was abandoned for a cane; then the cane was left behind. When it finally appeared, her face was a very lovely one, finely chiseled, with large, dark eyes and a flashing smile.

Mrs. Red will never be really skinny. Her normal weight is probably about 140 pounds or so, not bad on someone who is about five foot six.

Yes, she married the bandleader at the end of the season. Red broke up the group after the last cruise, and the musicians may be making life lovable and miserable for their own bands by now.

It would be nice to say that Red is living off the fat of the land somewhere in California, but it's not true. Felicia, who is still following my diet, is only slightly stocky and very attractive. Red's fiery temper has been sublimated into a warm, glowing love for his former Quarter-Ton Lady.

Jeraldine boarding the Niew Amsterdam, *the
flagship of the Holland-American Lines.*

chapter fourteen

HAVE BUTTERFLY
NET—WILL TRAVEL

JUST WRITING ABOUT RED AND HIS SYNCOPATED SCREW-balls brought to mind some of the other ding-a-lings we had aboard at times.

There's almost always one way-out loveable nut on each cruise. It can be a he or a she, young or old, it doesn't seem to matter. In my memory, they never caused scenes or discomfort to other passengers; they just remain sort of unreal, like Dali's paintings of wavy watches and sharply bent fried eggs.

In the world of sameness and the organization man, it's refreshing to have a unique passenger on board, if for no other reason than to give the cruise staff inspiration for laughs at mealtime.

In some cases we agree that wealthy families find cruises a far less expensive way of caring for a nutty relative than paying the bills at a private institution. Cruise ships are remarkably reasonable if you think of what is given in exchange for the money paid. The quarters are luxurious and scrupulously kept. The food is the best, very carefully prepared, and elegantly served. The entertainment is varied and constantly available: night club reviews, the latest films, athletic games and contests, and discussions, lessons, and lectures by celebrity guests. Those who are sent on a cruise by their relatives are among the most fortunate of people, even though they may be somewhat addled.

One of the most unusual was a fellow who boarded our ship for the South Sea Island cruise. He was a distinguished looking man nearing fifty, who must have bought his accommodations on an impulse, for he arrived in the purser's square without any luggage. He carried the proper papers and tickets, along with a wallet stuffed full of money. He'd evidently been tailored on Saville Row; his tropical-weight suit was beautifully cut, his shirt dazzlingly fresh, and his Panama straw hat the kind that is expensive. However, he wore neither shoes nor socks and though he did not walk like a drunk, somehow he seemed loaded to the edge of stupefaction.

Let's call him Mr. Wilber. Cruise ships can refuse passage to anyone who seemed to promise potential disaster, but Mr. Wilber was so utterly charming there was never a question about his acceptance.

For four days, this man was the life of that ship! He was handsome, a warmly gracious host, and a charming conversationalist with a brilliant wit. He could not pad down the deck, barefooted, without being stopped a dozen times with the glad cry, "Hey, Mr. Wilber, join us."

He was not—repeat not—on the prowl for female companionship. He drank sparingly, though constantly, and there was much speculation about whether he ever went to his very small cabin, which he occupied alone. According to the watches and the night stewards, he stretched out on a deck chair under the stars for a couple of hours of sleep.

I can't remember which port we visited on the fourth day, but he went ashore with the passengers. He did not sign on for the sightseeing tour, so he was not seen until he returned to the ship. And when he returned he was sober—very, very sober.

Sober, Mr. Wilber recognized absolutely no one. Former buddies would clap him on the back and say they'd missed him ashore. He looked right through them as though they must be mistaking him for someone else. Ladies who had sought his company would approach and he'd stare at them coolly and wander off in another direction. We found out that he was a doctor, having trouble with his wife back home. For the rest of the cruise, he slept in his tiny cabin each night, ate alone, and stayed sober. When we docked he was the first ashore, having straightened up his accounts early and owning no luggage. Was Dr. Wilber pixilated? Just drunk? Or, as the English would say, potty? I'll never know.

There was another man, a smiling little round fellow, who constantly heard music. And he conducted it just like Arturo Toscanini, with attention to the proper entrance of the brass and the fiddles and the reeds. When he did this in the nightclub and one of the bands was playing, it was really quite nice. He'd jump around a lot, wiggling his fingers at instrumentalists, jabbing a forefinger to signal a solo, or staring up in rapture and delicately keeping time as he evoked some particularly lovely passage. However, he went through the same gyrations on the sundeck or beside the pool and there was nothing to be heard but the splashing of water. That could be a little disconcerting. Always smiling, he walked along the alleyways day and night, keeping time to music only he could hear.

At the party that marked the end of the cruise, he was elected by the passengers and cruise staff as the person who was "Most Fun to Have Aboard." He accepted this accolade with a modest speech, a shy bow and said, "Whatever you say I have done for you is nothing compared to what you have made for me in my heart." He gestured with his hand over his heart and I handed him a trophy. He turned and led an unheard fanfare—but this time we heard it!

Then there was the gal we nicknamed "Happy Bottom." The name started with the cruise staff but it was picked up by the passengers, and they renamed her "Fanny." She was a cute girl who must have owned a very big suitcase containing nothing but underpants—panties of every color, fabric, and design imaginable which she changed frequently.

This was because she loved to put them on public display. "Happy Bottom" always wore a fully gathered mini-skirt or a micro-mini-skirt, and it didn't take much to prompt her to lift it up to display her latest change. You could be standing at the rail (it was better if there were some men in the deck chairs against the bulkhead) and comment to Fanny, "My goodness, but look at the sunset." Fanny would yank up her skirt, and say, "Wow!" Any excuse would bring up the full skirt.

Fanny didn't dance with her partners, but opposite them. In order to get the proper freedom of movement, she had to hold her wee skirt up as she cavorted about. Strangely enough, she didn't seem to be in the least promiscuous. She got her jollies by showing off her panties. Many passengers got their jollies, too.

I also remember a man who was even stranger and more hipped on clothes than "Happy Bottom." However, his addiction extended from the top of his head to the soles of his feet. From southern California, Max was a large young man with an enormous black walrus mustache, a luxuriant head of black hair, and very pale skin. He shared an expensive stateroom with another man he had not previously known.

By the time Max got all of his luggage moved in, there was hardly room for his cabin mate to hang up a toothbrush because Max had the most outlandish collection of clothes seen anywhere in this blue-eyed world. His headgear ranged from Russian caraculs to Western sombreros. His jackets were made of fur, bottle caps and imprinted buttons sewed to burlap, woven metal cloth, overlays of exotic feathers, and elaborate crochets and crewel work. They all fitted beautifully. His pants were flared and skin-tight, of silk, leather, suede, cashmere, and fine broadcloths. His shoes were an incredible assortment; he even had a pair that had curled-up toes in the Turkish manner with tiny wind chimes suspended from the ends of them.

The minute the cruise staff became aware of this cuckoo, we had an ad hoc meeting. How in the world could we manage to integrate him into our relatively conservative passenger list? We were really feeling sorry for him, thinking no one would talk to him and he would be our burden.

But maybe Max wasn't so all-fired cuckoo after all. Everyone on the ship wanted Max to dine with them, have a late snack, play cards, go to the shows, have a swim, play deck tennis, accompany them on a tour, get drunk, shoot craps, play bridge, gamble on the horse races, play bingo—you name it. Max changed costumes almost as often as "Happy Bottom" changed panties. He'd even disappear from the dining room between the entree and dessert to get into another outlandish getup. His wardrobe cost him a fortune in both money and imagination, but he got a lot of mileage out of it. The ship's photographer almost made a killing. Every one of the passengers wanted his picture taken with Max. It would be the only proof they'd have for the folks back home; otherwise no one would believe such a man could exist.

Come to think of it, clothes or the lack of them seem to be common manifestations of aberration. Certainly costume parades, always a very heavy item aboard a cruise ship, were a study in mass hysteria for passengers and staff alike. They also served to disclose those with hidden desires. People change slightly by donning different hats but put them in a completely kooky costume and they really become uninhibited.

We may have more than 200 men and women dressed for a costume parade, all trying to become most original, most outlandish, or most beautiful. The cruise staff tries to make a professional production out of this, always without success. The contestants mill around on deck, getting off highly hilarious remarks. We try to line them up in some sort of order, listing number, name of contestant, and what they want to call themselves. The orchestra leader is standing by so the proper music can be played when each contestant makes his or her appearance to walk around the dance floor.

The cruise staff may be trying desperately to organize but these are vacationers who have no intention of being organized. They're having fun, and mad confusion is an essential ingredient of their vacation spirit. In my rush to prepare the costume participants' list I'm frequently slowed down by unexpected remarks.

*Top executives let their hair down on board
one of my favorite ships, the Noordam.*

Me, to a lady wearing a vast assortment of beads and bangles: "Name, please."

Contestant: "Oh, Jeraldine. You know perfectly well who I am."

I look up from the list.

Me: "Oh, hi, Mrs. Thromtiddle. What have you called yourself tonight?"

Contestant (coyly): "Can't you guess?"

Me: "No, darling. I know it's something very clever."

Now Mrs. Thromtiddle turns to the horde awaiting their turn to register. They are all invited to guess. More highly hilarious remarks. The show will be late if we don't hurry so I'm going out of my mind. She finally confides she represents some TV character. But the cruise staff never heard of this character—we never have time to see TV. And so on, ad infinitum, ad nauseam.

Occasionally, a passenger is nice enough to make it easy. Once, a man in line was wearing a robe with a ribbon on which he'd printed his name plus his title, "Peter Pan." I thanked him and wished him good luck. When his turn came, as the orchestra played a selection from the Mary Martin musical, he took off his robe. He was wearing nothing but a tin pie plate affixed in some fashion to cover his privates. Peter Pan indeed! The passengers, who always pick the winners, named him "Most Original Costume" by acclamation.

Another time, a lady registered for the parade in a terry cloth robe and said she was "Miss Nothing to Wear." There was general bedlam, and I should have suspected something, but I didn't. When it was her turn to show her costume she took off her beach robe and paraded around, naked as a jaybird. One shocked lady objected that there were children in the audience. The unclad contestant retorted, "Well, that's their problem, not mine." I don't recall that she got a prize, but flashbulbs were flashing until someone had the presence of mind to haul her off.

And I'll never forget the cruise when three executives from the head office came on board. These fellows would spend their evenings listening to our very talented singer-musician in our beautiful lounge with its high glass windows looking out over the shining sea. The entertainer was Valerie-Jean Hume, who sings and plays the autoharp superbly. These execs were captured by her talent and the atmosphere of this lounge.

One evening, however, they went partying after her show. One of them awoke the next morning, still in his tux, far from his own cabin. Sunlight streamed all around as he quietly gathered his disheveled self together to escape back to his own quarters. Suddenly, he remembered a secret door to the theater that could help cut time, distance, and visibility in his sneaky journey. He tiptoed down the alleyway, pressed the secret door, stepped through, locked it behind him and turned around—to find himself on stage with a priest, right in the middle of morning Mass!

chapter fifteen

ROMANCE, MUSIC, AND MERCHANDISE

THE HISTORY OF THE CARIBBEAN SEA IS STUDDED WITH violence. Smugglers and pirates like Hawkins, Morgan, Le Vasseur, and "Peg-leg" Le Clerq ranged the sapphire waters, raiding under the flags of various nations or the skull and crossbones. Drake, Penn, Raleigh, Venebles, and Heyn laid waste full-rigged merchantmen with cargoes of precious metals and rare spices. The slave trade flourished; the islands provided a hundred thousand hiding places on the approach to the North American slave marts.

The nations competing for the wealth of this new land established footholds in the Caribbean, and their imprints are still strong. Off the northern coast of Venezuela, Aruba, Curacao, and Bonaire have extraordinarily trim and orderly ports with tall, narrow, neatly kept buildings packed side by side along the quays. This is the Netherlands influence. The Dutch were looking for salt to use in packing the fish they caught back home; they found the salt, and some lovely islands in the bargain.

French is the language of St. Bethelmy, Guadeloupe, and Martinique; and of course Spanish is the language of Cuba, the Dominican Republic, and Puerto Rico. The natives of the far-flung string of islands from the Bahamas off our Florida coast clear to Trinidad, only a few miles from the northeastern-most tip of South America, can spout as elegant an Oxford accent as someone strolling down Saville Row in London.

As a result, a Caribbean cruise is a whole bunch of experiences rolled into one, but the outstanding impression will be the music and dancing, if you're anything like me.

All sorts of cultures have combined themselves in Caribbean songs and dances. The African influence is strong, but modified by Western cultures and restrictions.

Because the use of jungle drums (a basis of tribal and voodoo rites) was banned, the steel drum was developed. These instruments are fashioned from fifty-gallon oil or syrup barrels. The sides are left long for a bass range, shorter and shorter as the instrument approaches the high tenor. Then the steel head itself is carefully hammered so that different tones can be created by banging different spots on the round pan. A band of a dozen steel drums can create explosive and compelling musical effects. American and European dance forms are invitations to the feet alone; the music of the West Indies makes you want to dance all over, from the hair on your head to the very tips of your toes.

If you embark on a Caribbean cruise from Europe or one of our seaports on the Eastern Coast, you will of course miss sailing through the Panama Canal. Our cruises originating in Los Angeles called first at Acapulco, allowing a visit to that lovely place, then entered the Canal from the Bay of Panama.

The Panama Canal is a startling experience. The approach is through stunning blue water amid an encirclement of beautiful greens of every shade. The day is spent almost entirely on deck, and luncheon is served there. A government lecturer boards our ship at the crack of dawn and relates the history, the politics, and the engineering marvels of the building of the canal. Passengers can hardly force themselves away from the railings of the ship because there's not a moment when there isn't something going on. Captains and pilots maneuver liners, tankers, and vast cargo vessels to take their turns entering the long series of locks. Ship's bells ring and whistles toot, adding their contribution to the melange of sound. We have to give repeated warnings about sunburn on this day because the time seems to go so quickly you don't realize you have been out and exposed so long. A bad sunburn can ruin the rest of your cruise.

If your ship stops at the Panamanian city of Colon, a shopping expedition is in order. The commerce that flows through the Canal is from all over the world, and so are the offerings of the shops. They can be fabulous buys: beautifully embroidered linens and cottons; transistor radios, computers, video cameras and tape machines; appliances of great ingenuity; jewelry and perfumes; beautiful little trees, flowers and figurines of jade.

But a few words of warning. These cities are not safe for a woman at night, and the favorite method of purse-snatching is to snip the straps of a handbag and race off with the bag itself. There are a lot of houses of ill repute and a lot of poverty, in Panama City especially.

And this is a good time for another word to the wise. The winds of freedom are blowing through the Caribbean islands you will visit, in some places even more briskly than the ever-present trade winds. The people guard these new-found liberties jealously. It is not only mannerly but intelligent to preface a request with "please" when shopping or ordering a meal, or even asking directions. You'll be glad you did.

The first ports we visited were Aruba and Curacao. Willemstad is the capital of Curacao, and it is a remarkable little city. Dutch Colonial buildings face the Breedestraat, a busy avenue on the water. There is an enormous refinery near the city that processes Venezuelan crude oil, and the town runs like a well-oiled machine. A beautiful club and small resort hotel overlooks Piscadera Bay and is worth a visit. Vendors have their carts and staffs lined up under the prows of ships that are nosed into the berths along the waterfront, providing a shaded and unusual background for a stroll.

The Indonesian food in both Caracao and Aruba is an epicure's delight. Spitzer and Ferman operate fabulous jewelry shops in both places—I love looking at their expensive jewelry. The clothes, especially in Willemstad, are unique. One of the best establishments there, Devi Devi's, wouldn't think of allowing a customer to walk out with an improperly fitted garment. They have as many as thirty tailors and seamstresses standing by for the feverish activity that goes along with the ship's stay in port. Devi Devi's is in the alley behind Spitzer and Ferman's.

Barbados has turquoise water, and beautiful Paradise Beach seems to shelve forever toward the distant horizon. It is possible to swim for miles, touch down and feel sand as smooth as powder beneath your feet, stand up and find yourself in five feet of water. This is not advised for people who are four feet tall. I got a bad surprise once when I stepped into sea urchins there. That did hurt! Both my feet were completely covered with black spots where the urchins' spines had broken off. It was so painful that I could hardly swim back to shore. I was alone so I asked the natives at a soft drink stand on the beach if they knew what to do and they said, "Oh, yes, mom, you need soft wax candle."

"What is that?" I asked.

"Here, we have some right here. Come sit down and we will show you how it works, you can't pick them out or they just break off." They then proceeded to light the soft wax candles and let the hot wax drip on my poor aching feet.

Well, forget it! That hot wax treatment is worse than the pain from the sea urchins' spines! I thanked them and told them I couldn't stand it anymore. I hobbled over to a taxi and asked the driver to take me immediatly to the emergency hospital.

As we were driving along he said, "You know it's closed today, it's Sunday."

Good heavens, I was going out of my mind with pain. I explained what had happened to me and he said, "Don't try to pick them out or they break off!" Then he said, "Oh, my cousin has something that will take care of that. He lives near here, would you like me to take you there?"

"Heavens, yes," I screamed, "I can't stand the pain!" When he got to his cousin's house he ran in and came out with the cure. Soft wax candles!

So as not to hurt his feelings I said I would use them back on the ship and asked him to take me there. When I got to the ship's hospital I showed the doctor my black spotted feet.

"Oh," he replied, "come sit down and I'll try to pick them out!"

I said, "Thanks, but no, thanks." He never before encountered sea urchins. Next, I went to the assistant cruise director's cabin for help, but he was ashore, too. I left a note for him to please help me as soon as he returned. I wrote that I would wait for him in my cabin. Well, I waited and waited and then it was time to start the evening's activities. I couldn't get my shoes on so I wore beaded elastic things that just went around the ankle down the top of the foot and around the big toe. I forced myself to smile at the passengers as I hobbled around on my heels. I wore pretty chiffon palazzo pants, so no one much noticed my plight.

When I saw the assistant cruise director I said in bewilderment, "I really needed help—why didn't you come help me? Didn't you see my note?"

He replied, "Yes, I saw that note and when I saw how you spelled sea urchins, I got so f—king mad!"

I felt stabbed in the heart to think he wouldn't help me just because of my stupid spelling.

The next morning we docked in Martinique and I hobbled over to another doctor's office. He gave me some salve for my feet. No help. The following morning we were in Haiti so I again hobbled over to another doctor's office. I'm afraid I lost my faith when I saw the dirt floor and a chicken on his desk. He gave me antibiotic powder to put on my feet; the only problem was, it wouldn't stay on. Besides, I knew I didn't have an infection, I just had sea urchin spines in my feet, hundreds of them. The next morning we arrived in St. Thomas. I hobbled over to the big hospital there. The only help they offered was a tetanus shot. I didn't want one so I told them I'd already had one. I hobbled back to the ship. As the days wore on I guess my body absorbed the spines because eventually they went away.

A doctor on the last ship I was on told me that a ship's doctor needs to keep an exotic medicines book on hand. He said, "A passenger came back from a swimming party ashore and was writhing in pain from being bitten by a stingray. I had to give him massive doses of morphine but absolutely nothing touched his pain. Finally, after more and more morphine and no relief at all, I decided to look in the exotic medicines book. Applying hot water was supposed to be the cure for stingray bites. Questioningly, I tried it. Like a miracle the passenger felt immediate relief and his pain went completely away."

I remember so many of the experiences we had at distant ports— like the one in Cartagena, Colombia. We tried having a nightclub tour there one night. I say "one night," because we never wanted to try it again. The show was so corny and the drinks so bad that I had to hide in the ladies room at the club, locking the stall door and standing on the seat of the toilet so the passengers couldn't find me. I was afraid they would lynch me for spending their money on this tour. I stood up there until I felt the buses had taken all the passengers back to the ship; then I peeked out carefully to make sure it was safe and that no Godzilla was lying in wait for me. I took a cab back to the ship and hid until everyone had been given his money back.

When I complained to the people who put on the tour they were so embarrassed at having presented such a poor show they refunded the money. In addition they came on board the next day and entertained us with an authentic native dance show, free. It included some of the most agile dancers I've ever seen and everyone was happy again.

chapter sixteen

WATCH OUT FOR THE WATCHES IN TRINIDAD

TRINIDAD IS A WHOLE NEW SCENE. UPON DOCKING, THERE can be as many as five steel bands playing while groups of fellows and girls dance to the strange beat. We had a darling talented young singer named Cindy Hunter with us on one cruise, and when she was disembarking for the first time in Trinidad she burst into tears; she was overcome by the thrilling welcoming music.

Of all the Caribbean islands, I nominate Trinidad as the swingingest and most romantic place of all. While most of its sister islands have been strongly influenced by a single European culture, Trinidad is the Caribbean version of the United Nations. Americans, Spanish, English, Scots, Welsh, Germans, French, Italians, Swiss, Syrians, Lebanese, Africans and East Indians—more than a million inhabitants in all live, work, love, and play on this southernmost island of the Caribbean Sea.

Here, 700 miles north of the equator and only seven miles off the coast of Venezuela, this polyglot population pours out its woo and woe in the enchanting melodies and rhythms of calypso. It pours out the dregs from fifty-gallon oil drums, originally from those left behind by our World War II Seabees, and creates hauntingly beautiful steel band music on the empties. Calypso and other steel bands are heard throughout the entire Caribbean now, of course, but Trinidad owns the patent on both. Nowhere will you hear more original, more polished performances of these captivating forms of music derived from such diverse cultures.

Oh! the Caribbean, how passengers love to shop there, but I remember two who didn't. They fell in love when we were doing our season in the Caribbean. Their romance was not a fantasy but the real thing. Before they met, each said they wanted to see the island of Trinidad, so I arranged separate transportation for each of them. The man, tall, slender, and good looking, was Gordon Douglas. Douglas left the ship first and soon thereafter the lady when her taxi arrived. I told each of them to have a good time as I helped other passengers to board the buses for the shopping tour.

How would you like to have a song composed "on the spot" and sung to you by a talented Trinidadian, all against a backdrop of radiant foliage and dazzling sea? This romantic happening, worthy of the finest Old World troubadours, charmed Gordon, who later told me it is one of the most flattering things he's encountered in a lifetime of travel.

The taxi in the Port of Spain drove him ever to Maracus Bay, one of the loveliest, and loneliest, beaches in the Caribbean. Trinidad is a very hilly island and the road dips and sways over rolling green landscape from the harbor to the far side of the island. Maracas is truly a honeymoon haven, hidden from the rest of the world.

Gordon told me he wanted to see as much as he could in the eight hours the ship would be in port. However, he couldn't resist the brilliant flora and spectacular views at almost every bend of the road. A mile or two out of town, Gordon said to his driver, "Oscar, stop at a roadside pullout so I can take a quick look at the waters below." Obligingly, Oscar slammed on the squeaky brakes near the edge of a promontory. Gordon had hardly emerged from the vehicle (a battered old Chevy) when two black men sprang from the surrounding brush. But Gordon wasn't about to be mugged, he was about to be serenaded.

The pair, armed with guitars and smiling broad grins, approached Douglas. The spontaneity and originality (and you might add, salesmanship) of what followed left him slightly agog. The composer-lyricist of the duo, his partner accompanying him on a well-worn guitar, strummed a calypso beat and sang the following song extemporaneously to our hero:

> *Sir, I sing my welcome to you*
> *In your lovely shirt of blue.*
> *You stand so straight and fair,*
> *Just like a U.S. millionaire!*

Realizing that he had fallen into the makings of a dandy travel feature story, Douglas whipped out his notebook and started scribbling furiously. The singer, with hardly a full note rest after the first stanza, immediately continued with:

> *And, Sir, I'd like to tell you this,*
> *You look exactly like a journalist.*
> *An' furthermore, the smile your face upon*
> *Make you look just like James Mason.*

Without straying from the musical pitch, the calypso man went into another kind of pitch, the final verse of his song, which ended:

> *...I hope the gentlemen will keep me alive*
> *with a crisp, brand-new U.S. five.*

Ah, yes, always the commercial. Enchanted though he was by the flattery and originality of the whole scene, Gordon Douglas was of

Scots ancestry and no Scot is going to tip a calypso singer five whole dollars. Remember, this happened when a crisp new U.S. five still bore a resemblance in value to the portrait of Honest Abe on its face. So Gordon, in keeping with the spirit of the occasion (and keeping a close eye on his wallet), composed a verse of his own as he climbed back into the cab:

"You have the wrong millionaire, son, I'll keep you breathing with a U.S. one." With that, he dropped a dollar bill into the singer's outstretched hand and grinning his thanks, waved farewell. Oscar sped off up the winding road, his engine coughing and sputtering, on the way to further adventure.

The drive from Port of Spain to Maracas Bay is no more than fifteen miles. But to Laura Thompson, the pretty and youthful school teacher from Spokane, in the other taxi, the trip was like a miniature world tour. Indian mosques sparkled in the noonday sun, residences with tiled roofs showed the Spanish influence, on other dwellings the shutters or wrought iron accents or weathered wooden balconies reflected the architecture of other lands. Entire villages were crammed with residents of Chinese descent.

Laura oohed and aahed at the landscape, entire hillsides of orange pumice, the great pui trees with their six-inch, trumpet-shaped yellow blossoms, variegated silver hibiscus seldom seen elsewhere in the subtropics, many-hued oleander, flamboyant trees festooned with flowers, and flaming red poinsettias. The poinsettia, usually blooming only at Christmas in the U.S.A., knows no season in Trinidad.

Laura told me later in the cruise that, despite the beauty surrounding her, she couldn't take her mind off the first thing she saw as she went ashore that morning. It was a handsome man's wristwatch that she was tempted to buy on the spot.

The dockside vendor said, "I'll give you a special price of $25 because it is the last one I have. My wife wants me to come home. She's sick. And I can't leave until I sell the watch and have money for her medicine. Besides, you know what an Omega sells for in the United States. I wouldn't sell so cheap but I need the money."

It would be nice, Laura thought, to make a gift of it at the end of the cruise to that nice reporter with whom she had struck up the semblance of a shipboard romance. He had gone out of his way to be nice to her, to ask her to dance, to tell of his travels to other corners of the world and to rescue her from a persistent, obnoxious male passenger with more sex than culture on his mind.

Meanwhile, in the taxi a few miles ahead, the nice reporter and Oscar were communicating well. "Pity you not here for Carnival," said Oscar. "The island, she go mad."

Pre-Lenten Carnival time is when Trinidad gets its heaviest invasion of visitors. It throbs and sways with calypso, steel bands, voodoo drums, feasting, merrymaking, and romance. But, as Laura Thompson and Gordon Douglas separately were discovering that day, Trinidad is colorful any time of the year. Besides singers who pop out of the underbrush to extemporize at the drop of a dollar, small boys lurk at many a turn in the road to proffer their own exotic wares. Oscar slowed down for a hairpin curve and a youth thrust a handful of nutmeg pods through the open window. Douglas tossed back a quarter and pocketed the red, marble-sized fruit.

At the next curve stood a tiny, pleading vendor laden with huge grapefruit picked from a nearby roadside tree. Again, Oscar slowed. "Hey, boy. Drop 'em in," cried Oscar. The youth obliged by plopping three into the car, gladly grabbing the fifteen cents that Oscar thought was a fair price for the fruit. If, later, the tiny grapefruit vendor consulted his competition down the road, he would probably decide to go into the more lucrative nutmeg pod business.

Oscar fished a Boy Scout knife from his array of tools, cut open one of the pink-fleshed delicacies, and Douglas and he happily slurped their way to the top of the mountain.

Here, the trade winds blow cooler, and cocoa palms and bamboo shade the tender cocoa pods coming to maturity on pocket-sized plantations. Large black and yellow birds wing in and out of pendulous, teardrop-shaped nests in the aptly named bird nest trees.

The taxi laboriously crested the mountain, unfolding a grand, beautiful panorama. Slowly, the car wound down to a seven-mile stretch of road paved by the U.S. Seabees during World War II. At its terminus, seemingly the terminus of the world, a half-mile crescent beach was guarded by jungle headlands. Tall palms rustled and the slight surf foamed on the clean, sugary land. A solitary couple snuggled on a straw mat in the afternoon sun, happily oblivious to everything. Here is where the off-duty cruise staff comes for privacy and a chance to unwind before being on their best behavior again.

Today was no exception. I had taken a lift here from the local land tour operator. Douglas walked by the palm tree I was resting under and I yelled, "Hi, isn't this a beautiful place?"

He was glad to see me and agreed it was truly a heavenly beach.

"Are you here alone?" I asked.

"Yes," he said.

"Would you mind giving me a lift back to the ship when you are ready to leave?"

"I certainly would just love that," he grinned.

Douglas surveyed the peaceful scene. Then he took a few photographs, and said that Maracas was easily the equal of any beach he had seen in Hawaii, or elsewhere for that matter. "Why the solitude, Oscar?" he asked.

"Only on Sunday many people come here for picnic. But, no tourists. Too far from everything, so you have it all to yourselves today."

"Why didn't you bring Laura, the girl I saw you dancing with last night?" I asked Douglas. I had seen them on the open deck last night and they seemed to be enjoying being alone to gaze at the stars that appeared to dip down to human reach.

"Yes, I should have brought her," Douglas agreed.

Then it was time to get back to Port of Spain, perhaps do a bit of shopping and make it aboard by the 6:00 P.M. sailing. Oscar urged the taxi over the ridge, and we careened downward, negotiating turns with tires screeching and horn honking. No time for vendors now.

"I don't think maybe these brakes too good," worried Oscar. "They cry going down hill."

Despite the uncertainty, the brakes, and the rest of the Chevy, made it down the long, exciting hill. Soon, Douglas and I were deposited on Frederick Street, where the melting pot population of Trinidad again manifested itself. An intersection roundabout reminded me of England's traffic patterns. A helmeted "bobby" as well as the nearby Anglican church helped to complete the picture of a tropical, languid London.

Trinidad is an interesting place for shopping. The population is a great stew of different nationalities, and there is a large colony of people from India. They were first imported as indentured slaves by the French, who were then in control, and promised land if they survived a five-year period of slavery. The East Indians survived the slavery hardships somewhat better than the Chinese and Portuguese who were also caught up in the scheme. Today there are Indian shops where you can find the most beautiful saris imaginable. I think they are one of the most flattering and practical styles a woman can wear. Gordon wanted to buy something nice for Laura but concluded that at this stage of their romance, a sari might be considered too daring. He was, after all, a conservative guy, playing it cool. He settled for a small water color of Maracas Bay that he found in a gallery run by Roy Galt, and we headed back to the ship.

Unknown to us, Laura Thompson had traversed practically the same route as had Gordon and I. She and some other women had lingered for a swim at Maracas and had no time for shopping on their return to town. Cruise ships don't wait for any laggards ashore.

Later, Laura told me that she was still pondering the wristwatch that she'd seen earlier as she was hurrying toward the gangway, when the same vendor who had approached her that morning emerged almost magically from the dockside throng and called to her, "Lady, I still have the watch, you like to buy it now?" He handed it to Laura for her inspection. When she hesitated, he poured on his final pitch, "Business no good today. I still need to buy medicine for my sick wife. I give you very good special price. Twenty dollars. Twenty dollars for a Omega! How can you go wrong? Your man will love you!"

Laura said she was just about to succumb when her school-teacher thoroughness prompted her to fish her reading glasses from her purse and examine the face of the watch more closely. Her gasp of disbelief turned to momentary anger then, sighing in relief, she handed the watch back to the waiting vendor. "It says O-M-E-C-A," she told him with a smile, "shouldn't that 'C' be a 'G'?"

Without a word, the vendor retrieved his fake luxury timepiece, turned, and melted into the crowd.

The 6:00 P.M. departure was a fortuitous one, because Trinidad reveals its seamier side after nightfall. Gordon, Laura, and the others who had gone ashore that day might have been less impressed had they been exposed to the waterfront dives and what passes for night-clubs in Port of Spain. Drugs and sex are peddled openly. Still, the music of the steel bands and calypso singers in the club makes a visit worthwhile. On other cruises if we didn't sail until midnight, the more adventurous of the passengers would insist on doing some-thing after dinner. The only available night clubs on shore were a couple of real low-down dives which had great music, fully equipped B-girls, pimps who could make the arrangements, peddlers of drugs, and the rest of the attractions of waterfront bars. We were always honest in describing these places, but added that if we stayed together it was safe. It was a rare chance to see the seamier side and we told them slumming is the thing to do in Trinidad at night (and it is). This was like offering catnip to a bunch of Siamese kittens. We often had to form the eager applicants into three or four groups so that the clubs wouldn't be inundated. Passengers would join in the limbo dances, competing with topless girls and muscled boys as they slithered under a limbo bar held not far above the dance floor. Sometimes our passengers would get drunk and noisy and careless about their money—and declare the next morning they never had a better time in all their whole born days.

But back to our current hero and heroine. I met Laura and Douglas as they hurried up to the main deck after freshening up in their cabins. Aft, on the fantail, the Carib Steel Band, fifty drummers strong, was playing songs of farewell to the ship, its passengers, and crew. Most of the passengers lounged against the ship's rail or relaxed in deck chairs, drinks in hand, as they were serenaded. Most, that is, except the bridge foursome I had spotted at their customary table in the lounge at 9:00 that morning, wheeling and dealing in their non-stop tournament. I had learned about bridge by now. The first cruise, I had named the wrong tournament winners. I thought they were going to hang me, draw and quarter me, and then throw me over the side while doing some kind of ritual dance. Bridge players are smart, intelligent people, but I was so surprised when I learned they take their game very seriously!

As sailing time drew near, the Carib Steel Band stood, bowed to the applause and filed down the gangway to the dock. There, they reassembled and stood at attention. Precisely at 6:00 P.M., as the equatorial sun began its daily dip into the deepening blue horizon, the ship's whistle gave a mighty farewell blast. The last of the hawsers holding the vessel to the dock was hauled aboard. Imperceptibly, our beautiful, joyful, passenger-laden ship started its drift away from shore and toward the awaiting sea. At this dramatic, romantic moment, the steel band struck up "Finlandia," one of the most stirring renditions of music that I have heard anywhere, anytime. I have thrilled to Sibelius' masterpiece by symphony orchestras and it has been sung in schools and by innumerable choirs, but never had it moved me as it did now. I still get a lump in my throat when I think about it. It makes me wonder about the tremendous spirit of man, able to take some discarded steel drums, rework them, and then give us this heavenly music.

I looked down the ship's rail a bit and saw that it got to Laura and Gordon, as it did to me and others also—tears running down their cheeks, they waved fervent thanks and farewells as the ship faded slowly away from the music and the lovely shores of Trinidad.

This emotion-filled event did not move the bridge foursome, literally or otherwise. Oblivious of the inspirational moment they were missing, they stayed at their battle stations as they had all day, skipping the shore excursion, the music, the magic moment of departure, but doubtless not missing a trick.

Oh, well, different cruises for different uses, different strokes for different folks. Some passengers sign on a cruise to eat and sleep, others to read all the books they've meant to read all their lives, still others try to drink their way around the world. Some, of course, find the Love Boats the perfect place to pursue sex and use the ship as a giant, ocean-going waterbed.

Later that evening, Laura told me that she and Gordon met on the promenade deck and as they strolled in rhythm with the sea, they exchanged stories of their day ashore. Unabashedly, Laura said she had told Gordon of her near purchase of the phony wrist watch. Then she said Gordon recited from his notebook the custom lyrics sung to him on the now distant promontory. When she remarked about the beauty and solitude of Maracas Bay, she said Gordon excused himself momentarily and returned with her small gift, the water color. Her eyes sparkled with delight as she told me this and I could sense she was in love. She asked me to read her palm and yes, she had a long-lasting marriage due very soon.

Not long ago, I received a nice note from Laura Thompson Douglas. A few months after the end of the cruise, they had married. For their honeymoon they had gone back to, where else? Maracas. She never did say what kind of wristwatch she gave her husband as a wedding present. Nor did she say whether they heard the Carib Steel Band again. If they did, I'll bet these words, which could apply to Trinidad as well as Finland, still are music to their ears:

> *Where candid skies and waters blue aglowing*
> *Come from above, their tribute to pay, and*
> *Nature's God is beauty rare bestowing,*
> *May it endure Finlandia for aye.*

chapter seventeen

Resistance to Tyranny

North of Trinidad lies Grenada, southernmost of the Windward Islands, and what I consider the most beautiful spot in all the Caribbean. I think Grand Ansa beach is the most beautiful beach in the entire world. Strung out above Grenada are the Grenadines, scores upon scores of islets and reefs almost always within sight of one another. There are so many coves and inlets that smuggling is very simple and isn't considered very hot potatoes as a crime. I'm told that is one of the reasons liquor is so cheap in the area. On every cruise to the Windward or the Leeward Islands a dozen passengers will always be busy with fantasies about buying one of these little islands for some sure-fire way of making a fortune.

Barbados lies over the horizon to the east from St. Vincent's in the Windwards. Its capital is Bridgeport, and the town reflects its British heritage with narrow, ordered lanes between hedgerows of gaily flowering shrubs and small, well-kept manor houses something like a typical English countryside. The Barbadians, like the Grenadians, are friendly people, not at all inclined toward surliness, as are some of the others in the Caribbean. Like Grenada, it is a relatively quiet place and its beach is a splendid one.

I'd rate the Virgin Islanders as medium sullen, but its city, Charlotte Amalie, is the place to shop. There's a little place in Creeky's Alley where you can buy blouses, shirts, and carvings made in Haiti at real bargain prices. This alley also has the best designer shops.

I won't go into the details of Haiti. The memory of the poverty there is too painful for me. Puerto Rico has virtually everything you probably took the cruise to get away from: television, radio, condominiums, tall buildings, lots of traffic. However, there are more than enough compensations so you can overlook the annoyances. The natives are very friendly, and the island has an undercurrent of excitement and optimism that is contagious. Puerto Ricans are talented and adaptive people who know how to handle any situation. Years ago, when San Juan was overrun regularly by buccaneers, the citizens would head for the hills with their valuables at the first sight of freebooters' sails on the horizon. If they couldn't arrange a ransom for the city, they would wait until the inevitable dysentery drove the raiders off.

The pleasures of San Juan are not those of the distant past but of the present. Of course old San Juan is now almost completely restored to its former picturesque state, but the modern arts in all their forms loom large among the activities of the islanders. Drama and the dance are performed regularly by superb troupes. Painting, sculpture, and the poster arts are boldly imaginative and there are constant showings in the city's galleries. I have seen some of the world's most talented Spanish dancers in the clubs in Puerto Rico.

The joys of traditional Puerto Rico are not far away, either. The hill country begins only a few miles out of San Juan. At night, the air is heavy with the unforgettable scents of night-blooming jasmine and frangipani, and resounds with the clatter of insects and the sounds of toads and frogs. At dawn, while the perfumes still linger and the sun breaks up the towering rain clouds into lovely puffs of white, the birds take over and sing their brains out for an hour or so.

Jamaica, favored though it may be by awesome mountains and forests, lovely beaches, and handsome towns, wins the Sullen Sweepstakes, especially Montego Bay. When I was last there, Kingston was actually dangerous. Shopkeepers were closing their stores at four in the afternoon in order to get home before dark.

The feeling of the Jamaicans toward visitors was typified one afternoon when a large group of our passengers took a land tour in Montego Bay. The group required three big buses, which were supposed to be air-conditioned, but the equipment had failed through neglect. The passengers were supposed to be driven to Ocho Rios, a trip through the most scenic parts of the island. I decided to take a taxi and catch up with the tour to make sure our passengers were treated right and given the full tour.

As I drove by the local tour office on a small square, the buses were still sitting in the broiling sun, the passengers near heat prostration in the pitiless glare. I had the cab stop and got out.

I didn't dare go directly to the buses and confront my passengers. They would have handed me my head. Instead, I went across the street into the bus tour office in one of my courageous, red-headed temper moods.

There were eight Jamaicans seated in the shade inside the office, with revolving fans blowing the air about. When I entered, they merely looked at me, not stirring from their chairs.

"Have those passengers been sitting out in those hot buses for more than a half-hour?" I screamed.

"No doubt," one of them said without expression. I knew I was outnumbered and I didn't want to hang around another second.

When I got to the buses, the passengers were furious and with ample reason. No explanation had been offered, nor had they been told of any place where they could wait in some comfort. They were still chewing me out ten minutes later when the drivers finally did appear.

Actually, we shouldn't wonder why these recently freed people act this way; after being dominated by the British for so long their favorite saying is "I'm a free mon, mon." I'm sure the Irish sympathize with them—after all, they know the tyranny of British rule. Who was it who said, "Resistance to tyranny is obedience to God?"

It's Nothing but a Hangnail, Doctor, I don't Need a Pelvic

SHIPS' DOCTORS ARE CAST IN THE SOMEWHAT LARGER THAN life adventure-romance mold.

They are by no means the same, but they have a certain kinship with the rest of the men who become ships' officers: a liking for the unusual as opposed to the expected, and faraway places rather than the familiar by-ways of home. Or it may be these medical sailors are not turned on by the ownership of a Jaguar or they play lousy games of golf. You can be certain of one thing: the ship's doctor will be a skilled practitioner of his science, with a special talent for surgery under less than ideal conditions. He is an employee of the ship's owners and keeps an eye on the health of both passengers and crew. Frightful accidents can overtake seamen, either because of the violence of the sea, or the enormous power under control in the engine room. The owners of a multimillion-dollar liner, the life of which is in the hands of the crew, are hardly going to entrust the care of these men to an unqualified person.

The ship's doctor is an officer of the ship. His working quarters generally are composed of an office and examining room, a small surgery, and a hospital with beds for patients who need constant attention. He is generally assisted by two nurses (male or female) and on some of the very large cruise liners, there may be a second surgeon and four or five nurses. As happens with all doctors, most of the emergencies seem to occur at night.

On some ships, when it comes to bookkeeping, the ship's doctor is his own boss. Should a passenger's needs require services beyond the ordinary, the doctor is free to make his own arrangements with the patient. On some ships his fees are apt to be quite reasonable. However, someone whose health would benefit from an ocean cruise, but who would need special skilled medical attention, should complete such arrangements with the company and the ship's doctor ahead of time. In that case, the doctor may have to supplement his medical stores. Only the Army and Navy run real hospital ships.

But strange things can happen in the antiseptic world of the ship's surgery, the residence of a strange species I call the "white-coated medicine bird."

This critter can be identified by its mating call of "I assure you nothing will happen to you but pure pleasure," murmured in a low, comforting tone.

Usually these birds aren't married, and halfway through some cruises the hungrier dames have gotten to the stage where they're ready to chase the waiters up the stacks. So the medicine birds may feel they have a right to strut around the aviary a little.

Dr. Frith, our ship's doctor, had been assisted by two nurses, who were extremely proper and well along in years. Both nurses left the ship at the same time, though for different reasons. One got married and went to live on land, the second had a daughter who had become ill and the nurse, a very nice woman, felt it her place to care for her daughter and her grandchildren.

The company had been prepared for the one who got married, but not for the loss of the second nurse, so on the trip following their departure, Dr. Frith was aided by only one new nurse, a big, dark-haired girl with a rather long but attractive face. Her name was Lucille. A young Italian fellow who was normally a busboy was pressed into service to do clean-up work in the surgery and examining room. He was called Willie by the cruise staff because his name was Guilliermo, and he was trying desperately to learn English.

The selection of Willie for the job was not just a happenstance. He had been a pre-med student in Italy but had been forced to drop out of school because of lack of funds. He had no intention of returning to his studies—his ambition now was to become a head waiter.

Lucille turned out to be just exactly what the doctor ordered— for himself. You must have heard of couples who look at one another in a way that says as loudly as words that they can't wait to get their hands on one another. One evening this need apparently became too much to bear, at least for Lucille, because she told Willie to keep an eye on things for an hour or so. She was going to be otherwise engaged. Willie asked where Dr. Frith could be reached in case someone came to the surgery complaining of illness. It appeared that Dr. Frith was also unavailable for this period.

The nurse was supposed to be on duty, but she had a way out of that cul-de-sac. She set out two large vials of pills and told Willie that since he didn't speak English and so wouldn't be able to understand any of the passengers—we had only American passengers on this cruise—that he could help them if he would watch where they pointed on their bodies. If the complaint was about a headache, they would be pointing to or holding their head and the medicine in one vial was to be handed out; if it was an abdominal problem, they would be pointing to their abdomen and the pills from the other vial were the ones to give. In this way the passengers wouldn't realize that he didn't understand a word they said.

Unfortunately, the first caller at the dispensary a half hour or so later was a passenger who really had a pain in the gut. In the meanwhile Willie had kind of lost track of which bottle went with which area of the human body. While he tried to figure this out, the passenger lost patience and realized this kid didn't know what he was doing. The passenger went right to the purser's office and complained. The nurse lost her job.

Dr. Frith was replaced by Dr. Horne, who must have gone to medical school at Pelvic U. This bird would have a girl on the examining table and her feet in the stirrups before she'd finished detailing her symptoms, but he was a real loser in the Nokkie Stakes.

During his brief regime on this big beautiful ship, we were on rather long cruises that lasted over a month. On one cruise, we had aboard Diane, a scrumptious gal who'd been employed by the company's advertising agency to pose for photos for a new brochure. She was to accompany us one way, pose for photographs by the famous photographers William and Melba Figge, then take a plane back home. She asked me if I had been a fashion model and when I answered yes, I became the receptacle into which she poured every bit of news and information about herself. Diane held nothing back.

At the very first sight of Diane, Dr. Horne's eyes started to pinwheel. He played every card he had, reshuffled, then played them again. Diane didn't give him a look, though the things she said to me about him must have had his ears ringing like carillons.

At the same time, Diane met and went ape over the athletic director, Clint, a handsome devil, built like some sculptor's idea of what Charles Atlas had in mind. Clint was also very sweet and devoted to a pretty little girl back home he'd gone with in college and was going to marry.

After one week Diane had moved into his cabin and introduced him to all sorts of pills, I suspect, and maybe pot, too. During the day, Clint could just barely power a Ping-Pong ball over the net. When the time came for Diane's flight home, she said the hell with it, and exchanged her first class jet fare, plus some cash, for a ticket so she could remain on ship for the return voyage.

The idyllic arrangement continued, therefore, until Diane was forced to call on Dr. Horne in his surgery for private consultation. I am in no way breaching the good doctor's privilege of confidence between him and his patient.

I got the word from the other side when Diane came to me almost in a state of shock. "Jeraldine," she said, "that doctor is too much! I have to tell you what his solution to my problem was. I can't tell Clint or he'll kill him, I'm afraid. I told that doctor I was suffering a good deal of discomfort in a certain area of my body and wanted some sort of ointment to relieve it. It wasn't a dire problem, just a soreness from staying in bed too long with Clint and making mad love too often. Do you know what that doctor did? He put me in the stirrups for a pelvic examination, and when he saw how sore and chafed I was, he said, "Oh, you are sore there, my dear. Let me kiss it and make it better."

Jeraldine's senior portrait,
"I'm out of school—I wonder what my future holds?"

"I wonder if my first job as a photographer's model sold any of these dolls?"

GLENDALE NEWS-PRESS

Women
IN THE NEWS
Betty Preston, Women's Editor

THURSDAY, APRIL 8, 1965   **PAGE 1-D**

Model Makes the Grade in London

When Jerry Saunders went to London, she didn't meet the queen.

But she did meet the queen's favorite dress designer, and she did land a job as one of his models.

Jerry, who has been a top Southern California fashion model for several years, spent last year in New York in an executive post at the World's Fair.

Shortly after the fair closed for the season she left for a trip to Europe, visiting Germany, France, Switzerland and Denmark.

And then came London, where she met Norman Hartnell, the man who had designed Queen Elizabeth's wedding and coronation gowns, as well as most of her "every day" wardrobe.

Until she returns home this month, Jerry will be modeling in Hartnell's shows and for his fashion photographs.

Jerry, whose home has been in Glendale for many years, writes that the famous designer's "very posh" salon is hung with crystal chandeliers, and is frequented by London's fashionable women, who all love his clothes.

A "Model" Career

"I love modeling Mr. Blackwell's gowns."

A Cruise Director's Life...

...Introducing
Passengers to the Captain

Captain Guido · Susan August · Captain Beautier · Jeraldine Saunders · George August · Junior Sandello

Teaching the Can-Can at the costume parade rehearsal.

Conducting shipboard pool games.

Jeraldine doing a
South Seas dance
in Vava'U.

Shipboard Fun!

Jeraldine giving "Spoon Diving Champions" their prizes.

Palm reading for Ila Britton,
Cruise Hostess on another ship,
one of the few times that their
ships were together in port.

Going ashore while her ship is in the port of Ketchikan, Alaska.

Jeraldine enjoying a few moments to herself before welcoming passengers in Bora Bora.

Travel to Exotic Lands

"Biggie" used to wait for Jeraldine's ship to arrive so she could sneak him some filet mignons.

"These were my darling playmates during rare time off in Fiji."

With just a hint of the Greek flag behind them, companions on the fantail of the *Royal Odyssey* are Quique Jourdan, Captain Gregory Avdelas, Jeraldine, and world-famous movie star Louis Jourdan.

Dancing with the pursers on the Greek ship *The Orpheus.*

This is one of the photos Jeraldine's cruise line used in their advertising and publicity.

This photo was taken when Jeraldine's publishers sent her to New York for TV interviews.

The Glamorous Life

Life after cruise directing, Tahiti revisited on the "QE2."

Henry Miller congratulating Jeraldine on her success with "The Love Boat."

Jeraldine with philanthropist Buddy Rogers.

Jeraldine with
Florence Henderson
on board
"The Love Boat."

Jeraldine with Angie
Dickinson in port.

Charlton Heston with
Jeraldine at the Motion
Picture Christmas
party, 1993.

Jeraldine with the "new" McCoy, Patricia Klous.

Love Boat Buddies

Ted McGinley, Jeraldine Saunders and Jill Whelan.

With Ted Lange, "The Great One."

With Gavin MacLeod.

With Aaron Spelling.

Jeraldine Saunders
with Bernie Kopel.

Jeraldine and her husband, Arthur Andrews.
Happily married and lecturing at sea.

Happily Ever After!

Jeraldine and Arthur
in Puerto Vallarta.

Cruising with Arthur near
Morea in French Polynesia.
"Life is perfect now as we sail
into the sunset."

chapter nineteen

ENTERTAINERS WANTED

WE WERE IN THE PORT OF MIAMI AT THE TURN-AROUND
point during a Caribbean cruise when Pete, the cruise director, asked me to watch the rehearsal for the evening program. This was usually his job but he had a rotten hangover
and wanted to sneak in a quick nap. I'm afraid that I didn't
pay too much attention because a passenger came in and
begged me to read her palm. I usually give my palm reading
lecture the last day at sea; otherwise I have everyone putting
their hands out to be read and I can't get my work done.
Anyway, this passenger had my attention instead of my
watching the rehearsal, which I should have done.

Cruise directors are encouraged to fraternize with the
females and they are given unlimited bar credit. So, like the
cat who liked the water and jumped into the well, they

frequently overindulge in wine, women, and song and within a few months, practically have to be carted off in a basket. I would then be asked to train a new one. Anyway, that evening Megan, who had been flown in from Los Angeles to join our ship as a singer, was introduced to the audience by Pete. Much to his chagrin she couldn't sing a note. She was young and sort of cute. When she came backstage after her song Pete really let her have it. He also read the riot act to me for not having listened to her at rehearsal. Then he turned to Megan and in a gruff voice said, "Why did you tell the home office that you could sing?"

She was crying by this time and then she confessed, between sobs, "I have...(sob)...never traveled, never been on a plane or a ship and I heard your company wanted a singer to fly to Miami and cruise all the way through the Panama Canal...(sob)...and it all sounded so utterly fantastic...well, I guess I just wanted to make this trip."

"Good God!" Pete screamed. "Now we have eighteen days until we get to L.A. and we have no singer! Dammit!" He stormed off, and Megan ran to her cabin crying.

However, the next day, instead of hiding in shame Megan went around to all the passengers and apologized for her lousy voice. Instead of complaining about the lack of entertainment, passengers tried to comfort her. She became the hit of the ship. Everyone loved her. She was an adorable character. In Acapulco she was coming back from nightclubbing with some passengers and as she tried to step from the tender to the ship she slipped and fell into the water. As she was going down a crew member tried to catch her by the hair; but was left holding her hairpiece. Megan screamed, "Help me! Help me!" as she went down.

Pete was in the same tender and was just about ready to step onto the ship when she fell. "Oh my God!" he yelled as he jumped in to save her. As he grabbed a hand line and wrapped his other arm around her waist, something phenomenal happened: he kissed her—and then she kissed him back. Both soaking wet, they started laughing hysterically and embracing.

Meanwhile the passengers on the tender, who all knew Pete was angry with Megan during the whole cruise, started clapping. Some were misty eyed to see that Pete had succumbed, as had they, to her magnetism.

chapter twenty

If My Garden Club Could See Me Now

On one cruise we had an entertainer, a singer, who literally dripped animal magnetism. He was so damned charming he was unreal, and when he saw a pretty woman, steam spurted out of his ears.

On the same cruise we had aboard an extremely attractive woman in her mid-thirties. She was accompanied by and shared a cabin with a female companion who was also good looking, but not quite in the same ethereal way. The cruise staff had been briefed on Mrs. Carroll before she came aboard. She had lost her husband in a tragic accident several months before and the trip was an attempt to restore her shattered nerves.

The singer's name was Al. Like all the other entertainers he took his instructions directly from the cruise director. As a rule the cruise staff is always glad to have our entertainers spend time with the ladies—it keeps them happy—so we had all encouraged Al. But this time Al was told bluntly to leave Mrs. Carroll strictly alone because we felt she wasn't ready for this treatment. Also, Mrs. Carroll had friends in the home office so highly placed that the whole lot of us could find ourselves on the beach if she made the tiniest of complaints.

There was nothing wrong with Al's head. He not only played it cool so far as Mrs. Carroll was concerned; he declared a moratorium on prowling throughout that whole cruise.

Mrs. Carroll was an ash blonde with finely chiseled features and large, widely spaced gray eyes. The weather was far too warm for widow's weeds, but she clothed herself in a substitute by keeping to herself through most of the day. She often stood on deck watching the wake of the ship, as if intent on things forever in the past.

The woman with whom she shared her cabin, Nedra Speer, was a friend and not a paid companion. Restrictions were self-imposed by Mrs. Carroll, but though Nedra had a good time, she was not overt about it. She was a divorcée and became friends with the very attractive second engineer.

During the meal sittings, Nedra was attentive and sympathetic to her subdued friend. In the early hours following dinner, usually a fun time aboard ships, Mrs. Carroll was present but not a part of the jollity. Al invariably made an appearance with their particular little coterie, joking with them for a while. He had to. He was enormously popular and to have failed to join them would have been a pointed snub. However, Mrs. Carroll generally excused herself early, probably in the belief that she was putting a damper on the party.

When we began the homeward leg of the cruise, however, Mrs. Carroll started to emerge from her protective cocoon. She sat in on several of the horse racing sessions and won tidy little sums. She played deck tennis with Nedra, then the two of them split up and were joined by two young men for a rousing game of mixed doubles.

She spent part of the afternoon at the pool. We found that she had a bubbling, infectious laugh, and that her first name was Barbara.

The next to last day before making home port is the time for the Captain's Farewell Party, which is always fun for the passengers. It's like graduation day—and graduation night. People are selected as "Most Fun to Be With on a Cruise," "Fanciest Dresser," "Girl I Wish I'd Been Shipwrecked With," "Man Ditto," and so on. The beauty shop is a madhouse for twenty-four hours prior to the event, because everyone really gets dressed to the teeth.

Mrs. Carroll stayed through the show after dinner and for the dancing that followed. She was quite a different lady from the subdued soul who had boarded the ship several weeks before. She danced with several of the men in the group that had more or less adopted Nedra and herself. At other times, she watched the swaying couples appreciatively.

Later I saw her standing in an aisle that led between the tables to the exit from the nightclub. She was talking to Al, who towered over her. Her head was high, her pretty mouth compressed, and the glint in the corners of her eyes had to be tears. She turned and went out abruptly. Al looked around uncertainly, like a boy who thinks he may have been seen with his hand in the cookie jar.

Al had indeed been seen, by Nedra Speer and me. Al didn't look guilty nearly so much as he looked mystified.

"Just what happened, Al?" I said in a very concerned tone.

"I'll be damned if I know," Al said.

I had visions of being transferred to cruise director on that rickety launch that goes to Yelapa. "What did you say to her?"

"I didn't say one word to her," Al exploded. "She said to me that I hadn't asked her to dance. Then she split."

"Oh," I said. "I understand, Al. You've played it too cool!"

Nedra cocked her head to one side and looked up at Al. "I don't think there's anything you can do but go down to our cabin and apologize," she told him.

"She'll spit right in my goddamn eye!" Al objected.

"I still don't know of anything else you can do," Nedra insisted, and gave him the cabin number.

Al looked at me and I nodded encouragement. He shook his head doubtfully, but he went.

Those farewell shindigs can run right up until dawn. This one was no exception. Nedra danced the night away. She obviously was making a point of staying away from the cabin she shared with her friend. Mrs. Carroll did not appear, nor was Al seen again for the rest of the night.

The next day there were no complaints to our head office. As for Mrs. Carroll, she made a point of giving me a personal good-bye. "Jeraldine, when I came on board I was a grieving woman watching others dancing and having fun, and I have to confess I looked back and felt my life with my dear departed James had been a cheat. Frankly, although I loved him dearly, I thought maybe I had been missing something."

I made a gesture toward her.

She said, "No, don't stop me; allow me to finish. You see, Jeraldine, last night I decided to find out once and for all if my love had been real or wishful thinking." Her eyes narrowed as if looking inwardly. "You know something, Jeraldine?" she said. "I had a liaison with Al last night. I suppose that is a polite way of putting it."

"Please, Mrs. Carroll," I interrupted, "you don't have to tell me anything."

"I know it," she responded, "but even though I've known you for such a short time I feel you are someone I can talk to and God knows I've needed someone to talk to for a long time." Passengers were departing in a flurry of activity and the noise level was rising; her words were barely audible. "I'm going to say good-bye, but I feel I want you to know what happened last night."

By this time I was looking around in embarrassment, not wanting to hear what I felt was a very private affair, but she had my arm and tugged me down to where she could talk directly into my ear.

"Jeraldine," she whispered, "I know now that my years with James were not wasted, not in any way. Do you understand?"

She must have read my bewildered look; she started to smile, then laughed lightly, then guffawed. The laughter must have been infectious; in minutes the two of us were holding our sides, doubled over in laughter. The other passengers were too busy departing to notice the tears streaming from our eyes. For survival we both heaved breath-catching sighs. I couldn't control my curiosity any longer.

"Just what are we laughing at?" I implored.

"We're laughing laughs of celebration, Jeraldine, dear. The celebration of a woman who knows that her past was one filled with love and satisfaction. My doubting self-pity is finished. I have this cruise to thank for it and I suppose poor Al in particular."

"Poor Al?" I responded, startled.

"Yes, Jeraldine, I was going to go with it no matter what. I had to find out what I had been missing all those years with James. Do you know something?" she asked. "I hadn't been missing a damn thing. You know what Al did for me last night? He made me laugh. Personally, Jerry, inexperienced as I am, I think that 'sex symbol Al' is probably the poorest lay in L.A."

Gads, I thought to myself, if only the gals back at the garden club I belonged to before I went to sea could hear this!

"Don't ask me why," she went on, "but suddenly the whole thing seemed ridiculous. After the crucial moments, I laughed, and Al's anger changed to understanding, and we spent the rest of the night talking. His search is much the same as my own. He felt he had been missing something all these years. He felt he wanted someone ladylike like me and that would be the answer to his promiscuousness." As Barbara departed, the cruise ended and I felt I had learned something more about the human dilemma.

The only beef was from Al himself. Like a true Flame-eyed Tailchaser, he grieved over the lost potential of those two golden weeks. "Greatest lover in the whole goddam world," he mumbled to me all through breakfast the next morning. "This cruise could have been the sex experience of a lifetime and I had to wait until the last goddam night to make her. What a waste! Oh, well, I'm taking the next cruise too, Jeraldine. Maybe I'll find another one just as good." He got up from the table mumbling, "Two whole weeks I could have been balling her," etc.

If he knew I was told he was "the poorest lay in L.A.," the guy's ego would never recover.

chapter twenty-one

THE MYSTERIOUS, VIOLENT SEA

I HAD LITTLE EXPERIENCE WITH THE SEA UNTIL I CAST MY lot with cruise ships. I have learned to love the sea, respect it, and fear its awesome power.

Most of its moods are beguiling, even those I have seen when I stood in the protection of an overhang, out of the wind and well protected by a heavy raincoat, and watched torrential showers sweep across great, leaden gray waves. The ship surges against them, sometimes taking a whole turbulent cascade over the bow. The wind sighs and whistles. The whipping rain stings your face.

I have stood at the bow of the ship during a dead calm and thrilled as I gazed up at the Southern Cross, the humidity so high my body dripped as though I were in a light rainfall, yet cooled slightly by the light breeze from the ship's movement through the calm, phosphorescent water.

Then of course there are the times, those pictured in the ship's brochure: ideal weather with a warm, sparkling sun and a feathering of clouds in the sky, and highly paid photographer's models posing at the deck games and by the pool.

In all truth, the latter situation is the rule rather than the exception, though the actual passengers are not usually replicas of the photographer's model. There are times, however, if you go to sea regularly, when you have to wonder how the early settlers had the sheer guts to take off on voyages across the treacherous Atlantic in small wooden sailing ships, as my Irish ancestors did.

The liner you board today is really a miracle of engineering. It is structured so that a 1,000-foot ship, which is almost one-fifth of a mile long, can be lifted high into the air by a gargantuan sea—so far that both its bow and stern are actually hanging free in the air— without structural damage. This is sheer magic! A ship can actually be driven through by another ship, and the safety factors built into it will seal off the damaged area and keep the hull afloat, unlike the *Titanic*. Even fire, the ultimate terror of the sea, is controllable now.

I am very serious about this. I know that a ship's passenger runs less risk than a driver on any freeway in California, but there is a peculiarity about ocean travel that must be recognized. The most modern of ships will move around a bit underfoot, despite the complicated and efficient stabilizing gear. In a really heavy storm, they'll react to the battering of the swells. Acquiring your sea legs is an important part of ocean cruising, and it happens more quickly for some than others. When the sea is rough it's best to hang on to the rails while running up and down companionways until your body has acclimated itself to movements of the ship, infinitesimal as they may seem. Usually the larger the ship, the less movement.

Should you have the poor luck to run into a real storm, follow the advice of the captain and take no chances. Don't trust yourself to an open deck during a bad storm, exciting as the prospect may seem. The crew must venture out onto the decks, but they know what they are doing and they are extremely careful. That's why they have to be "able-bodied seamen" and have it drilled into them that in precarious situations it is "one hand for the ship and one hand for yourself." A misstep aboard a pitching ship can have tragic consequences.

During the Alaskan run, there are two places where the going can get pretty rough. One of these is Queen Charlotte's Sound; the other is the open sea off the ocean port of Sitka which, unlike most of the harbors in that area, is not protected by big windward islands to the west.

Early one season in Alaska, one of the oilers was promoted to the job of fourth engineer, which made him an officer of the ship. He was a tall, very good-looking black man, a native of Jamaica—so his accent was almost like that of Oxford. He'd been very popular with his shipmates and quickly won the liking and respect of the cruise staff and the passengers. Now that he was an officer, he was allowed to be in the public rooms to drink and dance. Though he was naturally proud of having achieved officer status on sheer merit, he didn't make a big thing of it.

Heavy weather came up during the day we were in Sitka, and when we left for the next port of call, the ocean was beginning to behave like a mad thing. We sailed at midnight. After an hour and a half at sea, a report came from the bridge that our new officer had slipped on the rung at the top of an inspection ladder in the bowels of our ship and had fallen to the steel deck below. He had died almost instantly.

The captain turned the ship in the wild sea, and we went back to Sitka, where the body was taken ashore. On our next trip to the port eight days later, the entire crew of the ship attended the man's funeral. It was so sad. He was buried there on Baranoff Island, under a cold, snowcapped mountain, a long way from the verdant mountains and blue, cloud-piled, warm skies of Jamaica, and an even longer way from the goal he had set for himself of becoming a chief engineer.

One Christmas Eve in Acapulco, we had both a mystery and a tragedy, one involving a girl, the other an elderly woman. The woman, a pleasantly cheerful passenger, elected to stay aboard rather than spend the evening doing Acapulco. The woman with whom she shared the cabin returned to the ship, and found her cabin mate had taken a whole bottle of sleeping pills. The doctor was unable to bring her out of her drug-induced coma and she died.

Christmas cruises are the bane of all cruise staffs. It's when we get society's rejects and more Godzilla types than all the rest of the year, and this Christmas cruise was even worse than most. The cruise staff feared we were really going to get rotten comments on the forms the passengers fill out on the last day of the cruise. So when this sweet little old lady died, the cruise staff was very sad because she was practically the only passenger to be appreciative of our efforts to make the cruise a happy one. The cruise director, who was also a comedian, said, "If only we had known she was going to kill herself we could have asked her to first fill out a good comment form for us. It would have gone something like this, 'Being of sound mind, etc. etc.'"

The mystery involved a tiny Asian girl with a flowerlike face and glossy, jet-black hair that hung well below her waist. She was the photographer's assistant, a skilled technician who worked in the darkroom producing prints of the films he snapped day and night. Her home was in Los Angeles, in the Chinatown just east of the Civic Center; she was the first one ashore when we made our turnaround and the last one back on ship. During the cruises, we seldom saw her, possibly because of her workload in the darkroom.

After we sailed from Acapulco, the cruise staff and the entertainers tossed a real bash after the show on Christmas Eve. The epicenter of the party was in the cabin of Chuck James, one of the singers on board, who has one of the best voices on sea or land. There was some runover into the neighboring cabin, which belonged to another entertainer, but we all kept crowding into Chuck's place, and it soon was ankle deep in popcorn. The line of champagne bottles kept lengthening along the bulkhead of the alleyway, for everyone—cruise staff, entertainers—all who could get away had been invited.

We were well out to sea and it was long past midnight when the photographer came to me. His assistant was not to be found.

"Maybe she went to a private party with some passengers," I suggested.

"She doesn't know any of them," he said.

"What about the party in the crew quarters? She knows some of those fellows."

"I called there. They haven't seen her."

"Maybe she was just tired and went to bed?"

He hesitated. "I checked there. Jerry, she's cut all her hair off."

I stared at him. "Cut all her hair off? I don't believe it!"

"It's all over the place."

I went with him to her cabin. Long black hair was scattered over her bunk, in the tiny bathroom, in the wastebasket, in her opened suitcase. Her clothes were there, as was her purse, her expensive camera, and her money.

I called the captain. "*Pronto,*" he answered.

I said, "The photographer's assistant has disappeared and she cut her hair off."

"Cut her ear off?" he screamed.

"No, her hair off," I said.

He found out that she had been seen on board after the ship had sailed, so she hadn't stayed on in Acapulco. The only other thing we found out from all the questioning was that she must have gotten LSD in Acapulco and cut her hair off because of the crazy effect of the drug and then jumped overboard. Unless, well, unless....Lots of other explanations could be imagined but we will never know just why or how she vanished. Sometimes I look down from the rail at night and see the dark, silent ocean, and I wonder if it holds that dear Chinese girl.

The next day, the captain interviewed us. He asked everyone where they were the night before. He found it amazing that thirty-two of us said we were in Chuck James' cabin, which could hold only six comfortably. That was not an ordinary cruise. Most are filled with happiness and gaiety.

A passenger complained to me and said, "Jeraldine, don't you think that two suicides on one cruise is a bit much?"

The poor, hard-working cruise staff gets blamed for everything. She must have thought that I sat down to make out the daily program and said, "Let's see, I think we will have two suicides today."

After staying at resorts, riding buses, flying on airplanes, or staying in hotels, have you ever heard of people having reunions and keeping in touch with each other? No, I don't think you have. It happens frequently with passengers who have sailed together on a cruise ship. They often correspond and many have tender, loving reunions. This is one of the reasons I say that usually something beautiful happens on cruise ships.

In these turbulent high-tech times, being on a cruise ship will draw you into a much kinder, gentler ambience of old world elegance, pampering, physical and emotional comfort, and contentment that is inaccessible on land. No small wonder I have seen so many passengers fall in love again with each other, or if they are traveling solo, sometimes they find a soul mate.

Nothing is more romantic than a cruise—you can find the once-upon-another-time that you longed for but thought was gone—the romance of the sea. It is proper etiquette to introduce yourself to fellow passengers as though you were at a private party. You may safely smile at everyone, as in the old days of life in a small town, except on a cruise there is the magic of the sea to add to the spice of your experience.

chapter twenty-two

WHY L.O.L.F.P. SHOULD WEAR TENNIS SHOES

WHEN YOU GO TO FARAWAY PLACES ON A CRUISE SHIP YOU are going to be offered a variety of tours at the ports of call. These tours will vary in length from a few hours to all day. You may be aboard a boat or a bus, and you may explore byways of the adjacent coast, or venture into the back country away from the sea.

The tours are not a part of the cruise. They are like optional equipment when you buy an automobile, not really essential but they add a great deal to the overall enjoyment of a cruise.

The tours are a sound buy. They are sometimes set up, "pitched," and supervised by the cruise staff. The experiences on a tour will be an important part of the cruise, and weigh heavily in the passengers' judgment of its overall worth. Any cruise director worthy of the title wants people wishing that their vacation would never end, not thanking the good Lord that it's over.

However, it is important for the cruise director to explain what the tour is going to be like.

Usually there are tours to places which are quaint, unlike anything you've ever visited before. They are sometimes primitive and may be hidden deep in the tropical zone, so they are hot and subject to torrential downpours. They are invariably reached by rough roads, in transportation that may wheeze, clank, sputter, drip nuts and bolts, and finally expire miles from civilization. I sometimes tell the passengers that one of the unique features of our trip is the fact that they are not next door to a neighborhood service station with a mechanic on duty.

If you're prepared for this sort of thing and are a good traveler, not just a tourist, you'll have a delightful experience. If not, you can be pretty miserable.

This is why I say L.O.L.F.P., or any one else for that matter, should have tennies as part of their wardrobe when embarking on a southern cruise. L.O.L.F.P. means, as you've undoubtedly figured out, little old ladies from Pasadena. L.O.L.F.P. are very proper and swear by shoes with heels on them, but a wooden sidewalk in Alaska will chew the heels off a pair of shoes quicker than a teething Great Dane puppy. A cobbled street in Puerto Vallarta can render dress shoes useless within a hundred yards. A forced march beside a disabled bus for a quarter of a mile will make a mess of your prettiest country walking shoes, while a good, sound pair of tennies laughs such things off. Dunk them in suds, a good scrub with a stiff brush and they are ready for the next foray into the back country.

The cruise staff makes the very best arrangements possible and makes sure that you get back to the ship on time. The ship never sails until the scheduled land tour is back. But a couple who go flitting off by themselves to explore a port of call are taking a chance unless they have some prior knowledge and a good command of the local tongue. Their ship will wait for an entire tour that has been held up for some reason, but it will rarely delay sailing for a stray passenger or two. This is understandable. The missing person probably won't even be missed until time for dinner or breakfast the following morning.

Tours are seldom included in the package price of a cruise, but passengers should consider them a part of it and budget themselves accordingly. The tours offer a nice change from the routine of ship-board life, pleasant as that may be. Tours can even provide the material for entertaining letters home.

I was asked to take a group of our passengers on a tour that we would be offering for the first time. Our ship would be in Acapulco for two days each cruise and so this would be a one-day tour that left the dock at 7:00 A.M. heading to the airport for a flight to Mexico City. We were to return to the ship that night at 8:00 P.M.

There were thirty-five enthusiastic souls in our group. We were to see all of Mexico City in one day. I mean everything from the pyramids to the museums and the *Ballet Folklorico*.

When we arrived at the Mexico City airport, I told the passengers that we would travel five each per taxi and they complied, even though some twosomes had to be separated.

On one of our quick stops I explained to my group that this is the theater where we will see the Ballet Folklorico, but there was just one disadvantage. They could stay in the theater for only twenty minutes, then we were to meet out front by the taxi stand where we would then dash on to our next attraction.

It was really interesting but also kind of crazy to try to see so much in one day. Anyway, my dear passengers were very obliging and met me at the appointed time. I then controlled the loading of five passengers to a taxi. I was trying to hurry the loading when the next couple I tried to separate, with our arrangement to load five passengers to a taxi, just wouldn't comply. I guess I became a little impatient when they wouldn't get into different taxis. I even tried to pull their hands apart, but they simply refused to separate.

Finally, after trying to explain to them my need for their cooperation, the bewildered young man said to me, "Who are you?"

"Good heavens," I exclaimed, "aren't you from our ship?"

He said, "Ship? Hell, no, we're here on our honeymoon!"

Oh dear, was I embarrassed. On the following tours there I had my passengers all wear hats with a balloon on top so that I could find them in the crowds.

When one works on the ships too long, we say the same passengers embark that just disembarked from the last cruise, they have just changed their names.

Weather can always be a chancy thing unless you elect to stay sealed up in your house. When our ship docked at the island of Tonga, in the South Seas, where not many cruise ships stop, the evening before our arrival the elements had elected to go on a spree. I had given a glowing description of the tour available—almost all the passengers took my advice and bought tickets.

The all-day sojourn had been planned to start at nine the next morning and was to include a bus trip to the far side of the island, an inspection of plantations where bananas, papayas, coconuts, and taro were raised, and a great feast and entertainment after swimming and sunning on the beach at O'Holei.

When we were docked at Nuku'alofa, it was raining heavily, but sometimes a rainfall in the South Seas can be over in a twiddling. The tour passengers were undaunted, provided themselves with raincoats and hats, and got onto the three garlanded buses at dockside promptly at nine o'clock. I just took an umbrella; it was too humid to wear a raincoat. I go along to keep the morale up and to see that the tour owners give and do all they promise; besides, the home office wants me to go. Of course, this means no nap, and I never finish my work the night before until 1:00 or 2:00 A.M.

By the time the buses had reached Captain Cook's Landing and the village of Ha'amoaga, the downpour had become a deluge. Nevertheless, the passengers got off to bargain with the gathered natives about the handicrafts for sale. They figured they might as well, because the roofs of the buses had long before begun to leak like sieves.

One of the three buses, not the one I was on, fared slightly worse than the others. The crew on each bus consisted of a young driver, who explained the technical aspects of the scenery (mostly rain falling down), another young fellow who was a general helper, and an elderly man who sat at the rear of the bus and shouted through a megaphone to provide the historical background of each area. The driver of one bus elected to use a road that was less traveled than the regular one and possibly not so chewed up.

But it was worse. After a while, the bus skidded off sideways into an enormous mudhole. There was no help in sight, so the driver spun the wheels furiously, causing the bus to sink deeper and billows of smelly blue smoke to rise up through the thundering rain. The smoke brought fifteen curious onlookers from a neighboring village, half of them children who were entirely naked. They were truly adorable nature children.

Palm fronds were thrown under the wheels and the villagers shouted and grunted as they shoved at the bus, which went deeper. Someone then declared that all the men must alight. The bus went even deeper. Now everybody got off.

That didn't do any good either, except that the passengers learned that the village was called Lavengatonga, one of our stops for an inspection of a typical island village. It was a very slipshod inspection that day. The tourists huddled in the thatched huts to escape the solid walls of water slamming down from the heavens, and the hospitable, loving, generous, happy natives gave them gifts of exquisite shells they had gathered at the beach.

The beach where the afternoon and evening festivities were to take place was less than a mile away, so most of this rain-drenched, mud-soaked group of passengers elected to walk there rather than wait. Some were very elderly and some were grumbling about watches and purses being ruined by the rain. The path led through the jungle and they met an occasional horse, pig, or scrawny mongrel, also wet. "Less than a mile" turned into almost three before they were met by one of the other buses, which had come looking for them. In the downpour, the walkers had missed the turnoff to the beach.

Their problems were by no means over. O'Holei Beach is ringed by a cliff, in which there is an enormous ceremonial cave, one of the spectacular features of this place. The cliff is normally descended by steps cut into the steep bank, but these were engulfed by a cascade of water. Instead, the group was assisted down the steeper incline of grass and weeds by a human ladder of powerful local men who handed them from one to the next.

They finally met the rest of us in the cave, a vast, beautiful cavern where traditional dances and songs and an enormous feast of South Sea island food were presented. Upon seeing the gal who talked them into this tour (me) they were torn between anger and gratitude for having reached a dry haven.

I shared their yearning for a warm, dry feeling. For some reason the name "Burt Bacharach" played through my head. The reason became obvious. Raindrops were starting to fall through the top of the cave and splatter on our heads!

Two of the passengers on that particular bus were on an extended holiday in the South Seas, New Zealand, and Australia. When Mr. and Mrs. Sterling Ensign returned to their home in Terra Bella, in the heart of California's citrus country, they were interviewed by a reporter from the local newspaper. Of everything that happened during their thousands of miles of travel, the only thing they talked about at length was their experience in Nuku'alofa. Mrs. Ensign sent me a clipping of the long story that appeared in the Terra Bella News.

Land tours can do that for a person. They're something special. I had to give the same glowing sales pitch for that same tour on the next cruise.

However, weather is not the only thing that can lift a land tour above the ordinary. On rare occasions, just keeping a tour intact until everyone is returned safely to the ship can be a hair-raising adventure.

During one stop at Puerto Vallarta in Mexico, I had the responsibility of the tour to Yelapa, a tiny spot up the coast, which involved taking a small sightseeing yacht onto which a lot of people could be squeezed. At eight that morning, 200 of our passengers were transferred by tender to the tiny yacht. All had been advised on several occasions to wear tennis shoes or other comfortable walking shoes, and the women in particular had been told that they should dress very casually. Some paid no attention and wore high heels and stockings. One dressed as though she were having lunch at Sardi's.

Yelapa is normally an attractive spot well worth visiting. It is a tiny place in a cove that provides the escape to the sea for a little river. The village itself is utterly primitive. Pigs, dogs, and burros wander around without a care in the world. The residents subsist largely on fishing, some small gardens that cling to the steep hillsides, and the income derived from the sale of local curios to sightseers about to climb up the tortuous trail to the waterfall.

The waterfall is attraction *numero uno.* There are places, such as Alaska, where you can get blasé about waterfalls, but in Mexico they are scarce. People will go far out of their way to gaze on one.

Difficulties began the moment the yacht anchored offshore and dugout canoes moved out to meet us. Docking facilities at this spot were unable to accommodate even a motor boat. The passengers must be paddled as close as possible to shore, then wade on in to the dry, sandy beach.

Lady Passenger One (heatedly): "You didn't say anything about this, Jeraldine. Look how my shoes are ruined!"

Lady Passenger Two: "She did so, Mabel. At the Puerto Vallarta lecture yesterday. I was sitting right next to you. She told us just how to dress."

Lady Passenger One (still hot): "Well, I didn't hear it."

Lady Passenger Two: "And she made a specific point of it over the loudspeaker this very morning! Twice."

Lady Passenger One (still grumpy): "I don't know how I was talked into this. That's all I can say."

Lady Passenger Two (smugly): "Well, I've got *my* tennies on."

We all sat on the beach and started to eat the box lunches provided by the ship.

The village is interesting and its inhabitants pleasantly cordial. However, Mexican dogs and pigs must migrate to this spot, having heard via the grapevine that there is a special sideshow of tourists set up purely for their entertainment and feeding. The dogs are so miserably thin it hurts me to look at them. They gather around and eye the travelers suspiciously, some baring their fangs when they think they can produce a proper reaction, at other times going into an unearthly bedlam of yapping. None is very big and they are all hungry, so the total effect is unnerving. I'm sure they sit around at night and, between sessions of howling at the moon, regale one another with tales of how that lady jumped when she thought she was about to have her calf nipped if she didn't share her lunch. One passenger ran screaming out of the ladies room. She found a pig in there with her.

Now it was time for the visit to the waterfall and this day had become unbearably hot. I led the way, feeling I was going to die at every scrabbling step since I had been working late the night before, but I was responsible for their taking the trip in the first place, so I had to pretend I was in seventh heaven. I kept reassuring my faltering followers they would be fully rewarded for their effort when we reached our destination.

But something had happened. When we got to the spot where we could view this spectacle of nature, what had only a few weeks before been a pretty respectable waterfall was now nothing more than a puny little trickle. "Jeraldine! Is this your idea of humor? I thought this was a rival to Niagara Falls?"

I turned around with what I knew must have been a sheepish, sickly smile. To myself I said, "Jeraldine, what have you gotten yourself into now?" But as I am wont to do in times of emergency,

I laughed blithely when I should have been crying. The words poured out of me like the torrent that should have been waterfall.

I told them they were witnessing a rare occurence—what had been from time immemorial a raging waterfall was now a trickle lovely to behold. My words continued to pour even though the waterfall did not. My eyes flitted across that sea of belligerent faces which by now were being transformed into amazed expressions. I knew they were thinking: Is that girl daft? But nothing could stop me now.

I said, "This is really something to write home about. We are probably the luckiest people in the world. We are witnessing a miracle. By the time the next cruise arrives all they will see is an ordinary waterfall. Everybody sees that." The faces now became mobile; incredibly, there were nods of appreciation. A few shutterbugs even began snapping photographs of absolutely nothing. Mabel, the Godzilla, made her way up to me and adoringly asked how we could be so lucky.

With a sigh of relief that must have been heard around the world, I looked Mabel directly in the eye and said, "Seek and ye shall find." What I was saying to myself, however, was "Thank God I kissed that Blarney Stone." (To be good at this job it helps to be Irish.) We turned around in the hot sun and skidded and slid back down to the village and the beach.

In the meantime, due to a storm far from land, a really heavy sea had come up. We were able to get from the dugout canoes to the little sightseeing boat without mishap, but when we returned to Puerto Vallarta, there was no way the transfer could be made from the tenders to our big ship. The ugly swells were up to thirty feet. I was on the first tender to approach the ship. When we lay off from her, the tender rose and fell alarmingly. The hull of the ship flashed up and down past us as though we were passengers in a berserk express elevator. We had to turn back.

At this point I transported my 200 charges to the end of the pier on the beach in Puerto Vallarta, where we were joined by another 100 passengers who had been wandering around the colorful town. I was now responsible for 300 persons, it was getting late, and there was no telling when the sea would subside enough to allow us to board. And Puerto Vallarta was full—there was no room at the inn!

Then I remembered that a lovely new hotel, The Dolphin, was being built at the end of the pier, but was not yet completed. I took my problem to the manager.

I told him that my company would gladly reimburse the management for the expense involved, but that it was absolutely essential that I get these poor people something to drink for morale purposes. I added that if they got involved in a singalong, they wouldn't mind the discomfort too much so would he try to get a mariachi band for me right away. There were no phones in the hotel yet, so they never did find the band, even though they ran all over Puerto Vallarta looking for them.

Fortunately, some of the new hotel's liquor supplies had already been stowed in the wine cellars. The cooperative manager enlisted the townspeople to serve as bartenders. These nice natives knew nothing about measuring booze, and it wasn't their liquor anyway. The dollops they poured into those glasses would have stunned an ox. I had already told the passengers during my Puerto Vallarta lecture the previous day that they were not to drink the water in this port, so some little old ladies had no choice but to drink the liquor and beer, even though they had never even tasted it before.

After a couple of hours, we were all still outside on the beach, and things were going fairly well except that it was starting to get cold. Some of the passengers in wet bathing suits were sunburned and sandy and hungry. I figured the company would kill me if I fed all this horde. Then a couple approached me to ask what was being done to rescue them and when would the water calm down. I guess they thought I had contact with God. I banged on something to get attention and announced that the captain was arranging to pour oil on the water, which would smooth it all out, and we would be back aboard in about an hour. I don't know how they thought the captain and I were getting messages to one another, but they were satisfied. From then on, I kept telling them every hour that it would be about one more hour.

Exactly four hours later, well after our scheduled sailing time, everyone was cold, hungry, and drunk, and we started the transfer to the ship. I had them all singing "Row, Row, Row Your Boat" together with rousing sea chanties, as we made each transfer from the tender to our ship. The sea was still wild, and if they hadn't all been looped I couldn't have gotten them into the tenders.

When I got aboard with the last group, the captain was waiting for me.

"I'll be damned, Jeraldine," he said wonderingly. "I thought they'd be ready to string us all up. They're happy as larks. What on earth did you do with them?"

"Oh, I just gave them all a little morale juice," I told him. "They're all looped."

So when you go on a cruise, take along tennis shoes.

A cruise hostess needs to be well-educated, radiate warmth, have a friendly personality, good sense of humor, and a natural gift for conversation. It's a tall order, but can be a very rewarding way to make a living.

chapter twenty-three

GETTING A JOB ON BOARD A CRUISE SHIP

YOU WILL FIND THAT THE PEOPLE WHO ARE MOST IMPOR-
tant to you when you're off on a cruise are the members of
the cruise staff. They are the ones who most desperately
want you to have the best time you ever had in your life.
This is not just that they'll find their employment of very
short duration if you have a lousy time, but they are initially chosen because they like people and like to make
them happy.

The cruise staff is an entity unto itself, with its own rules
and responsibilities. I have beside me a sheaf of these
instructions which fill six legal-sized, single-spaced, typed
pages. It was written by my former cruise director, and if a
cruise staff member even bends one of these regulations,
he's in trouble. The person who metes out the punishment
is the cruise director, the boss.

I was the hostess, second in the pecking order. The job requirements for social hostess read:

> She needs to be sophisticated and well-educated, radiate warmth, have a friendly personality, good sense of humor, and a natural gift for conversation.
>
> One moment she may be teaching a craft class. Later, she may be leading a karaoke contest. In the evening she hosts the captain's cocktail party, then she helps backstage with the evening's show, all the time while assisting the cruise director, and looking out for passengers who may be traveling alone and need help in meeting new friends.

These are just the tip of the iceberg of the list of duties assigned to the hostess. It gives you an idea of the multiple roles that the hostess will be expected to play.

Next in rank are the assistant cruise director and the athletic director; then comes the assistant hostess (if any) and the permanent entertainers. When entertainers are not doing shows, they're supposed to be helping with the bingo games and horse racing, handing out costume supplies for the parade, and generally helping the cruise director with most activities and land tours. There are a hundred little details each day. Special acts such as singers, comedians, or magicians are generally booked for limited runs because of other commitments; they only perform in the shows and then have the rest of the cruise off, just like paying passengers. All of these jobs are a lot of work, but the job of cruise director is particularly tough. Cruise directors usually become a little squirrely after a while and some crack up and have to be carted off for good.

If you are looking for a job as a cruise staff member there are two things you had better know all about: comportment (behavior) and etiquette. You must know which piece of silverware to use and when. Of course, you must eat whole fresh fruits with a knife and fork. Start practicing now with an apple—no fair using your hands!

On some ships we have all our meals with the passengers and on others we have to eat with them only during open sitting, tea time, meals on the open deck, and the midnight buffet.

I may not have known foreign languages when I talked my way into this job, but my mother was strict about impeccable manners so I didn't have that hurdle.

There are times when comportment goes out the window—as long as it isn't in front of the passengers, if you are the cruise director, you may get away with it.

Early in my career, while I was still a hostess, I was working the Mexican Cruises with a cruise director named Bill. He was a charming dynamo but he'd been a cruise director for too long and was more than ready for a long vacation. When he did have a few hours to relax, an application of rum or tequila would help him unwind.

Just such an opportunity for relaxation presented itself during a stopover at Puerto Vallarta. You remember, I hope, the site of the waterfall at Yelapa. Members of the cruise staff regarded assignment to this tour as a fate worse than death. The trip was interesting, but we had to find something for the passengers to do in Yelapa so climbing the waterfall was inevitable. This was very nice for the passengers. They were on holiday and the heat and the exercise were good for them, but the cruise staff worked at least fifteen hours a day, seven days a week, eleven months of the year. The assignment to Yelapa meant a lost opportunity for goofing off at the beach or just staying in your cabin and trying to catch up on correspondence or sleep. Naturally, the cruise director assigned this duty to the member of his staff currently in the doghouse.

I don't recall who got stuck with Yelapa on this particular day, but as sailing time neared, the members of the staff gathered with the entertainers for an early dinner. We thought the cruise director had wandered off about some business of his own.

We had about finished dinner when Bill came rolling in, accompanied by Jill, the shop assistant. They were both stoned, but Bill had sort of wall-to-wall eyeballs. We could just about make out the pupils under his upper lids and he was happier than a kid in a chocolate factory. Jill looked as though she'd just emerged from the wind tunnel at the Air Force testing grounds.

"We found the best little old beach you ever saw," he announced. "You cats gotta go there next time. Waiters wade right out to you in the surf with the Margaritas. Waves knock 'em on their ass, but they keep right on serving! What a blast!"

It must've been. He was really looped.

"Where is it, Bill?" I asked.

He managed to find me after looking around; then he came over, arms wide.

"Jeraldine," he said, "I love you."

I was seated with the assistant cruise director. "Surely you love Bruce, too," I said.

"I love everybody," he proclaimed.

However, he clearly intended crushing me in a bear hug. I wouldn't have minded, except his nose was starting to drip so I gave his chest a teensy little push with the palm of my hand. "Oh, Bill," I said, good-naturedly.

Well, Bill tripped over something or passed out, I don't know which. He went flat on his back, his head slamming against the floor, bouncing once, and he was out like a light.

Everyone jumped up. Jill grabbed a big pitcher of ice water and dumped it on his face and chest, then knelt above his head and began to slap his face violently with the palms of both hands so that it rocked back and forth. Our Italian waiter, a nervous hyperthyroid, rushed up and looked down at Bill.

"Is he dead?" he asked excitedly in Italian.

"No. He's just unconscious," I told the waiter.

However, the waiter had heard the old wives' tale that the way to bring people out of the unconscious state is to press on their eyeballs. So he shoved Jill aside and knelt to give Bill the treatment with his thumbs!

Amazingly, it worked! But Bill came off the floor swinging and in his immediate line of sight were Bruce and me. He caught me in the side with a wild, open-handed wallop.

I hadn't really pushed him that hard. I hadn't thrown the ice water on him, or whaled away at his face, or tried to jam his eyeballs against the back of his skull, but I was the one who got belted. I yanked up my dress and pointed to my side. The red welt of his hand print was already beginning to appear. "Look what he did!" I screamed.

He yelled even louder. "You, Jerry, and you, Bruce, you're both fired as of this minute. And more than that, goddam it, from now on, you both have to go on the Yelapa tour every cruise." We put him to bed and covered for him during the evening's activities so that the company representative couldn't get him in trouble.

When he got rid of his terrible hangover, we were able to laugh over it, but that was not until the next day, when he had to agree that firing us at one moment, then keeping us on so that he could send us out with the Yelapa tour, cruise after cruise, was really funny.

Relationships between the cruise staff are essentially love-hate affairs. The quirks of human nature become noticeable under the confinement aboard ship.

Staff members live closer together than brothers and sisters with much too much propinquity. We are not in any way independent; on the contrary we must be completely interdependent if the staff is to operate as a successful unit. Except for a few hours of sleep, we are together day and night. A smoothly running cruise is the result of the meshing of many efforts. If even the tiniest of them breaks down, it means confusion. If one of us is even five minutes late, it can foul up activities for the whole day. Events are scheduled every hour and must go off on time. If we try to sneak in a quick ten-minute nap and forget to set the alarm, a mess ensues. The staff cabins are all next to each other on the top deck and we do not go to the crew quarters down below. The result is that each of us knows just about all there is to know about the others. It is impossible to keep any secrets and we share our triumphs and our tragedies as regularly as we do our meals.

We all look forward to our mail but when we are out at sea it's sort of "out of sight, out of mind." So, mail is scarce. Except for our assistant cruise director, who always received so much mail. We were jealous of this until we learned that most of his mail consisted of unpaid bills.

I always love the ship on which I am working. It's a strange kind of feeling—being dazzled and familiar at the same time. One feels proud when showing it off as though it is one's own home.

Upon returning from shore I feel I have left an etheric part of me on board that welcomes me back into the ship's arms.

Sea Mood

As we stood at the rail
Our hands on the rough teak wood
Readied for varnishing
The evening star already high
And the moon ascending to its apogee
Our closeness felt as of another time
Unspoken words we knew need not be said
Though, seemed not real, the time itself
Allowed us to share this sparkling night,
When sea and stars gave us
to share unspoken moments, to remember,
As we were there.

—Patrick Stiven

chapter twenty-four

THE BOUNDING MAIN

ONE OF THE FEW CONFUSING ASPECTS OF A CRUISE SHIP IS its chain of command. It is especially important to the members of the cruise staff to have this properly sorted out, because requests for services by other people working aboard cannot be made directly to that person, but should come through his own boss.

The head of the whole shebang is, of course, the captain. However, there is even a small distinction here. Some companies specializing in cruises lease the ships from owners. This means that they hire the ship and the people who run it, which includes the officers and crew, but not the cruise staff or the entertainers. The officers and crew—like the ship—are always from a country other than the U.S.A. (unfortunately, because the U.S.A. union wage is more) and seldom speak much English. Because the passengers are usually Americans an American cruise staff is needed. The operating company provides and pays for the cruise staff and entertainers. Shops, personal services such as beauticians and barbers, and the like are concessions. Therefore, although the captain is indeed the master of his ship and responsible for everything that goes on, the cruise director is, in a manner of speaking, the captain's direct contact with the organization that is paying his salary. In this situation, captains get along very well with cruise directors.

On occasion, those who lease a ship for cruising will control all functions other than the actual operation of the vessel. Far more often, though, these are in turn leased out to specialists in their fields as concessions. There are catering companies which provide the food and beverage services aboard liners, maintaining their own staffs of chefs, cooks, maitres d'hotel, chief stewards. The operating company always keeps direct control over the cruise staff and expects us all to be public relations experts. This is very important in determining the success of the season. If the passengers don't have a good time they don't return and they don't send their friends. Fortunately, most of the luxury ships I've sailed on have over fifty percent repeat passengers, and the others have sailed with us because of the good time their friends or relatives had with us.

The regular return to home port is such a devastating time for the members of the cruise staff. If your family is in the area you try to see them. The stay is short—barely long enough to disembark one set of passengers, replenish supplies, do a bit of clean-up, and welcome the next 700 or so passengers. We usually get in at 8:30 A.M. and by the time we get through customs it's 10:00 A.M. and we sail with a new bunch of passengers at 8:00 P.M. the same day, but the cruise staff must be back to welcome them aboard at 5:30 P.M.

This brief period is the only time that the brass itself take a good close look at the cruise staff, so you'd better appear pretty perky—and that's hard to do when the prior night's gala farewell lasted until 2:00 A.M. There is inevitably a problem at home that must be solved, and the dash to the cleaners, the bank, and home, with a million things to tend to, may be a five-hour round trip. After a mad day of rushing around home, you're even more delighted to be back at sea, even with the fifteen-hour daily grind. Nothing is as hectic as this "turn-around day" in home port.

Though the pay is not excessive, we are without expenses. The company even gives us money for our tips to the steward and waiter. The passengers force gifts on the entertainers, but never tip the cruise director or hostess. We usually dress to the teeth because we have to and so I guess they think we would be above taking a tip.

Although the cruise route may be the same for a year at a time, each cruise is different and challenging. It's hectic work, but fun. Each group of passengers has its own uniqueness.

The cruise staff hears some of the most unusual personal secrets imaginable. Since I do not hear them in the confessional box, nor am I bound as doctors and lawyers are supposed to be by professional ethics (you should listen to their chatter sometimes), I see no reason for not sharing a couple of the crazier confidences, with the names changed to preserve privacy, of course.

A very attractive Parisienne once noted that I was often sought out by passengers who wanted their palms read or who wanted astrological advice. The serious way in which these conversations were held amused her, and one evening she drew me out about them. "What do the passengers seem most concerned about?" she asked.

I had to admit that the greater share of them wanted advice on their love life. Pinned down further, I explained that the unhappiest of those who sought my advice was a nice gal who'd finagled this cruise with her husband in the hope that it would reawaken some of the lust that had marked their early years together. Unfortunately, the poor guy found the job too much for him. She said, "Jeraldine, it's like trying to put a marshmallow in a piggy bank."

"After studying his and her birth dates and her palm, I gave her all the advice I could think of; but somehow I feel this woman needs more help," I told the Frenchwoman. Then I asked, "What would a Frenchwoman do if her man had this problem?" Well, it seems I asked the very question she was hoping I would ask her.

"I will give her a present," the French lady said. "You give it to her and she will find that it will correct this temporary problem her poor man is having." From her purse she took a small black jar with a crimson plastic top. "This is a very special cream that is devised by a scientist in Toulon," she explained. "She should tell her husband that it is very expensive and rare, but very potent. She should very carefully apply a thin film of it to his member. He will be assured the most pleasurable time he has ever had."

I turned the little jar over in my fingers. "It really works?" I asked.

She looked at me archly. "Do you think it does not?" she asked.

I wished I hadn't asked that question. She had the chief engineer so out of his mind he was cooling off by bathing in live steam. He usually went from one female to the other, but on this cruise he was devoted to just this one Frenchwoman.

I sought out the lady with the problem and gave her the instructions. She was doubtful, but was willing to try anything.

Two days later, the deprived lady phoned me in my cabin while I was rushing to change clothes for the evening. She had called twice before she got me, but I was in the shower. Her voice shook a little with anxiety. "Jeraldine, dear, the cream worked just great, but the jar is empty. I desperately need some more. My husband is hooked on the stuff. Could you possibly get some more for my poor husband?"

I dressed, then called the French gal. Fortunately, she was also in and dressing for dinner, so I could tell her of our desperate need for more of that amazing, wonder-working French cream. She made a couple of sympathetic sounds. "I understand, and fortunately I have a bit more of my supply. If you will get the empty jar and bring it to my cabin, I will provide a refill for this emergency."

The lady was almost tearful in her gratitude when I phoned her back. "Jeraldine, please tell her I'll be glad to pay her for it, no matter how expensive it is." Though she had to walk the length of the ship to reach my quarters, she was at my door within minutes to give me the tiny jar.

I stopped off at my French friend's cabin, which was on the main deck. When she let me in, she looked exquisite—in her slip. She had left off her gown for the delicate operation of refilling the little black jar.

She drew open her dresser drawer and as she reached in she said, "And here, my dear, is the very effective French sex stimulating cream that works miracles. The power of the mind." She drew out a giant-sized jar of Pond's cold cream.

"Witchcraft," she said as she refilled the tiny jar. "But it has afforded me a great deal of pleasure I would not otherwise have had."

So now the secret is out.

Another helpful and fantastic piece of information was given me about a variation of this sexual problem, this concerning the frigidity of women who are otherwise genuinely interested in sex.

The lady in this instance was an attractive American girl of twenty-eight or so who, though quite modern in her attitudes about sex, was obviously as enthralled by her husband as he was by her. They were a very handsome, loving young couple. We were chatting one evening while her husband played poker with a group of fellows in one of the cabins. It wasn't showtime yet so I had a few minutes. It was a lovely night, with an undercurrent of suspense about it. We sat on the deck, and though there were stars directly overhead, lightning played constantly on the horizon on all sides, and there were the occasional growls of thunder from afar.

Abruptly, she asked me how often I had heard girls complain about an inability to reach a climax during the sex act, a problem which she had had. She was obviously ecstatically in love, so I was a little surprised. I told her that I'd heard of this a great deal, but that in some women it is quite normal and they seemed happy.

"I was ready to kill myself about it," she said. "Really. Take a ton of sleeping pills, cut my throat, anything—until I was cured."

"So what did you do?" I asked. "You always look like a gal that's eaten the canary."

"My husband's brother-in-law is a doctor. I went to my sister-in-law and we went together to see him. A regular appointment. After he'd examined me, he said there was an extra layer of skin over my clitoris that prevented me from enjoying the full pleasure of love-making. He suggested a female circumcision."

"Redheads like you and me are supposed to be missing a layer of skin. That's why we sunburn so dreadfully," I said.

She giggled. "Maybe that's where my missing skin went. Anyway, I had the operation."

"And happily got your jollies thereafter?" I said.

"Not right away. The healing process was much slower than the doctor predicted. I can still remember the sight of my sex-starved husband one night, frustrated, armed with a flashlight and looking between my legs to see what had happened to his 'lovely little thing.'" She and I got to laughing at the thought of her husband with the flashlight and we laughed till tears streamed down our faces.

The entertainers who work cruise ships are always fun people. The specialty acts are really special. Since they appear before the same passengers a number of times in a single cruise, they have to have a great variety of skills. All have traveled extensively and lead exciting lives, so they are full of interesting tales.

One of the really great acts I remember very well was the Carlssons. They are husband and wife, Ruth and Carl, and they danced, juggled, played Swiss bells, and did ESP tricks on several of the Caribbean cruises I worked. When I see acts doing ESP tricks I am always glad if the performers announce before or after their act that just because there is trick ESP doesn't mean that the real thing doesn't exist.

On a cruise to the Mediterranean I was working with Carl Carlsson, although it hadn't exactly been planned that way. This was a special cruise, since the Italian-owned vessel was being taken to dry dock in Genoa for a month of refitting and overhaul before being returned to the West Coast. We had a full complement of passengers who embarked in Los Angeles and Florida for this highly special cruise; they would spend the time the ship was in drydock making various land tours in continental Europe.

The Carlssons, who always put on such a great show, had been booked for this cruise, but at the last moment, Ruth Carlsson was unable to make the complete trip, since she was called to do a part in a motion picture, so she flew back to California from Fort Lauderdale. Carl didn't turn a hair over this development.

"You've seen the act fifty times, Jerry," he said. "You'll assist me."

We hadn't time to rehearse before the first show on the second night out, but we managed to go through the routine for only a few minutes so he could point out where I would foul up a whole trick if I missed a cue or handed him something the wrong way. Not only was I terribly busy with my own duties, but a lulu of a storm, which was to plague us during most of the crossing, was brewing.

By that evening, things were becoming wild. The ship rolled and pitched in the heavy seas and the wind howled topside. Sailors rigged ropes in the public rooms so that the passengers had something to hang on to as they made their way about, but there was no thought of canceling the show. If anything, putting it on became even more important as the storm grew more violent, to keep the passengers from panic.

Carl Carlsson took this right in stride. His performances were even more inspired than usual. In one spot we actually improved a comedy bit.

He had this very funny routine in which two things were to happen simultaneously in the middle of the dance area. A small table equipped with eight rods of varying heights was set in the middle of the dance floor and a smaller table was put off to one side. Carl, who was a marvelous juggler, then set eight dinner plates spinning atop eight rods, then rushed off to the other table to perform a feat of magic. My job was to keep an eye on the spinning plates and

*Jeraldine
entertaining on
the Bounding
Main.*

*Watch out for
the s-s-s-s-snake
in the basket!*

holler at him when one of them began to wobble. He would rush from the other table, where he was in the middle of the magic routine, and get the plates going again.

It was a funny piece of business because it was impossible to set into a routine. Sometimes, three or four plates would begin to wobble at once. The audience really got involved with watching Carl keeping all the plates going until he got the other trick finished. And on this particular night another element was added: the crazy tables wouldn't stay in one place. The pitching of the ship had them dancing around that floor like a bunch of teenyboppers. Though hardly able to stand myself, I'd be chasing the plate table around as he chased the magic table, and the audience began to join in my screams for attention whenever the plates started to fall. The act was wildly successful, but of course there was no way for him to incorporate this hurricane feature into his act.

Sometimes a chance remark by a passenger will set the entertainers off on an evening of mad improvisation, particularly if you have a talent named Jay Price aboard as the starring comedian. Price is an uncontrollable comedian who starts saying outrageously funny things when he comes out of his cabin in the morning and doesn't stop until bedtime. He's heavily muscled, so he looks heavier in a dinner jacket, and he has huge shoulders, curly hair, and bright blue eyes. It's difficult to have lunch or dinner with him, because you laugh so much you can't get any food into your mouth. Paul Lorenz was the cruise director during the cruise Jay was on. Paul was also a professional entertainer who did marvelous impressions of people—not just famous stars, but people aboard the ship itself.

What set this bunch of clowns going one night was a remark by a passenger that she really hoped we had something planned to celebrate the Fourth of July properly. We'd overlooked this so far as the show was concerned—the decorations at lunch had been properly patriotic—but that remark was all Lorenz and Price needed to make them dream up a whole bunch of nutty blackouts for the show.

In one of them, Betsy Ross (Paul, looking a little bit like Jonathan Winters as Auntie Fud) was sewing the American flag, but when she stood up to proudly display her handiwork, her bloomers fell off. Jay led the singalong of patriotic songs and the passengers loved it.

Jay is a beautiful mixture of black and white blood and he likes to tell his audience that "It really confuses the bigots when they see my blue eyes."

The show was a fantastic success. It seems as though when we Americans are away from our beloved U.S.A. on the Fourth of July, we become even more patriotic than when at home.

chapter twenty-five

OH, FOR THE CAREFREE LIFE OF A SEAGULL

THERE ARE SEVERAL NICKNAMES THAT HAVE COME INTO general use among the crews of passenger ships.

One of these is "Godzilla"—and it refers to a passenger who is unusually quarrelsome and critical. It may be used on either sex, but the term is most generally applied to a woman who just can't be pleased, no matter how hard we try, and there is usually at least one aboard, sometimes more.

The second appellation with worldwide currency is that of "seagull," but not the Jonathan type. This is an entirely different kind of bird.

We had a two-day layover at our home port of Los Angeles because of some necessary refitting. On the day of embarkation, our ship was to be moved from the temporary work dock to her regular berth so that passengers could board. I left Glendale at 4 A.M. to drive to San Pedro, hoping to get there before five. There were a number of things I wanted to stow in my cabin, and I planned to do it before the short move was made because there was so much more to do before we sailed at nine that morning.

It was not yet dawn when I slid my car into a space near the gangway of the ship. I had carried a load of dresses and gear up to my cabin, thinking how quiet it was on board with no passengers around. As I walked down the gangway to return to my car, an enormous figure appeared from the shadows of one of the dock-side buildings. It startled me, until I realized he was one of the longshoremen.

"Hey, baby," he growled. "Is this your car?"

"Yes," I said.

"You can't park your car here overnight. Just because you go with some officer doesn't mean you own this place," he hollered.

It was too early in the morning, and I was at my low ebb. "How dare you talk to me like that," I said. "Don't you accuse me of following this ship around, you big baboon." My red hair must have stood on end.

He could have pinched my head off with a thumb and forefinger. "You still can't park that car here," he said. "You seagulls are all alike."

Now I really got mad; my Irish temper was ready to explode. "I can park my car on deck if I want to," I snapped. "I happen to work on this ship, and if you had any manners, you'd help me get my luggage on board to my cabin. And don't you call me a seagull," I snapped.

The eastern sky had begun to brighten. The jumble of winches and derricks, packing boxes and tarpaulin-covered gear that cluttered the work dock was beginning to emerge from the dusk. The water gleamed a steel-silver color. The man must have remembered me vaguely, because he grunted and waited until I got the trunk of the car open. He handled my four big bags as though they were hand luggage. After he'd put them in the cabin, he apologized for not having remembered me as the cruise hostess.

"We get them damn seagulls all the time," he explained. "Pain in the butt, leaving their cars parked all over the place at night while they sleep with the officers and crew."

I forgave him. After all, at night all cats are gray to some men.

A seagull is a female who has chosen a certain cruise ship to follow to the various ports at which it stops. She haunts these ships for one reason: her quarry is the ship's officers and crew. There is a group of seagulls each time we dock. It can be embarrassing sometimes when the fellow one of them is waiting for has another seagull on board. How he tries to disembark one before the other sees her is fun to watch. Sometimes they ask me to help get them out of the mess by talking with one while they get rid of the other.

The seagull can be as intrepid as a big-game hunter trekking into the jungle of Africa, except that she is armed with no more than contraceptives.

The first night at sea on an extended cruise is always extremely informal. Most of the passengers are tired from the journey to the ship, sometimes slightly bombed from bon voyage parties, and they have bags full of clothes to be hung in closets and put away in drawers. The bars get some activity, but generally everyone is locked away in their cabins by midnight and the ship is relatively quiet.

The seagulls specialize in crew members, virtually ignoring the passengers. They mean for their alliances to be temporary and without regrets. Male passengers also have plenty of opportunities to play it fast and fancy—there are almost always more enthusiastic female partners available than the men can readily handle. After the single male passengers have been taken, the really avid lady passengers sometimes forage among the officers and cruise staff, the waiters, stewards and busboys, even the oilers, if they hate the idea of sleeping alone. Not that there is anything wrong with busboys and oilers. They are usually young, handsome, and have their sights on becoming a maitre d' or marrying a wealthy young passenger. The home office encourages the hiring of good-looking crew members as a sort of stud service—politely advertised in brochures as "come sail with us and be shamefully pampered by the handsome Italian crew." I remember one cruise when the oilers were taken, so the cab drivers got lucky when we were in port.

Honestly, it is so normal for fairly well-to-do ladies to go on cruise ships wanting to fall in love that I can think of only a few cases unusual enough to be worthy of recording at this time.

On a voyage I made from Miami to Genoa, Italy, we took a full complement of 750 passengers aboard in Florida. When we arrived in Barcelona, Spain, they were divided into groups for conducted land tours to various parts of the Continent while the ship went to dry dock in Genoa. The passengers were to rejoin the ship a month later when she sailed back for her next season in the Caribbean. This company doesn't want to be empty for the long crossing, so they offer the round trip at a fantastically low price, which includes the land tours and hotel and meals while the passengers are ashore.

We celebrated our departure from Miami with a swinging party, the kind that makes sailing on time a real challenge for the officers and crew. The carousing kept flaring up at intervals even after we were well out at sea. Merrymakers would explode onto the decks from the cabins, raise a little hell, then disappear—only to be replaced by new groups. It didn't entirely quiet down until dawn.

Only the hardier and more reserved passengers appeared for breakfast. The others began to drift into the various bars for medication about mid-morning.

Just before lunch, my attention was caught by a young woman who was at the main bar with a group that was just getting up a head of steam again. She was wearing an exceptionally smart outfit that went so well with her coloring. I complimented her on her choice of the shades of lavender that seemed to really flatter her. "Thank you, I'm a summer," she said.

"Oh, you know about the four seasons color concept," I replied. Then I went on, "Isn't it amazing that there aren't any two people in the world who have the same group of pigments that make up their skin tones? We are as unique as our fingerprints."

We talked some more and she said she had attended my lecture on astrology this morning and wondered if I would have any time on this cruise to give her a private "reading."

"No, I don't, but give me your birth info: month, day, hour, year and place and I'll look it up for you. What is your cabin number?"

"I really would appreciate that because my world seems to be falling apart. I left my husband and I took this cruise to get away to try to think straight." She turned her face to hide a tear. I had to dash for our next activity but I could sense this girl really was looking for some guidance.

I really didn't have a free minute but I ate my lunch in my cabin so I could look up her birth information in my ephemeris. No wonder she seemed so eager for the reading. She had at this very time the planet Saturn in opposition to her Zodiacal sun in the 10th house and making hard aspects to some of her other planets. I would have to find time to explain to her what she was going through.

Jeraldine teaching the passengers astrology.

When we went ashore on our first port of call. I asked about her husband's birthday and we talked at length. I helped her to understand that the feeling of discontent she was experiencing was only temporary as the planets always keep moving. Then I said, "Please, this is not the time for you to make a big decision. Ride loose in the saddle of fate right now."

She had a great time on the cruise. I saw her dancing and drinking with several young men and she attended all my lectures. When she left the trip she gave me a big hug and said she would write me. She left with the young man she had danced with each night on the ship.

Time went by and a year later she wrote me that she could never thank me enough for guiding her. She had taken my astrological advice and postponed the divorce until the date I gave her and she said that, sure enough, by the time those bad aspects were over, her feelings changed and she had fallen back in love with her husband again. She said she loved him all the more because he had been so patient with her during her confused cycle. To this day, they send me Christmas cards and they now have two lovely children and seem so very contented, and are leading constructive lives. She writes that she is enjoying being a homemaker (true to her Cancer Sun) and is a student of astrology.

I continue using astrology on every cruise. When passengers who are sailing unattached come to our singles party, I place signs at the tables so that the air and fire signs sit together and the water and earth are next to each other. If nothing else, it makes for a good conversation ice breaker. These parties probably have started more romances than Cupid's arrows.

chapter twenty-six

THE PHONE CALL
I SHALL NEVER
FORGET

I KNOW IT ISN'T FASHIONABLE TO TRY TO MAKE ENDS MEET by hard work when one can freeload off the government but my mother always said, "The harder one works the luckier one gets." She always kept President Lincoln's quote on our ice box. It read:

> *You cannot strengthen the weak by weakening the strong.*
> *You cannot help small men by tearing down big men.*
> *You cannot help the poor by destroying the rich.*
> *You cannot help the wage earner by pulling down the wage payer.*
> *You cannot further the brotherhood of men by inciting class hatreds.*
> *You cannot build character and courage by taking away a man's initiative and independence.*

You cannot help men permanently by doing for them what they could and should do for themselves.

Mother always had the perfect maxim to fit the situation. Those that helped us kids the most were: "The crime is not in failing but in failing to try." "Where there is a will there is a way." "A stitch in time saves nine." The one that helped me most was "There isn't any use in crying over spilt milk."

I had my test of strength when the beautiful ship I had been working on for over two years went to drydock. We sailed from San Pedro, California, to Genoa, Italy. On the way, we off loaded our 750 passengers in Ft. Lauderdale, and, within a couple of hours, filled the ship with new passengers. The new passengers were to be taken on various land tours in Europe for three weeks while the vessel was in drydock, then reboard our ship and sail back to the U.S.A. When we arrived in Barcelona my duty was to be in charge of three busloads of passengers through Spain and Portugal. By this time I was pretty good at faking Spanish so when a passenger would ask me what certain signs said, I would make up something that I thought sounded logical. Many Spanish words I had never seen in print and the words on the signs looked like Chinese to me.

I kept a head count each time our bus stopped, and I panicked when I lost a passenger at the Prado Museum in Madrid. He was an elderly gentleman with a big mop of white hair. I had the passengers wait in the buses while I went back to find him. Now, how did I go about that when my Spanish was so poor? I remembered that when our ship was in Caracas, Venezuela, we used to buy false hair called *peluca* for our costume parties, and I assumed that was the Spanish word for "hair." I knew that white in Spanish is *blanca*, so I proceeded to run frantically throughout the vast rooms of the Prado asking everyone, "Have you seen a *hombre* with *blanca peluca?*"

No one could help me. They just gave me strange looks. Finally, I found my passenger sitting on a bench.

He said, "I got lost but I knew if I just stayed put you would find me."

Only later did I find out that "peluca" doesn't mean hair in Spanish, it means "wig"! I was asking them if they had seen a man in a white wig!

We went all over Spain and Portugal. Our bags had to be packed and out in the hallways of our hotels every morning at 6:00 A.M. One morning the alarm clock went off and I thought to myself, These early mornings are killing me. I went to the shower in a zombie-like state, brushed my teeth, put on my makeup, fixed my hair, packed, and put my bags out in the hallway. Much to my surprise, there weren't any other bags there—then I looked at my watch. It was 2:00 in the morning!

In Lisbon we went on a nightclub tour and our guide asked us if we would like to go up to the hills to see how the Gypsies live and see them entertain. We all agreed that it would be of interest to us. These Gypsies live in home-like caves, with their polished pots and pans hanging from the ceilings. While the passengers were enjoying the passionate music and the dancers, our guide said, "Would you like to go to the next cave where there is a Gypsy fortune teller?" I agreed and he interpreted for me. I don't remember much except that the fortune teller said that in less than three weeks I would be receiving a very important message. Having Sagittarius as my rising sign is most helpful when it comes to positive thinking and so I was eager to hear what the good news would be. We would reach the end of our land tour in three weeks.

The news came the night before we were to sail back to the U.S.A. I was awakened during the night by a phone call from my brother who lived next door to my daughter Gail. He was sobbing, and I could barely make out what he was trying to tell me—I just heard unintelligible words. Finally, I understood what it was he was trying to say. My precious, my only child, my beautiful, brilliant Gail had passed away. I screamed, "Run over quickly and you can save her! Hurry!" He could hardly talk for crying, he said, "Please, Jerry, if you crack up the whole family will, too."

After that call from my brother telling me of my daughter's death, I felt my life had ended because we were so close. I don't know how I managed to pull myself together to endure my grief and get home on a flight that took my last penny. I remember when our casino manager got word that he had lost his father, we saw him take a drink for the first time. He drank until he passed out because the ship's authorities told him he would be fired if he went home to his father's funeral. I recalled how greatly he suffered because he couldn't attend the funeral.

So, when I had to make the decision to fly home, I wondered if they would fire me? Where could I possibly find another ship's hostess job? What would my family do without my financial help? All the while my heart was being wrung dry.

Somehow, I managed to endure the funeral. I had to hold myself together for my family's sake. My daughter had separated from her husband so I was back in the apartment where my precious daughter had passed on. My family was in almost complete depression and then the doorbell rang. I had a telegram in my hand saying I had been replaced by another hostess. The cruise line was sorry, but they needed someone right away and my gear would be sent home to me. My first thought was, How will I be able to help support my mother? Actually, I had no idea how I could support myself.

Right here I'd like to tell you why my daughter passed on. I'll try to condense the book I later wrote about it with the help of the brilliant Harvey Ross, M.D. *Hypoglycemia: The Disease Your Doctor Won't Treat* was published by Kensington Publishers in New York. It is considered the definitive work on hypoglycemia. I feel Gail's death was not completely in vain because the book has been a phenomenal success and has helped more than one million readers who have identified with her plight.

Hypoglycemia is a "do it yourself" disease. There isn't any patented drug that the pharmaceutical companies can sell for it, so it is known as "the stepchild of medicine." Most young people have it, to some degree, when they don't eat enough protein but eat processed foods that have added sugar. Medical schools are just now beginning to teach a bit of nutrition. Doctors mostly study disease, not how to prevent it. The medical students should have tattooed on their foreheads, so they will see it every time they look in a mirror, "We are what we eat—and what we think." Dietitians are still counting calories; they should be replaced with nutritionists who know that it is not how many calories but what kinds of calories that are important. Very few people die from hypoglycemia (low blood sugar). Usually they just suffer symptoms ranging from unexplained tiredness to asthma, attention deficit disorder, insomnia, obesity, headaches, crying spells, dizziness, mood swings, hyperkinesis, etc. There are over forty symptoms—you may have one or any number of them. There are so many ways to react to it that most doctors can't find anything in the usual tests. (It is now a fad to say hypoglycemia is a fad disease.)

So the doctors send the hypoglycemic to a psychiatrist. "It's all in your head," they say. Only the minority of doctors who are informed realize that in some individuals who are sensitive to refined carbohydrates, the blood sugar either goes too low or drops too rapidly, causing reactive hypoglycemic symptoms. The only way to prove it is to take a blood sample every half hour at first and then every hour for five more hours. I don't recommend this because it can be a traumatic test for some patients. The other way to test for it is to try not eating refined carbohydrates, have frequent snacks of complex carbohydrates and protein, and use no coffee or alcohol for one week. If your various symptoms go away you will know that you are one of the biochemically challenged individuals who shouldn't eat refined carbohydrates. For these individuals, coffee and sugar lower the blood sugar after giving an initial false lift. This false stimulation whips the adrenals and eventually takes its toll.

I wish I had known about this when my child was growing up and I was trying to be such a good mother. I would bake cakes and cookies, thinking I was a good parent. As my daughter grew older, doctor after doctor told me my daughter's symptoms were all in my head, that I was just becoming a "health nut." A teenager by this time, Gail listened to the real health nuts, those who don't realize we are what we eat. After a child reaches her teens, it is impossible to control her diet. Kids eat sugar-laden food at school and also in restaurants. My daughter's death was caused by ignorance of this particular aspect of health. You mothers and fathers who have children with health problems may now find even less help than I did. Ritalin, a drug to keep a poor child quiet, is often prescribed. It stunts their growth and the long-term effects are yet to be discovered. The armed forces won't take recruits who have been on Ritalin during their childhood. When will we teach young people the importance of whole foods so that they can raise their children to be healthy and keep themselves healthy?

My daughter would have been twenty-seven years old if she had lived two more weeks. In college she was a straight-A student, exceptionally beautiful, and no one could believe she wasn't in perfect health, but she had suffered from insomnia since she was an infant. When I told her pediatrician about this (during World War II when doctors were so busy and overworked) his reply was, "Infants don't have insomnia." Period. That was all the help I got from him. Her allergies and highs and lows in energy never kept her sick enough to be in bed, but never really well enough to utilize her gifts.

I feel Gail's lasting gift to humanity is the book Dr. Ross and I wrote about her illness's prevention and cure.

With the funeral over, I had to pull myself together and find another job. I still couldn't type and my spelling wasn't any better. I wrote letters to the few cruise lines in existence then, but the odds of finding a job aboard a ship were one in a million. Most cruise lines use foreign crews because American unions have priced our skilled workers out of the market. The only Americans used on cruise ships are the cruise director and the hostess, who both need to communicate with the American passengers. There was only one hostess on each ship; you can imagine how few cruise hostess jobs there were.

Gail

My daughter passed away at the end of November. A month and a half later, alone in the darkness of a very early winter morning, I was awakened by the loudest noise I had ever heard. I don't know why, but I thought to myself, This must be the end of the world! In a reflex action I ran down the stairs to my mother's apartment. The whole world was rocking, but I had to see if she was all right. It was the worst earthquake in California in fifty years. My mother's apartment was a mess, mirrors down, broken dishes and everything all over the floors. After calming her down I began to feel a pain in my back. I asked her to look at my back to see if I was hurt. She looked and said, "No, dear I don't see anything."

Back in my apartment the telephone was ringing. In my still-quivering state I lifted the receiver. It was the owner of a cruise company replying to my letter asking for a hostess job. He said, "We need a hostess right away. The ship is in Los Angeles' San Pedro harbor. Can you be there tonight for the 5:00 P.M. sailing?"

"Thank you, dear God," I said to myself. To the man on the telephone, I said, "I know you are calling from Miami, but have you heard about the terrible earthquake we have just experienced?"

He said he hadn't heard of it yet. So I told him, "I can't get into the room where I have my cruise clothes and my cruise supplies because the bookshelves have all fallen and I can't get the door open. But, I'll manage somehow to be there in time to greet the passengers."

I was so elated about the job offer that I almost forgot about my backache. When I looked around my bedroom, I wondered how I got out of that bed alive. The free-standing bookcase with heavy shelves, books, and a TV set on it tipped over onto my bed, right where I had been sleeping. When I took my shower, I couldn't believe the black and blue marks on the front of me. One bruise on my hip was as big as a large grapefruit. I called a chiropractor, dashed over for an adjustment to my aching back, then dashed back to start packing.

Being a neat Virgo, it was hard to leave my smashed-up apartment and just lock the door and rush off to the ship.

The first night aboard this Greek ship, after I had finished my hostess duties and fallen into an exhausted sleep, I felt myself walking and smashing right into the bulkhead alongside my bed. After the passengers have fallen asleep, the captain sometimes orders the ship's stabilizers to be retracted; the ship goes faster that way and saves money on fuel. When that first big wave hit my side of the ship, my sleeping mind forgot that I was aboard ship and it seemed like another earthquake. Bam! I almost broke my nose.

The next day, it was business as usual, activities scheduled every hour on the hour for the passengers, and, of course, preparations for the Captain's Welcome Aboard Party and a show.

I found myself functioning well in the public rooms, both the forward ballroom and the aft observation lounge, supervising activities all day and most of the night. I think I was able to play the jester so well because, as I went from one end of the ship to the other, I had the long alleyways to myself. This was the only time I could release some of my grief for my daughter. To my surprise, I would hear myself moan all the way from one lounge to the other.

Sounds must be healing in some way. I don't know how long I mourned in this way, but the necessity of having to work probably played a constructive part in coping with my grief.

chapter twenty–seven

My Off-Broadway Ship

I MANAGED TO WORK PRETTY WELL ON THE NEW SHIP. Keeping busy helped me cope with the loss of my daughter.

While I was the hostess on this large Greek ship, we had just finished the winter season on the Mexican Riviera and the Caribbean, and were about to sail from Los Angeles to Victoria, B.C. I was asked to come to the ship-to-shore telephone because "the home office wants to talk to you." The boss in the home office said, "How would you like to become the only female cruise director in the whole wide world, Jeraldine?"

Well, I thought, isn't that wonderful! "Okay," I said. "Great! Give me the details."

He said, "The ship is waiting for you in Victoria. When the ship you are on now pulls in, you get off and as soon as you board your new ship, they will sail. You will arrive in about two hours and they are waiting for you. The passengers are boarding now."

The first thing I had to do was quit my hostess job. The cruise director had a fit because I really was a hard worker. Quickly, I packed all my gear—that wasn't easy because I had a cabin full of clothes. During my few hours off when we docked in Los Angeles, I would sometimes dash downtown to Mr. Blackwell's showroom where I used to model. He is famous for "The Ten Worst Dressed List," but in real life he is a greatly talented couturier. His beautiful gowns, dresses, and suits are classics. He and his partner, Robert Spencer, let me buy his model's samples for just about what they paid for the buttons, so I had the greatest wardrobe!

I was so excited about the job offer that I could hardly think straight. It all seemed so fabulous! To think after all these years of my being a hostess and taking orders from various cruise directors I would be one myself. Directors often didn't last long. They were being carted off the ship every few months from too much work and too much play, then I would have to train a new one. Now I was actually going to be a real, live female cruise director. What a break for women's lib, and especially for me!

As soon as we arrived, I boarded the waiting ship, a pretty white one that was very expensive, very exclusive, and held only 475 passengers. It was about 10:00 P.M. when we arrived. Because the passengers had flown in from long distances, most had gone to their cabins to unpack, and gone to bed to rest up for this eagerly anticipated cruise to Alaska. I was shown around the public rooms by the chief purser and the first officer. "Well, I had better get to work," I said. "Introduce me to the hostess, please."

"Oh," the chief purser replied, "didn't they tell you? You are the cruise director and the hostess, too."

I thought to myself, Good heavens, I can't imagine! I had to work so hard just being the hostess, how on earth can I be the cruise director, also? However, I was in no position to object so I just swallowed and tried to act nonchalant. I said, "Okay, please introduce me to the entertainers so we can get tomorrow's ' Welcome Aboard Show' ready."

The purser looked at the first officer and said, "Entertainers? What entertainers?"

I couldn't help it, my voice raised a bit to reveal my shock when I said, "Don't tell me you don't have any entertainers aboard!" I couldn't believe it. I said, "Well, who does the show?"

They said, "The cruise director does."

Well this certainly was an "off-Broadway" ship. It reminded me of something Ricardo Montalban said whenever he found himself in a "B" movie. "Ask not what this role can do for me but what can I do for this role." Oh yes, that really applied to my job on this ship.

I thought to myself, Well, I have faked my knowledge of languages to get my job at sea, but how do I fake singing? I knew how to do the hula but in Alaska it didn't exactly fit in. At least we had this Yukon orchestra. The next night I told the audience at the "Welcome Aboard Show" that because this ship would be on the South Seas the next winter, I would do the hula to give them a preview, and perhaps they would sail with us down there. I got the passengers to join me and we had a fun show. Later, in desperation, I took a familiar melody and wrote new lyrics for a "Yukon" song to get passengers in the Alaskan mood.

Each cruise was eight days long. We went to KetchiKan, Juneau, Tracy Orm, Endicot Arm, Skagway, Prince Rupert, and back to Victoria. We never had an overnight anywhere. We sailed from Victoria the same day we got back, having only a few hours in port.

Eventually, I put together a fun time for the passengers. Because we had no entertainers I had them do Robert Service plays, but I had to triple cast them because I never knew who would get drunk, seasick, have cold feet, or just plain forget to show up. The shows were more fun than professional entertainers because the passengers became involved and almost everyone has some "ham" in them. They had so much fun that we had return passengers lined up on the dock waiting to sail with us again, hoping for a cancelation. I was a success, but I was also amazed. If you knew the hardships some of these passengers endured on that ship you would understand my amazement that they would want to return to the ship I later called the "Leaking Lena." We had a lot of things go wrong. We didn't even have anyone in charge of the hospital. I asked during the first emergency, "Where is the doctor?"

I don't know a Totem Pole Dance so I'm doing the Hula to entertain passengers on the Alaskan cruise.

They said, "We don't have one because when a ship is less than two and a half miles from shore it isn't required to have one."

I said, "What do you do if someone gets sick or needs first aid?"

The captain looked me straight in the eye as if he was making a logical statement as he said, "That's the cruise director's job."

Good heavens! I thought. How can I fake first aid? I guess he could see I was apprehensive about this so he said, "We'll have a first aid man come on board and teach you how to do it when we get into port tomorrow."

He did and it certainly came in handy. You should have seen me running around that hospital trying to find medicine when everything was in Spanish—the ship had formerly had a Spanish crew.

My previous ships were all very posh. We always had a lovely chapel and a priest on board. On a long cruise, we occasionally would have a rabbi and a minister, too. During my first week on board this "off Broadway" ship, the days were moving so fast that I didn't realize it was Sunday already. I knew we would not be in port that day, so I asked, "Which do you have aboard, a minister, rabbi, or priest?"

The chief purser answered, "We don't have any minister aboard."

Before I could ask, "Well, who does the Sunday service?" he said, "The cruise director does it."

Well! Now I was expected to conduct a nondenominational church service—that really was a challenge. I had been in a Catholic church, but my mother said that it was some kind of sin— a mortal one, I think—if we went into any other kind of church.

I asked every crew member I could find if he had a Bible. I even went to the captain. No one had one so I went to my cabin to look in my astrology and numerology books for something that might be uplifting. I had taken a motivational course called PACE a long time ago so I jotted down some ideas about imaging which I learned there. Within a few minutes, I had made up my own religion.

The next challenge was to conduct the service without being terrified. We did have hymn books on board so I passed those out.

I had never heard these hymns before and I can't read music, so I had to try to get a passenger to volunteer to play the piano. The orchestra's piano player worked late the night before and wasn't about to lose his sleep for my early morning service, so I turned on the microphone and asked for someone to play. Since there wasn't any response, I continued, "You know every Sunday (it was my first Sunday) someone volunteers to play the piano for us." Silence. Then I said, "Every Sunday God always has someone volunteer to play the piano for us." I guess they finally felt sorry for me. Finally, someone volunteered to play. Silently I said, "Thank you, dear God."

I conducted the singing with the mike turned off so they would think I knew the songs as I pretended to sing along with them. And they really liked my sermon. The problem was, they all came over to me afterwards and asked me, "What religion are you?" Much to my surprise, a portion of my sermon appeared later in the book *A New Beginning*, from the Hazelden meditation series.

"Fear is only an illusion. It is the illusion that creates the feeling of separateness—the false sense of isolation that exists only in your imagination." Those were my first words in print. What a thrill! It is most comforting to realize that we are all a part of God. There isn't any separation.

I liked conducting the Sunday service. I think I would have liked to be a minister. It was really kind of fun once I got the hang of it. Later, I built it up to be a big event. I had the captain read a prayer to open the service. I called a friend and asked if he could send me anything, and he sent some very inspirational material from his Unity Church and some books from the Science of Mind. What I read in the books about imaging, I applied to helping me write and sell the first edition of this book you are now reading, my very first book. The more I learned to trust it, the more this philosophy of imaging what you want really worked for me. Since then I have studied "The Course In Miracles" and learned one can take quantum leaps in time by imaging or prayer. God's infinite mind can straighten out situations faster than we can with our finite minds. Of course, one must remember to ask for God's will to be done, because God only wants what is joyful and what brings an abundance of good for us. Sometimes we wish for what isn't best for us. That is why it's so important to say: "if it be God's will."

I am including for you here the music and lyrics of a song two friends of mine sent me that the passengers really loved to sing.

You Stand Tall When You Kneel To Pray

Words by
RALPH PORTNER

Music by
JOE RIZZO

We had a beauty parlor on board but no one to operate it, so there wasn't any way I could get my hair done. I was forced to tell a bit of a fib. "The passengers are complaining that our beauty shop is closed," I said to the chief purser.

He replied, "I'll try to get an operator and give it a try. If it pays for itself we will keep it open."

So I had to make sure this new operator would be successful. For the next cruise they put on a hairdresser, a very young, good looking kid named Tom Vercillo. When he was introduced to me I asked where he had worked.

"I'm just out of beauty school and I have been working in the beauty shop at Penney's Department Store in Tacoma."

I then asked him "Have you ever sailed before?"

"No," he said, "this is all new to me."

The mother instinct in me is very strong, and I desperately needed the beauty shop to be open, so I explained, "We will be crossing the Queen Charlotte Sound in the morning and it can be very rough water for a couple of hours. Please remember the secret to preventing seasickness: If the water is rough, keep solid food in your stomach and never put any liquids in it, not even things that turn into liquid, like Jello. Tomorrow morning be sure to eat your breakfast. OK?"

He nodded that he understood.

That night when I welcomed the passengers to our special loving ship, I said, "Ladies, our 'Captain's Welcome Aboard Party' is tomorrow evening, so you may want to try our new hair stylist. He is so talented. He comes directly from the studios in Hollywood. He got tired of the prima donnas and the smog so we are very fortunate to have him! Make your reservations early."

Well, it really worked, but it backfired the next morning as we were crossing Queen Charlotte Sound and I was giving one of my lectures in the Grand Salon. I heard "Jeraldine...help!"

It was a gasp from an ashen-white Tom, the hairdresser. "Please help me, I'm seasick. I just had to grab a lady by the hair and throw

Then there was the lady who took the cruise director's advice at the disembarkation talk. I had asked that all the baggage be placed outside the cabin by 2:00 A.M. the last night out. I tell them to pack everything except what they wanted to hand carry off the ship the next morning. After dancing all night this dear lady put her luggage outside her cabin for pick up, and then her cabin door swung shut. There she was, barefooted up to her chin. I guess she packed her jammies and decided to sleep in what Marilyn Monroe did—a little Chanel Number 5.

Passengers sometimes ask the funniest questions; often heard are:

"Does the crew sleep on board?"

"Is the mail picked up every day?"

"Is this island surrounded by water?"

I was asked, "Is there sea water in the pool?" When I said, "Yes," the reply was, "No wonder the water's so rough."

The one that really stumps me is, "What do you do on the weekends?"

*Geraldine Saunders introduces passengers to the captain
at the "Welcome Aboard" party.*

chapter twenty-eight

How to Look Happy 24 Hours a Day

Most of the ocean-going playpens I've worked on are wondrous things. They are sleek and graceful, their upper paint work sparkling white, their hulls and stacks of different colors according to the tastes of their owners.

When cruise ships depart from their first port with their new passengers, they are at their best. They sail from the harbor toward the open sea, their decks awash with lights, pennants fluttering in the breeze, sounds of music and laughter drifting across the millions of dancing bright pinpoints on the dark water. They exude a feeling of buoyant gaiety. Oh! It's all so very romantic!

There is also a practical way of regarding one of these lovely crafts. It is a monster of 50,000 to 109,000 or so gross tons and nearly 1,000 feet in length, made up of girders and plates of steel that have been riveted and welded, framed and braced, to form the main structure of the hull and upper works. There are acres of cabins, alleyways, galleys, and public rooms fitted together like a giant puzzle. Small forests of fine mahogany and teak have provided her panelings, and there are hundreds of miles of pipings and lead-encased conduits and cables snaked between decks and behind her magnificent bulkheads. Works of art, freight-train loads of plumbing fixtures, specially made furniture, fine china, crockery, utensils, bedding, and provisions have been fitted into her to provide for the needs of between 1,000 to 3,000 passengers, staff, and crew members.

The brain transmitting the orders which keep this complex organization running is, of course, the bridge of the ship. The heart lies in a pulsating area seventy or eighty feet below. This is the engine room, a place of endless clamor so deafening that those who work there must wear large ear coverings clamped to their heads or lose their hearing.

The point of all this is that when the heart, or the engine, stops aboard a ship, all else stops—for all else is dependent upon it. For this reason, the vigil in the engine room is never-ending. It is a place of constant movement, with engineers checking peepholes to the burners and studying air- and oil-pressure gauges, control valves, oil and water levels, generator output, and a multitude of other things beyond my knowledge.

These men who work deep in the sweat-drenched bowels of a liner must be thinking as much of themselves as anyone else when they take such severe pains to do their job properly. Should anything go wrong, they are certain to be the worst sufferers.

There is nothing so helpless as a great power-driven ship dead in the water. Its rudders are useless and it is at the mercy of wind and tide. Traveling at normal cruising speed, a liner will still go far more than a mile before it can be brought to a complete stop, even with full reverse power. Without power there is nothing to stop it, and even though a ship may weigh up to 109,000 tons and have a skin of steel, it has got to come off a bad second in a collision with a continent.

If what I've written so far is making you nervous about ships, it was not my purpose. Considering the realities of sailing the seas, plus the frailties of man in his struggle against the elements, I am stunned by the reliability that has been engineered into these wonderfully great passenger vessels. With today's ships, sea travel is far safer than air travel or surface travel.

In proof, let me tell you about twenty-four hours of continuous action in which it seemed always imminent that Davy Jones would have a whole lockerful of unexpected callers. There was no raging hurricane involved; there was never more than a light breeze on this cruise, and the air was as clear as crystal.

The cruise staff, of which I am a part, has nothing to do with the actual running of the ship, the maintenance of arrival and departing schedules, or the safety of the passengers, though we certainly pitch in willingly enough if there is an emergency. Our sole concern is to make sure the passengers have a good time. Of course, on this ship I called "the Leaking Lena," the cruise staff consisted of just one person, me, the cruise director. This series of misadventures occurred on the ship during an eight-day cruise through the inside passage of Alaska, a place of spectacular beauty. Vast mountains literally leap from sparkling blue-green straits and twisting channels more than a mile in depth, and they are deeply forested almost to their snow-capped peaks. Misty waterfalls cascade in veils from their steep sides.

On this cruise the captain of the ship was a temporary one—replacing the vacationing, very capable captain who was usually in command. Our regular captain was so competent that I always felt safe with him, but his substitute was unfamiliar with both cruise liners and Alaskan waters. These two facts were to contribute to his undoing.

Ketchikan is the southernmost of Alaska's cities, sitting on Revillagigdo Island on the Tongass Narrows. Until this point on our cruise from Victoria to the north, the sailing is fairly straight and open, though with many sheltering islands to the westward. However, tidal currents can do weird things in channels or straits along the Inside Passage. There the currents race from ten to twenty-four knots at full ebb or flow; the cruising speed of our ship was about twenty knots. Captains usually hate this run because it is so difficult to handle the current.

The approach to Ketchikan is a special event to the passengers, of course, for it is usually their first view of a genuine Alaskan city, even though it isn't really much more than a large, adorable town.

Most of the passengers had gathered along the starboard deck and at the bow as the top of Ketchikan's towering radio antenna appeared above a pine-clad outcropping. As we cleared the point and the rest of the town came into view across the glittering waters of the harbor, the remaining passengers joined them for the show. It was a dandy.

There was some confusion on the bridge, where the captain was being assisted by an experienced Alaskan pilot as the law requires. We suddenly went barreling along toward the pier, caromed off a docked Japanese freighter, and slammed into the wharf like a little old lady parking her car in the garage at a nice rate of speed—and without brakes. Pilings and pier plankings went galleywest. Passengers grabbed at supports to keep from falling. But we did manage to come to a stop.

When you start banging into freighters and shearing off portions of docks, there's going to be some talk, and Ketchikan was full of it for the rest of that day.

The passengers went ashore to look over the town while the residents looked them over. A number of the crew also got shore leave, evidently so they could fill in the regulars at their favorite saloons on what had happened. As cruise director, I had to stay on board to reassess our program for the evening in case the dockside accident should cause a delay in departure.

There was a delay, all right—quite a delay—but not entirely for that reason.

As I was trying to get some idea from the captain on our estimated departure time, the second engineer burst in and insisted
upon an audience with him. Several of his oilers had been drunk
and on the very brink of bloody fights since the beginning of the
cruise, and he asked that they be "logged"; otherwise, he could not
take responsibility for the engines.

The distraught captain glared at him, undoubtedly envisioning
what this entry was going to look like in the records. "Don't tell me
what to write in my log," he said coldly.

At that, the young second engineer, not noted for his ability to
control his temper, red-faced with anger, unleashed a string of invec-
tives that ended with the statement, "If this matter isn't put in writing
at this moment, I flatly refuse to take responsibility."

This comes close to mutiny; fortunately for the engineer, the
medic raced in at that moment to report that there was a knife fight
among some of the oilers below decks. The minor insurrection was
immediately overshadowed by this major one as the officers rushed
off to bring the fight to a halt.

The three oilers who had been primarily involved were a bloody
mess when they were finally taken ashore by the Ketchikan fuzz, a
police lieutenant remaining behind to fill a notebook with answers
to his questions.

Meanwhile, back at the busted-up dock (as the saying goes),
some of the passengers and crew had begun to return to the ship.
Among them was a very dear gentleman, the second mate, a ruddy,
hearty man of sixty who'd spent all his life at sea. To add to our run
of bad luck, just as he reached the dock, he fell and broke his hip,
requiring his removal to the hospital for a three-week stay before he
could be sent back to Seattle for further recuperation.

By this time, all the passengers had returned, but there was no way
we could leave. The sliced-up oilers were also in the hospital being
stitched together while the authorities decided which men were to be
thrown into jail, and which, if any, allowed to return to the ship.
Estimates of damage to the dock were being made and argued about.

Something had to be done to get the more nervous among the passengers calmed down, and this was my job. I decided on a community singalong, champagne on the house, and music by our peerless orchestra, called "The Yukoners." Jimmy King was the leader. I loved his voice, and Norm was great on the accordion. They knew just the kind of songs to help the passengers get in a better mood.

There was an enthusiastic response, dampened only slightly when the passengers began to study one of the waiters who'd been chosen to serve the champagne. He much preferred singing to serving. He'd been among those given shore leave, and he was fried to the eyes. With his being sent to the showers and his replacement working at full tilt, we sang along until well after midnight, when the ship finally pulled away from Ketchikan's harbor en route to the Wrangell Narrows.

I got to bed a little before 2 A.M., much too weary to sleep. I'd been awake and on my feet continuously since six the previous morning, but that wasn't what kept me tossing about on my bunk. I was thinking about the changes in program that would have to be made because of the delay. Chances were that we would have to improvise for several days to come.

I had finally fallen asleep and was dead to the world when there was an unearthly grinding sound, and I was thrown against the bulkhead of my cabin. The motors below me, normally almost inaudible, sounded briefly like a hot-rodder gone berserk, then stopped. The ship was completely quiet.

I tried the cabin lights, but they weren't working. I always keep a freshly batteried, very powerful flashlight clipped next to my bunk; I used it to dress quickly and find my lifejacket and tambourine. Then I opened the door into the alleyway. Others were venturing out of their cabins, lighting their way with matches and cigarette lighters. The beam of the flashlight disclosed that the automatic watertight bulkheads that separated the ship into compartments had closed. I rattled my tambourine to get everyone's attention.

"Oh, Jeraldine," a woman called, rather gratefully, I thought.

Behind me, a man growled, "What'd he do, Jerry? Go back and take another crack at Ketchikan?"

It was a blonde young giant of a guy having a honeymoon cruise with his wife, also blonde, almost as tall as he, and a former Miss Golden West if ever I saw one.

"If he did, he leveled the whole place, Pete," she said.

I had to laugh. "Follow me, everyone, I'll show you where the fun is," I said.

Crying, a little old lady said, "Did you say show us where the front is, Jeraldine?"

"No—I said show you where the fun is."

At that moment, the emergency lights came on and I had them all follow me to the Grand Salon, gathering more passengers with us as we went.

I looked out the portholes in the Grand Salon—it was very dark, for the moon had disappeared behind the mountains. Over part of the ship was a canopy of something you seldom see aboard a liner and I hope never to see again. Trees! Touching our ship! Not little, ordinary trees. Towering hemlocks that rose a hundred and more feet above the upper deck and bathed it in needles and a refreshing scent of balsam. We were hard aground in the Wrangell Narrows, where at times the water races like that in a log flume, but it was impossible to tell whether we were in sand or on the rocks themselves.

Immediately after the impact, all the watertight bulkheads had been closed, electrical circuits cut off to prevent fire, and radio signals broadcast. Compartments near the bow that might present problems were still secured, but everything else was more or less normal. However, people who are prone to panic don't need much of a reason for it and this certainly was a pretty good reason.

Passengers were already beginning to appear on deck, dressed and questioning. The odd sight of the towering trees, faintly visible even with the blackness of the night, did nothing to reassure them. It was time to get back to work.

I called the musicians, who had worked just as late as I and been awakened just as rudely, and asked them to report to the Grand Salon, ready to play. I had a consultation with the purser's office and made arrangements for sandwiches, bouillon, coffee, and for those who might need it, the customary champagne.

I then called the bridge and was invited to the wheelhouse.

The bridge, which is never visited except on invitation, was dark except for a faint reflection from the open door of the chartroom just aft and the pinpoints of shaded light at the binnacle near the helm. The officers on duty were no more than shadowy figures. The complicated controls were invisible, though any officer could put his hand on any one of them in an instant, blindfolded, I'm sure. It seemed we had sailed on the wrong side of a lighted buoy. Suddenly an old ship's adage came to mind. It goes, "Red to red, green to green—for perfect safety, go between."

The captain and the pilot were in the chartroom with long faces, holding a guarded conversation with the chief engineer. There were coffee and sandwiches available, but I was too excited to eat. I waited beside the first officer while they decided whatever it was they were discussing. "I know we're aground," I whispered, "but how does it look? What shall I tell the passengers?"

The first officer didn't seem much concerned. "Can't tell. Not until we get her off."

"How will you know then? That water is too cold to go down for a look."

I could see his serious face in the faint light. He whispered back, "If it's damaged, we won't have to go over the side. The water will come right in. If it doesn't come in now, it will when and if we can get her off the rocks."

"I'm sure it won't be that bad," I said, though I wasn't the least bit sure.

"Well," he replied, "if it's messed up at all seriously, this ship is scrubbed for the rest of the season."

"Oh," I said, I think. Whatever I said wasn't very happy. A scrubbed ship meant my job was scrubbed, and just after I'd made it to cruise director. It's rare employment, and hard to come by, especially for a female. I do know I asked him if he'd ever been on a grounded ship before.

He told me that he had, during a cruise in the South Seas, and I asked what had happened.

"We finally had to abandon ship," he told me. "The only place we could land the passengers was at a leper colony."

This reassuring conversation was interrupted by the captain, who said to me, "Please tell the passengers (I had gathered them all in the Grand Salon by then) that there has been a miscalculation at a buoy and we are aground. There is no immediate danger, though as a precautionary measure, they should be prepared to abandon ship. The ship itself will not be lost, nor their possessions damaged; the major consideration is not only their safety but their comfort. The ship will hopefully be freed at high tide and until that time please continue the entertainment in the Grand Salon. Those who wish may stay there; the others will be quite safe in their cabins."

I replied, "Before I go down to the Grand Salon, may I ask you when high tide is due?"

He said, "It is due around 0800. It's now 0500, so you must try to keep them calm for three more hours. I'll try full reversing the engines at high tide and pray we can get free and that there will be no damage."

I thanked the captain and, falling on hidden reserves of energy and gaiety, got things started in the Grand Salon. "Listen," I told everyone as I grabbed the microphone, "this will be known in the annals of the sea as the 'Ship on the Rocks Party,' and instead of 'Bring on the Rain' dances as the Indians did, we'll do 'Bring in the Tide' dances." And they did, to "Balling the Jack," "Camptown Races," and the like as gray dawn began to break. They had so much fun they actually felt lucky to be on this cruise. As usual, I told them it was something not everyone can write home about.

This was by no means the end of the temporarily stalled odyssey. As the first of the tugs and fishing boats began to appear, I again went to the bridge.

Salvage and rescue can be an important business in those waters. Few owners of the squat little diesel-powered craft leave the waterways unmonitored. A distress signal, such as the one which had been sent out by our ship upon impact, gets them manned and underway within moments. A helping line extended to a disabled ship can net the owner of the rescue craft a large sum of money. A salvage that can be proved in intricate maritime law can come to half of the worth of the whole vessel, or more. It's a highly competitive business, engaged in by tough, hard-headed men.

There were three of these little bulldog-like boats standing off our port at the moment, and others en route. The captain was engaged in a conversation by bullhorn with one of the tug captains, who had made an offer of a line, and a haul. Our officers were taking a very hasty refresher course in salvage law in the chartroom.

Finally, one of them came out for a hurried conversation. It was decided that, since there was no agreement in writing as to the purpose of the offer of a line, the tug captain could still make a salvage claim. Our captain informed the tug that he was refusing the offered line and would attempt to get out of his problem under his own power.

Most of the powerful little boats turned for home with the announcement that we didn't want a line. Several, however, sought anchorage in small coves nearby and hung there, swaying like so many vultures waiting for our failure.

This reminded me of one of the saddest things I've ever seen at sea. Once, when we pulled in at Panama, there was a deserted English ship aft of us. It had been adrift at sea for nine days and when they got in to port the young captain, forty-two years old, had killed himself for having turned down the offer of help. Thinking they could get the engines started soon, he didn't want to salvage the ship. No other ships came by, and they were desperately looking for help as the days went by. For nine days they drifted without water and with only spoiled food because of the heat—they had no air conditioning or refrigeration. It was a real ghost ship when we saw her. So, so sad.

By eight, the Alaska morning was brilliant and utterly beautiful. Every passenger was alert, of course, for this moment of supreme effort on the part of the turbines would determine whether we were free or whether lifeboats would have to be lowered. If there was an announcement that the attempt was about to be made, I do not recall it. Suddenly, the liner, quiescent for so long, came alive. Water roiled under her stern. For a long time there was nothing, then the tiniest of movements, then a surging one.

We are off! And floating free!

The several tugs blasted their steam whistles from their anchorages and our own ship sent back a deep-throated message to them.

It was 8:00 A.M. I went to bed.

The captain called me an hour later to ask me once more to help the passengers.

The magnificent scenery sliding by on the port and the starboard was lovely to watch if you didn't know that the ship had nothing to do with it. We were without power, drifting on the current in much the same way that the Kennedys used to ride down the Colorado River. The Kennedys were in rubber rafts; we were in a large cruise ship. In a ship you cannot get oars over the side to make corrections in your movements through the currents of water.

The passengers—those who were not still sleeping off the late night—were aware that something was wrong; none of the toilets would flush, and none of the lights would work.

Nevertheless, our luck changed later. The engineers got things put to rights again, and we sailed into Scow Bay and anchored without incident so that local deep-sea divers, fully clad and helmeted against the icy waters, could go below and examine the bottom. They reported that it was scratched, but not harmed.

The temporary captain's luck remained lousy. In Victoria he was finally relieved of his command, and he was upset about it. I felt so sorry for him. He was a nice man and I hope that his future cruises—and mine—will bring a lot smoother sailing.

chapter twenty-nine

STARTING A CRUISE IN DRYDOCK

MY EXPERIENCE WITH MY "OFF BROADWAY" SHIP ON THE Alaskan cruise was an interesting one. The ship was a lovely thing, beautifully adapted to the Inside Passage since it was small enough to venture up the narrow fjords above Wrangell, but large enough to handle the often tumultuous crossing of Queen Charlotte Sound comfortably.

However, until the passing of ownership, the ship had been owned by a Greek shipping family and operated by Spanish officers and crew. The new crew was largely Canadian and English. I was the only American working aboard and, again, the only female.

We didn't know one another. And what was worse, no one knew the ship at all. All the instruction plates imbedded in the equipment were in Spanish, and these Canadians and Englishmen didn't understand Spanish. Any pamphlets or booklets about the operation of the vessel from hold to galley were also in Spanish. It was really something because no time at all was lost in putting her into immediate service. I was getting along pretty well with things Latin by this time, but I was of no help at all below decks. I wouldn't have survived a half hour down in the engine room.

The first few cruises on that ship (the Leaking Lena) were pure hell. So many things would go wrong that I was afraid I would have to prevent a mutiny among the passengers. The first morning at my "Welcome Aboard" talk I would try to squelch any discontent that some passengers might cause in trying to impress others by saying such things as, "When I was on such and such a ship we had such and such, etc."

To prevent this deserved comparison I would say, "Good morning, I'm Jeraldine Saunders, your cruise director, and I want to tell you a little about our ship. I know you all have been on bigger and better ships, but let me tell you this ship is very special. It has very loving vibrations. We don't know why, but it does. I'll guarantee that when you disembark in eight days I will be at the gangway to say goodbye to you and you all will say to me, 'Jeraldine, you are right, this ship does have loving vibrations.' and you will have had the best time ever!"

Even though they went through all kinds of hardships and emergencies, they had the right attitude and had a great time, and yes, they all thanked me as they disembarked. In fact, much to my surprise the passengers had such a good time that many would line up every time the ship returned to Victoria, just waiting in case a cancelation would make it possible for them to sail with us again.

A friend of mine, Ralph Portner, says to remember these three most important words: attitude, adjustment (you can't move into the cemetery), and appreciation. These passengers had the right attitude!

All ships must go into drydock once a year. It's a regular thing for them and quite necessary. I've only been in drydock once, and it was aboard this same ship with a full complement of passengers!

Mercury was retrograde and that can mean delays. We had left Victoria for the cruise that would turn around at Skagway, far up the Inside Passage. After we boarded our new passengers late in the evening, I was told that it would be necessary to spend the next few hours in drydock to replace a bent propeller. We had barely made it back from the last cruise because the ship could only make about seven knots after she had clipped an iceberg, so the repair was an urgent one. We couldn't tell the passengers this before they boarded, or they wouldn't have gotten on in the first place, and the company needed that revenue.

When the earliest risers among the passengers were up and about the next morning, can you imagine their surprised faces when they looked out and instead of seeing Alaska, they saw that we were in drydock and the workmen were busy at the task of changing the propeller. This is probably the one and only time that passengers have been on board a ship when it went into dry dock.

It is a strange experience. You are on the deck of a great seagoing liner, but you are not sailing the sea; you are poised in the center of a great metal and concrete box surrounded by towering steam winches. Looking down the sides of the ship is like leaning over the parapet of a skyscraper. Far below at the bottom are tiny figures seemingly as small as ants as they move around doing whatever has to be done. There are clangings and grindings, and an occasional blinding glare as an arc welder weirdly lights up the bottom of the drydock. There isn't any power, of course, no water, so there isn't any hot coffee, and the toilets don't work. There isn't any earthly way of getting off the ship and were there a way, it wouldn't do any good. There's nothing to see.

It had been estimated the job would take no more than three hours, but it was not until 2:30 the following afternoon that the ship was again afloat, and the passengers could flush their toilets. Can you imagine the job I had keeping that group happy and busy that day and trying to convince them that they were fortunate to be the only passengers to have the fascinating opportunity to be on a ship while it was drydocked? I didn't tell them that it's no wonder because it's against the law!

Another incident on this ship was a result of the crew's unfamiliarity with her inner workings. One day there suddenly wasn't any hot water available to the cabins, and since it was an Alaskan cruise, it was a bit chilly. The hot water boilers were operating and the ship was going along in fine style, but the hot water had just stopped running. For more than a day, engineers below decks blindly turned valves this way and that way, attempting to discover the malfunction. No one was able to take a hot bath or shower—the water was freezing—and the complaining was continuous and bitter, and guess who was in charge of keeping up morale?

Late in the evening, I heard this man yelling as he came into the purser's office. "I demand to know why the hell no one told us the hot water is back on."

It hadn't been announced because it had happened so recently no one knew about it. All the cabins of the ship, which previously had been in the Mediterranean service, were equipped with bidets, small fountains that are widely used in the southern parts of Europe for bathing the area between the legs. Because the water was icy cold, the man's wife had been using this facility in place of a bath. Except this time when she had turned it on, the water had been steaming hot! She got medical treatment at the first port, but for several days the poor woman certainly walked funny.

Actually, the passengers got a good deal of fun out of the situation when the ship was having her initial break-in with the new crew. The crew was learning a zillion little things about her shortcomings or things in need of repair, and it was not considered desirable to broadcast each fact to the passengers, so the crew developed a code. Almost continuously through the day, therefore, there would be announcements on the public address system: "Don Beeman, go to so-and-so immediately. Urgent." The passengers became very curious about the popular, mysterious Mr. Beeman, but none of us gave them so much as a hint.

The day before we returned to Victoria at the end of the cruise, there was the much-looked-forward-to costume party. A few of the men entered themselves as the mysterious Don Beeman. Their costumes were very imaginative. Some passengers entered in the contest carrying signs reading "Who is Don Beeman?" One guy carried a burlap bag on which was printed "POT—MARY JANE'S—WEED—STICKS—HASH" in bold letters. Another had fashioned a surgeon's outfit, together with a face mask and stethoscope, and had added the word "Abortionist" to the card bearing the name of the character. One man hit it right on the button. He had managed to festoon himself with plumber's helpers, coils of wire, wrenches, and lots of other appurtenances of the handyman, and had "Don Beeman" printed on his back. Yes, we did have mechanical and plumbing problems on that ship, but as I said, it was a fun ship and the passengers still enjoyed themselves.

You may want to bring pen and paper when your cruise director gives the port talks. The cruise staff have been in the ports over and over again, and have searched for the best places to eat and shop. They want you to enjoy your time ashore because it makes their jobs easier. After all, if the passengers are happy they don't bug the cruise director. Cruise directors have to be well dressed, so they scout around to find some really great clothes. They don't want to have any complaints, so they will make sure you get a good deal. You can depend on these recommended places; after all, the cruise director is not going to tell you to go to a shop unless he or she knows it is the best. It saves his or her passengers the trouble of looking for such.

Since the cruise staff must work seven days a week, eleven months a year, they feel they better make each cruise worth the effort. It's great fun at first, living at sea and experiencing the thrill of seeing new ports and meeting all kinds of passengers, but after a few years you miss being able to live on land and do the things the average person takes for granted, like puttering around the kitchen when you feel like it, reading a fresh newspaper, watching

TV, visiting friends and relatives, driving your car, or just eating a peanut butter sandwich.

I used to look out my porthole each night during my first few years at sea and thank the Universal Intelligence for my good fortune at having found such a great job. I would thrill at the sight of my ship each time I boarded her, and I never dreamed I could become tired of living at sea. Even though I felt a little insecure at first, being at sea alone, eventually I got used to it, and of course the work was always so time consuming I really didn't have much time to be by myself. As I have said, I was lucky if I could find time enough to sleep. I have learned so much about human nature while working at this unique job. Maybe the reason people seem to throw caution to the winds when they are on a ship is because it's a little like being on a roller coaster. You don't go that fast, but you do get the feeling of losing your equilibrium, which in turn puts you in the mood for fun and helps get out of your earth-bound rut. It's nice to be employed for the sole purpose of helping people find enjoyment. Passengers have spent their money to enjoy themselves, and the fulfillment of their expectation was largely my job.

It never ceases to amaze me that the desire for love has no age limit. I've seen this love need just as strong from eight to eighty, or more. It's beautiful in a way—nature making us feel this need. After the astrology lecture I sometimes give, I often have time to give palm readings as well. I utilize palmistry, numerology, astrology, and graphology in giving a quick fifteen-minute reading. Sure enough, no matter how young or old the passenger is, almost invariably the most frequent questions asked are about their love life—or the lack of it.

So at times working on a cruise ship can be very rewarding, especially when I see that I have introduced passengers to one another and maybe love sparks are beginning to fly, because I am a Cupid at heart.

I also enjoy giving my "Vim & Vigor" lecture at sea. I'm past the twelve-mile limit where my ideas cannot be censored. I talk about how I hear the American Medical Association has the third most powerful lobby in the United States. I only hope this power can prevent socialized medicine in our freedom-loving country.

Our biggest concern now should be about "Codex Alimentarius," an international attempt to make over-the-counter purchases of vitamins, herbs, and nutrients by prescription only. "Codex" is a very real threat to your health and mine and must be fought at every point so that an international bureaucracy cannot take away our sovereignty and freedoms. Could this be like the old fable of the camel getting his nose under the tent?

On land I could never get away with exposing what I feel is a threat to humankind, the powerful sugar industry, and the deleterious effect that refined sugar has on the body and mind. I tell passengers how sugar can cause hypoglycemia (low blood sugar), which can manifest itself as alcoholism, obesity, ulcers, depression, mood swings, juvenile delinquency, asthma, migraines, insomnia, suicide, chronic fatigue, etc. What a shame to see sugar in the form of Coca-Cola (sugar plus caffeine—a double poison) being sold almost worldwide now and given to children. About the only port in which I haven't seen Coke was Tonga. Unfortunately, most doctors are taught so little about nutrition in medical school. Those who seek meaningful nutrition knowledge must study it on their own after getting out of medical school. I call them "The Magnificent Minority." If only there were more of them there would be fewer children who are hyperactive, or have learning disorders, behavior problems, attention deficit disorder, etc. Ritalin would be outmoded if parents were made aware of what they should and should not feed their children. I won't go on here about the FDA and how they play ball with the AMA and the big drug companies.

Yes, being twelve miles out has its advantages. The company can have slot machines aboard, I can criticize the powerful sugar industry, and maybe you could even get away with murder; more than one person probably has. No holds are barred out here. We are in our own little world, a fantasy land where the rules of landlubbers don't apply. No wonder we called one ship I worked on "Devil's Island." It was a floating penal colony—real cloak-and-dragger stuff on that ship. Everyone was trying to exercise his own power, which becomes a real struggle on some ships.

I have been so lucky to have this unique job—I've met and become friends with so many very warm, wonderful passengers and crew from all over the United States and other countries, too. For every Godzilla there are thousands of really dear passengers.

I truly feel that taking a cruise is the way to get the most out of your vacation dollar. Remember, you have your floating hotel (no packing and unpacking at ports), great food, service you can't match at any hotel, great live entertainment, continuous activities, and the option to be as gregarious as you want to be or to keep to yourself if that's your desire. You become a participant, not just an observer of life. It's no wonder so many passengers repeat cruises over and over again. I say this with all modesty, of course, but the most fun ships are those with the best cruise directors and staff.

chapter thirty

BEAR HUGS AND BARE SKINS

THE CONTINUAL BEAUTY OF A CRUISE THROUGH THE INSIDE passage of Alaska rivals the fjords of Sweden and Norway. It would be hard to choose between them.

It is a never-ending wonderment, because from dawn until dusk each day you feel that you can reach out on either side of the ship and touch some new revelation of nature's beauty. In a way, it affords a cruise director an easier time of it than a voyage in the tropics where the ship may be at sea for a day or two, far from the sight of land. In Alaska, the passengers are regularly topside, snapping pictures like mad, fearful of missing some previously unseen splendor.

A great many people who book themselves onto Alaskan cruises fly to Vancouver in Canada, and board their ships. The season for Alaska is from June until September, and these passengers are likely to pack a wardrobe attuned to the weather they are currently having at home—hot. This is not advisable. Days in Canada and Alaska can be warm, but sometimes it can be cool, and even downright cold.

Moreover, Victoria and Vancouver are cosmopolitan cities well worth an arrival several days before your ship sails to allow time for sightseeing. You will want to dress there as you would in San Francisco, New York, or London. Your very nicest fall wardrobe will not be out of place.

However, this is the last time you'll use these dressy clothes until you've returned to Victoria. The cruise itself is wonderfully informal. Everyone is too busy looking at the scenery to look at one another, so you go casual and warm. On these cruises no one tries to outdress anyone else. A parka is advisable, as well as warm sweaters and sturdy shoes. I would not recommend shopping for them in Victoria, though they will be on display and very tempting. You'll find wider selections and better prices at upcoming port calls, when you'll really need them.

Victoria is famous for its lovely Empress Hotel, "A little bit of England," they say. Though I am unable to get terribly excited about English food, the English custom of serving tea in this hotel lobby at four each day is so elegant. The bone china, silver services, flatware, and other accompaniments to the art of "tea" that are used there make this tea time a memorable expedience. I bought some exquisite china in Victoria for my home because I love to cook and entertain.

The towns in Alaska are small and cling closely to the mountainous shoreline. The buildings are set on pilings, and in some towns virtually all the walks are planks so you must have comfortable footwear. Any venturing from the prepared walkways is apt to earn you a shoe full of mud, for permafrost lies not far beneath the surface of the ground, and it allows little drainage for the melting snow during the short summers.

The things you will want to buy in Alaska are limited in range, but make up for it by being quite unusual, and fairly costly. Parkas and sweaters are good-looking and warm without being too bulky. Garments of seal hair are excellent too.

You will want at least a small replica of an Indian totem. The totem pole is mistakenly believed to have had some religious significance, but it is actually a type of historical document tracing the life of a tribe or a family or detailing some specific event. The poles are very impressive, particularly if someone who knows explains the story each one has to tell.

The Alaskan black diamond is a sparkling black substance called hematite. It is considered a token of friendship and loyalty. Skilled Indian silversmiths fashion the stones into rings and pendants. Examples of them are among the collections of royal families who received them as gifts from Lord Baranoff when he was governor of Alaska under Czar Alexander I. Incidentally, the baked Alaska that is on the menus of all cruise ships and most fine restaurants was devised by Oscar of the Waldorf to celebrate the United States' acquisition of the Alaskan territory from Russia.

Alaskan jade is beautiful. It is found in the Kobuk River region north of the Arctic Circle. Its colors range from dark green to very light green and it is often flecked with dark spots and streaks of a rich brown or rust. Sometimes it has a marbleized appearance, and it is hand carved into quite large objects d'art. I bought a pair of jade bookends I would not part with, no matter what the offer. Since Alaska is part of the United States you can ship purchases back home without paying duties or any other unnecessary fuss.

The first stop on the cruise of the inside passage is always Ketchikan. It's a nice place to visit when your ship doesn't knock half the dock into the water. The Chamber of Commerce is very active, and it has done well in maintaining the feeling of gold rush days. Their parkas are very good; they also have the best selection of native artifacts. You may want to get a parka in Ketchikan; you'll be sailing farther north and the winds off the glaciers can be extremely cold.

North of Ketchikan comes the true grandeur of Alaska. The breathtakingly beautiful fjords of Tracy Arm and Endicott Arm are on the way to Juneau and you'll visit both, one on the trip north, the other on the way back. Your ship will seem like a child's toy as it glides up the ice field channels between sky-high walls of granite. You'll never tire of watching the interesting shapes and incredibly blue icebergs. Herds of seals bask in the sun's reflection off the icebergs. The seals slide into the water at the approach of the ship, but they continue to watch curiously as this strange visitor glides by. Mountain sheep can be seen briefly on the high slopes, looking for all the world like scattered tufts of wool, and there will be an occasional band of elk. Because of the beauty of this passageway, one woman passenger told me she chose to empty her late husband's ashes overboard here. I've often wondered how she got by the customs officer with her husband in a shoe box.

Juneau is Alaska's capital city and the gateway to Mendenhall Glacier. This vast, ever-moving field of ice is so imposing that it seems unreal. Each long winter, the great falls of snow feed it as it inches its way to the sea, peeling off huge icebergs that raise havoc with navigation. On one trip we bent a propeller on one of them and had to limp back to home port.

Below Mendenhall Glacier, on the return to Juneau, is a log cabin church. If you don't become spiritual while seated there, you are beyond help. It is a simple place; where the altar and a stained glass window would usually be is an enormous sheet of glass so clear that it doesn't seem to exist. This window frames a scene of upward-reaching pines, a sparkling blue lake, and behind it all, the awesome glacier. It is thrilling!

In contrast, the Red Dog Saloon in Juneau affords a fine view of the back bar and honky-tonk pianist who'll knock your hat off with his ricky-tick improvisations. Even a clam would join in the singing after the first ten minutes in this place. All the crew hang out here until the last second they can be away from the ship before it sails. Oh, the hangovers they have the next day! One poor steward got sick and lost his false teeth there. Did the crew ever tease him the next day as he worked toothless.

Juneau is great for shopping, clothing, and jewelry. There are beautiful things to buy in the Irish and Russian shops.

Skagway is the northernmost port of a summer cruise. This town is icebound most of the year, and the Lynn Canal is navigable only from late May until late September.

It was in the long, lovely Lynn Canal that we had the "Incident of the Canned Mussels."

Mussels are a delectable shellfish. If you've lived there or spent any time along the northern coast, you know them well. They are shaped like slender clams and have black shells. They attach themselves to rocks and pilings, where they live if they're not being pried away for food by animal and human life. The Dorchester Hotel in London has the most delicious mussel soup in the world. (Love that hotel!)

Like everything else, mussels have to grow up from small beginnings. Mussels are speck-like objects that float about until they find a place to attach themselves, at which time the maturing process begins. On this particular cruise through the Lynn Canal, a whole lot of these little specks had found their way into the plumbing system of our ship, which was fed by sea water. They had attached themselves to the insides of the pipes and flush cabinets, and proceeded with their natural life cycle, which was to get a few hundred times as big as they had been. They played havoc with our toilets on the ship (we referred to them as "canned" mussels) and when we were on the way to Skagway the situation had reached a critical condition. Every toilet on the ship was stopped.

Something had to be done. All hands, even the engineers and deck officers, were enlisted by the plumber and given instructions on the technique of getting rid of them; then the crew was dispatched from cabin to cabin to take care of it. It was an all-night job.

The passengers weren't quite sure what was going on, but they'd been aware that the toilets weren't working and were glad to see them repaired, even if it meant losing a little sleep. The deck officers disliked what they were doing, but it was highly necessary.

At four in the morning, away down on C deck the chief officer, grumbling to himself that a man of his rank shouldn't have to do this job of toilet fixing, knocked on the door of a small cabin. A very drunk-sounding guy asked what he wanted and the officer, whose name was Jimmy, said he wanted to fix the toilet.

There was a moment of fumbling, then this loaded guy opened the door partway. "What you say?"

"May I fix your toilet?"

The door was swung the rest of the way open. "Go ahead, take a crap in it, if you want," the man said generously.

There was a naked girl on the bunk. She was drunk, but conscious. "Give him a drink, Eddie. They're supposed to be fixing the one in my cabin right now," she said.

Jimmy was an AA member and explained that he did not drink, which Eddie and the girl took as a great insult. So he accepted a full tumbler of whiskey and took it into the head with him. When he'd finished whatever he had to do and had the toilet working, he flushed the drink down it, then came out to report all was in order and the drink delicious. After trying to force another drink on him which he managed to turn down, the man gave him a dollar tip. The girl suggested he stay around for a good time. Jimmy had us all in stitches, telling us about it the next morning at breakfast. Like the Gemini he was, he had a great wit.

This case of canned mussels had not grown big enough to cause any more problems before the ship was transferred to the South Sea Islands for the next season. In the warm water on the way there the mussels all died at the same moment. It remained a beautiful vessel, if you were looking at it from a distance on the windward side so you couldn't smell the dead little creatures. We made an unscheduled stop just long enough to get the passengers and crew off in lovely Hawaii for an overnight stay at the Royal Hawaii hotel with its perfect beach while the ship was deodorized.

Skagway, like the other Alaskan towns, is friendly and fascinating. It can't take more than an hour to walk through the whole place for an examination of its false-fronted buildings. It's like stepping back into the good old days. There are windflowers to be admired and shops to look into. It is delightfully rustic and you will love it.

There is a narrow-gauge railway operated by the White Pass Railroad Co. The engines are brave little locomotives that handle steep grades with aplomb, and the cars are gaily painted and have open platforms that allow you to really see the countryside and enjoy the boundless fresh air that blows from the mountains. At the tops of these mountains big snowstorms rage at the height of summer. One of the trains out of Skagway goes to Lake Bennett, the other all the way to Whitehorse, in the heart of the Yukon. Pot-bellied stoves keep you warm in the train cars. Many passengers break their cruises here in Skagway to journey on into that part of Alaska, returning to Skagway to rejoin our ship on its return to Canada. I highly recommend this side trip.

chapter thirty-one

Secrets to Prevent Seasickness

We were crossing Queen Charlotte Sound, one of the few unprotected areas on the Inside Passage cruise to Alaska, and it was terribly rough. I was in the purser's office going over my bingo money in the safe, while the assistant purser, an extremely gentlemanly young man, handled the few passengers who came to the office with questions. He spent a little while with an agitated man, who then departed. The purser called the assistant over to ask what the difficulty was.

"His wife is pretty seasick. He wanted some Dramamine." This was "the Leaking Lena" and it didn't have a medic on board so we kept aspirin and Dramamine in the purser's office.

"We're out of the pills, dammit," the purser said.

231

"I gave him the other kind," his assistant told him.

"Did you tell him how they're to be used?"

"Sure. Take them with a little water."

"With water! Goddam it," the purser exploded. "Those are Dramamine suppositories. You'll kill the woman. Get the husband on the phone."

"I don't know his name."

"Well, get on the public address system and ask for the attention of the man who was just in the purser's office, dammit. Tell him what to do."

His assistant stared at him. "You mean I should say his wife should not swallow the suppository but stick it up her bottom?"

"No, goddam it," the purser screamed. "Jeraldine, you do it."

I was almost helpless with laughter, but I managed to say, "You mean I should tell the whole ship that his wife should stick it up her bottom?"

"No!" the apoplectic purser bellowed.

Fortunately, at this point the man with the stricken wife returned. I calmed down quickly.

"What was my wife supposed to do with this?" he asked in a puzzled tone.

"I'm so glad you came back," I said. "We were looking for you. It is a rectal suppository; be sure to remove the foil first."

"Oh," the man said, nodding and turning away shaking his head.

The assistant purser didn't hear the end of that one for a long time. We teased him unmercifully about it for months.

Finally the company decided to put a young pre-med student on board to act as our doctor.

For the first several days at sea with this young medical student, we had a spell of everyone throwing up all over the ship. We couldn't understand it until we learned that the medic was recommending a little orange juice for those first queasy symptoms of *mal de mer!* Taking liquids as a treatment for seasickness is the number one no-no. The trick is to keep solid food in your stomach and stay away from liquids, particularly coffee. It stimulates the digestive action of the stomach, and when those juices get to really swishing around, it's everyone to the side of the ship. When the sea is rough and you even suspect that you may be seasick, take a preventive such as Dramamine or Sea Calm (or any pill that contains 25 mg of meclizine HCL) before it strikes; otherwise, it won't stay down. Once you start to regurgitate, the Dramamine suppositories are effective, and most cruise ships carry them in their hospitals. In some very sensitive individuals the doctor needs to give an injection for quick relief. Just remember, you almost always can prevent seasickness by avoiding liquids if the sea is rough. You can determine this by looking out to see if the waves have whitecaps. Usually the sea is calm and even if it isn't, it doesn't seem to bother most passengers. However, if you are the more sensitive type, use the sea's whitecaps to alert you for preventive measures. Especially at this time keep solid food in your stomach. Before I got my sea legs, whenever I saw the whitecaps appear, I would just get a handful of peanuts from the bartender as I dashed from one activity to another.

During a storm, the larger the ship the less movement one feels. Today most ships are so stabilized and state of the art; passengers sail in such contentment that strolling on deck to catch a moonbeam can become almost a spiritual experience.

The cruise company wanted me to add some extra lectures on this very long cruise to the South Pacific, where we had lots of days at sea between ports. I decided to try to build an hour of entertainment around the Mantic Message Mat. I wasn't sure just how that would work. It is a device a bit similar to a Ouija Board, except that it is round, not oblong, and instead of just displaying the alphabet, it has frequently used words and even some often-used sentences. Where the Ouija Board would be very slow in getting a word spelled out, the mat is capable of fast sentences. It does not have the somber black background of the Ouija Board, but a light spiritual blue, and has symbols that attract loving spirits.

I took the mat to a party one night and this perplexed man kept asking what made the planchette move. As with the Ouija Board, you need to place the tips of your fingers on something that is moveable and it will move to the various words and letters on the mat, enabling you to receive a message from someone in the spirit world but there is no way you can verify who it is. It was thoroughly explained how we were able to contact spirits using the mat, and that energy from the spirit contact actually moves the planchette. The man listened eagerly, but after hours of enjoying playing with the board he said goodnight. Just before he closed the door, he looked back and asked, "But what makes the planchette move, is it a battery, or what?"

Anyway, getting back to my trying to entertain a whole auditorium of passengers on the ship with a gameboard that only four or five people can play at once was a challenge. As I looked over the crowd I selected four of the passengers who looked as if they were water signs, i.e., Scorpio, Pisces, or Cancer. They are usually more psychic than most. Then, so I could incorporate the whole room, I asked for anyone else in the room to ask a question for which we would try to receive an answer.

I had never tried using the Mat anywhere except in a home, so I was rather anxious to see if it would work on a cruise ship. This was in 1973 when Richard Nixon was president. The question asked by an elderly man in the rear of the auditorium was "Who will be elected president of the United States?" I then had the four passengers who had their fingers lightly touching the planchette try to get it to move. They were very surprised, as was I, when it started to wander on the board. The answer it gave was also a surprise: Ronald Reagan. At that time no one ever thought he might become president—Ford and Carter came before him—so the audience just laughed. Since there is no time in space the answer was really correct, but I had no idea that it was at the time. "Let's have another question," I said quickly. As the hour passed rapidly, the answers were surprisingly accurate. I announced that there was time for one more question. By this time the room was transfixed with this testing of the Mat.

A young jock of a man had been standing in the doorway all during the questioning with his hands in his jeans. He hollered, "What is the name of the person who is going to pick me up to drive me home when I get back to L.A.?"

The four looked intently at the Mat to see what message it would give. They all smiled as the name was spelled out because it was such a funny, strange name they thought it must be gibberish but they announced what it was.

The poor young man screamed, "Good grief! That's his name! This is really scary!" and away he bolted.

There is a continuum. There is a truism in science that nothing is wasted, that matter can be neither created nor destroyed but it can only be converted. It seems that we all have a spirit, soul, or personality, or whatever you want to call it, that continues on after death. Perhaps when we all learn this, we may be more careful how we live our lives.

chapter thirty-two

NEVER A DULL MOMENT

WE HAD SO MANY MISHAPS ON THE "LEAKING LENA." EVERY time something went wrong, like losing a propeller to an iceberg, going aground, or our motor conking out, the laundry overflowing so that we had no dry linens on one cruise, or perhaps the oilers down below would break out in a knife fight—any trouble would prompt me to order champagne on the house. Some cruises on this ship were so filled with emergencies of this sort that by the time the cruise was over the passengers were about to come down with cirrhosis of the liver.

Once a sweet little lady came to me and said, "Jeraldine, I hate to bother you, but my cabin roof is leaking from the cabin above me and I had to sleep under an umbrella last night!"

I don't know why, but on one of this ship's cruises we ran out of water; it was a nasty situation. A passenger with a sense of humor posted a notice outside the purser's office which read:

> • RETURN WATER FROM MELTED ICE CUBES TO THE PURSER'S OFFICE.
>
> • PRIZE FOR MOST WATER RETURNED!
>
> • SHOWER WITH A FRIEND.
>
> • DRAW ENOUGH BATH WATER SO YOUR RUBBER DUCK BARELY FLOATS.
>
> • WASH ONE HAND ONLY.

It was incredible how many things could go wrong and each mishap would foul up my activities schedule. It was always up to me to face the passengers and keep them calm during each added calamity. I was the walking complaint department. I would write the highlights of each cruise in my letters home, which were passed around to any interested family member.

My dear mother was the worrying type. With each letter she read she would say to me, when I phoned her, "You poor dear: you aren't getting any younger." She was of the old school and felt women shouldn't work. She was always hoping I would meet someone and get married, feeling that would solve everything. I never could get married just for security. I knew intuitively that doesn't bring happiness.

I certainly didn't want for attention from men but as soon as one started to show interest in me, and not wanting to spoil the cruise for him, I would warn him that if he wanted to have a good time on the cruise he had better not waste his time waiting for me to get off work because I never did. I would ask for his card, thinking that when and if I ever got time off, I would call him. I never got time off, and the cards started to build up. Finally, I got myself a card file and started writing on the backs of the cards something that would trigger my mind about the person, like "this is the handsome guy who won the spoon diving contest," etc.

The longer I lived and worked on the posh ships, the better I became at my job. The ship became like a womb. It can be a very seductive life: no dishes, no laundry, no bed to make, no traffic to battle on the drive to and from work, music, dancing, laughter at meal times, escargot, filet mignon, beautiful ports, the thrill of hearing the ship's whistle as we sailed from each beautiful port, a never-ending group of new passengers who may become lifetime friends—join the cruise staff and see the world! Oh, there were the good times, especially the music. Some of the most talented musicians work on ships and the violins, oh, the violins! But I love discos, too. One can accomplish so much on board because the pesky details of living are done for us. The Old World service is better than in the most expensive restaurants.

There is never a dull moment for the cruise staff. Most crew members, officers, and cruise staff agree with me about feeling secure, loving the ship life, and we are all a bit afraid to try our luck on land. For me it was especially so, since I didn't see how I could earn a living any other way except working on the ship—of course I always had the dream that the "Love Boats" book I was trying to write would sell, but I had no connections with any publishers and knew no one in the business. Meanwhile, my mother needed financial help so I tried to figure out how I could add to my income. I talked the company into giving me ten percent of all land tour money if I gave the land tour pitch for each port with added enthusiasm.

On my first trip to Polynesia, I hadn't any opportunity to enjoy one of the fabulous beaches until we reached Rarotonga, in the Cook Islands. This was well along on our cruise, so I could hardly wait to get out onto the dazzling white sands when we reached this paradise.

There were about a zillion little kids running around in the palm grove that lay inland from the strand itself, and a number of loving, chubby grandmother types caring for them, which led one of the men in our small party (all the officers on our ship knew of this place little used by our passengers) to ask, "Where do they hide the beautiful broad who posed for all those South Seas posters? They must have only one and use her for all the pictures."

However, I wasn't interested in his complaints about the female scenery. I was too eager to get into the lazy swells of azure water that curled into white foam close to shore. Beside, later this fella found out that the prettiest girls and best dancers are actually from Rarotonga.

I dropped the *pareu* I'd been wearing over my bikini and ran down to test the water. It was everything that had ever been promised—pure heaven! After I'd enjoyed it for a while, I came in closer to the beach to stand in the shallow, foaming waves. They washed around my feet as I looked around at the magnificent view.

I was slightly startled a few moments later by a brief, gentle pluck at the skin of my thigh. I turned swiftly. A dozen tiny children were standing on the sand behind me, dark eyes wide, faces aglow with curiosity. The one who had dared to approach me raced back to the others and there was a chorus of giggles. I laughed with them, and said hello and returned to my survey of the sea.

After a short while, there was a repetition of the touch, this time on my calf. It was a second little girl. The others had moved much closer to the edge of the water. When she returned to them and said something in Maori, the native tongue, there were again peals of laughter.

This continued for a while, the tentative touches at my skin when they thought I was not looking, the sudden retreat, and the gales of childish laughter. It wasn't annoying at all, for they were delightful little tots, but it was quite puzzling, and I wondered what kind of game they were playing.

Finally, an older girl of twelve came down and shooed them back toward the grove of palms.

"Do you speak English?" I asked.

"A leetle bit," she said, holding a thumb and forefinger about a half inch apart. I laughed and so did she.

"Why did those precious children keep doing that? Pick at my skin, then run away and laugh?"

"They find why they not fall off," she explained.

"What?" I said.

She then pointed to my skin and said, "The spots, they never see them before."

My freckles! Of course! They'd never seen a redhead before, so they thought the millions of brown spots that cover my body had been painstakingly pasted on as a decoration. Maybe the freckles are a decoration, but I never thought of them as such when I used to try to bleach them with lemon juice when I was a kid.

The incident is typical of virtually all the people of the South Sea Islands. They are warm, curious, loving, friendly, outgoing. They are seldom shy and never seem devious or sullen. The Polynesians, especially the Rarotongans and Hawaiians, I've found, are the most loving and giving people anywhere in the world.

On this run our cruises were of eleven days' duration, with a one-day turnaround at Suva, Fiji. Passengers jetted in from Australia, New Zealand, Canada, the United States, South America, the British Isles, and continental Europe to board in Suva. It was a very expensive cruise. We sailed to Nuku'alofa and Vava'u in the Tonga group, Apia in Western Samoa, Pago Pago in nearby American Samoa, the virtually untouched Rarotonga, then Bora Bora and Tahiti.

There was a stop of only eight hours at Papeete in Tahiti, though it marked the end of the cruise. This is a mad rush, for one shipload of passengers disembark and a few hours later another group that has jetted in from all over the world takes its place for the return eleven days to Suva.

The languages of our crew on this particular ship were every bit as varied as those of our passengers. Our officers were Scots, English, Dutch, and Spanish, our crew Canadian, Indonesian, and

Fijian. I was the only native of the United States working on the ship, and the only female. The greater number of the passengers were from the United States.

There is mystery about the South Sea Islands that is very hard to describe. The islands of the Caribbean are lovely and unusual, but they do not have this same beautiful feeling of exuberant lightness. There is something very spiritual in the air, as if the blue skies and castling purple, salmon, and white clouds, the sapphire waters, and the sweet people are showing the way the whole world should be. Maybe the islands won't remain that way when they become more civilized, but I certainly wish they could retain the feeling you get there when the trade wind caresses you and you feel at one with the Universal Intelligence.

In Fiji, as in Trinidad and the Caribbean, there is a vast population of people who originally were imported from India to work on the plantations. There are far more of them in Suva, Fiji than there are Fijians, and the beautiful saris that the Indian women wear there can be purchased in many stores. They are a simple and practical way of dressing for your entire stay in Fiji. The sari, which is comfortable and flattering, doesn't go out of style. After wearing, it's merely folded up, so it takes no storage room. An Indian shop attendant can instruct you in the proper way of wrapping it on yourself in only minutes.

Throughout the South Seas, you can leave your stockings and pantyhose in the dresser drawer, and the fellows can save their socks, jackets, and ties for the flight home. There will be occasions for dressing up, but these will be the exception, not the nightly routine endured by the colonizers, who felt that formal attire for dinner for the men and girdles for the ladies was a mark of superiority.

Fijian girls wear Zulus (skirts) which are plain or printed and come to the ankles—topped by colorful blouses. Fijian men also wear Zulus that come to about the knee. The police always wear spotless white ones. With these, they wear shirts or jackets open at the neck. If the Fijans wear shoes at all, they wear flat leather sandals, and I'd advise you to do the same. They are cool, well made, and not costly.

Suva, which is the capital and major port of the Fijis, lies on Viti Levu, the largest of about 300 islands in the group, only a third of which are inhabited. Viti Levu itself is about the same size as Hawaii, the largest of the Hawaiian Islands. If you should get there several days before the departure of your cruise ship for the Society Islands, you'll find plenty to keep you occupied.

The botanic gardens near the governor's mansion are an explosion of tropical color. In Albert park, teams play cricket and violent games of soccer and rugby.

The municipal market is near the business center of the city. Pearl and tortoise shell jewelry and other souvenirs are tempting there, but you'll probably do better on the way to Papeete. Don't pass up the sandals and saris, however. There are tailors who do splendid work, from measurement through final fitting, in less than a day.

Should you venture into the back country by taxi, you'll be warmly greeted, and be witness to a lot of skylarking. When villagers in Fiji have a heavy job facing them, such as repairing a road or putting up a building, they make a game out of it. Though it entails a good deal of horsing around by everyone involved, the task gets done in a surprisingly short time.

You will certainly come in contact with kava, a liquor made from the green root of the pepper plant. There is an impressive ceremony attached to making kava, with a master of ceremonies who supervises the whole operation by the kava maker. The root of the plant is grated with a knife, then worked into a ball. An assistant adds water, and the kava maker kneads the lump of pulp to extract the juices. The emcee determines when the liquor has reached the right consistency and issues a command, upon which the kava maker uses shredded hibiscus bark to clear the brownish drink of the shreds of root. The liquid is served with a great deal of ceremony in a highly polished coconut half.

There's no consensus on the effect of kava: our Fijian band members say they couldn't play without it, some maintain it will get you drunker than a hoot owl, others that it numbs the mouth and limbs, still others that it just sort of refreshes. I can tell you that the show of making it is an impressive one.

Tonga, the first port of call after leaving Suva on our cruises, is a wondrous place, a real kingdom that has never been subjugated by any foreign power. Tonga is different from Fiji, which has tortured mountains that sometimes are hidden in mists. Tonga is more like the world's largest and most continuous garden plot. The islands were named the Friendly Islands by Captain Cook 200 years ago (a turtle he captured off one of them is still strolling around Nuku'alofa). It is a gentle place. A shopkeeper seems more anxious to form friendship than make a sale, and I have known passengers to return to the ship stunned by the fact that they found themselves pressed to accept as a gift an item they had decided against buying.

Of course, Tongans can be tougher and more resilient than whalebone. They were fierce warriors, and I gather that they would occasionally set out in their great double canoes and spread a little terror around the neighboring islands in sort of a "this is for nothing, be careful" gesture. No wonder they were never overrun.

The approach to Nuku'alofa, on the coral coast of Tongatapu, is spectacular. The windward side of the island is protected by rocky ledges. There are hundreds upon hundreds of openings in these ledges that are large and small blow holes, through which the water surges to produce geysers reaching as high as a hundred feet in the air. I've never seen anything even close to it for nature just showing off.

One of the things I remember about Tonga besides its beauty is our officers' eagerness in using the barter system there. It wasn't until the last stop during our six-month season down there that the radio officer told me in a hushed voice, "Jeraldine, since this is our last stop here this season, we have to give the king of Tonga back all the pornographic films he's been trading us for his favorite Indonesian food." (We had Indonesian cooks on the ship.)

"Good heavens," I said. "Is that why you fellas never came down to the public rooms and would all disappear on sailing night from Nuku'alofa?"

There is much to see on both Nuku'alofa and Vava'u, the north-ernmost of the Tongan Islands. I was attracted once by a church of plain, white-painted clapboard. When I entered to pay my respects, I found the choir—and it was a large one of both children and adults—was getting ready to practice. Their exquisite voices turned that simple house of God into an absolute cathedral. Vava'u is so small that no cruise ships stop there regularly except us, so all the people come to greet us as we dock.

We asked for a conducted tour of Vava'u, but the natives were very poor and owned only one bus, so they decorated their open-air trucks with colorful flowers and greenery to carry us around the island. Now to get the passengers to ride in the trucks (beat-up trucks with no shock absorbers) was my job. I wanted to go on the tour to see the beautiful island and the display of native crafts and dancing, and I also wanted all of the passengers to go because they would be bored if they stayed on the ship; besides, I always had my ten percent commission from the tour on my mind. So I explained to them that this most primitive of all the islands had a really unique experience in store for them. No Hilton Hotel here, no posh buses; this is the real thing. This tour is for the courageous who want to see how the people really live. If you are a complainer don't come along with us. (This saves me from lots of ulcers.) We are going on trucks on bumpy roads, and if it rains we all get wet. We have one bus available for the few who don't want to have some fun roughing it.

Well, do you know almost everyone bought the tour tickets, and, much to my surprise, when I loaded the tour no one wanted to ride in the bus except a few who were lame. I'm telling you those people had so much fun, laughing at every bump in the road, and when it started to rain they were prepared to get wet. I told them to leave their watches on board and to wear their oldest or only drip-dry clothing. As they bumped around on each other with the rain pouring in, the laughter became hysterical. We all had a ball. I laughed till my sides hurt. People really lost their inhibitions as they ended up bouncing on top of each other's laps. There was one woman, though, who didn't crack a smile. She cursed the whole way. She had a rotten hangover—she and the maitre d' were boozing together the night before—and at one point, as the rain was pouring on her and we went over an unusually big bump, she yelled out, "Now I know why that damn maitre d' wouldn't come along with me. I'll kill him when I get back for not warning me." This only struck the other passengers as hilarious, and they laughed all the more every time she moaned. They had so much fun that the few passengers who didn't come along with us felt they had really missed something when they heard everyone rave about the tour.

A cruise director has to know how to prepare the passengers psychologically to get the most out of a tour. If you don't prepare them for the hardships of a tour, you are the one who gets blamed for the whole thing and you really get into trouble that way. When Bill was cruise director on his first cruise to Mexico, he didn't prepare them for the Yelapa tour, and they all came back so raving mad that the company representative called him to his office and told him he had better hide in his cabin for the rest of the day because they were all running around the ship looking for him with blood in their eyes, saying, "Where is he? Where is he? Let's lynch the S.O.B.!"

Getting back to Nuku'alofa, the flying foxes of Kolovai are certainly worth seeing, though you'll be almost deafened by the chattering. They are fruit bats descended from a colony that had been presented to a highly placed Tongan by a Samoan princess. They hang head down and royally protected in a small grove of trees in the center of the village.

And you must have tapa cloth. It can be found other places in the Polynesian group, but this is where it is at its best. Tapa is made from the inner bark of the paper mulberry tree, which grows in great profusion on these islands. It is gently pounded into intricately woven strips of fabric by patient women who use light wooden mallets and sing or chant while working. These strips are joined together by a special gum that forms an imperishable seam; then the whole vast fabric is painted in intricate designs with dyes concocted by the Tongans. They get a very effective deep reddish hue from plants. These works of art make utterly beautiful hangings and placemats, purses, etc.

The International Dateline runs right through Tonga, and there is an International Dateline Hotel that stands astride it.

The Samoas, our next ports of call, were not so fortunate as the Tongas in remaining free of foreign domination, but the experience has not marked them seriously. Western Samoa, the capital city of which is Apia, is now independent; the capital of American Samoa is Pago Pago (pronounced there as Pango Pango) and I think they are very happy with their association with the United States. American Samoa is a tiny place. Its harbor is strangely like a fjord in Alaska or Scandinavia, except for the humidity and heat, and an island protects its entrance. It was a great staging area for our fleet during the Second World War, which explains the treaty that made them our only possession south of the equator.

There are many lovely things about the Samoas, but the most remarkable is the *fale,* pronounced "fallee." This is the greatest structure ever devised for living, and is possible only in that sublime climate. The fale is round with a floor of crushed coral or stone, and a conical thatched roof is supported on regularly spaced columns of palm trunk. Rolled-up blinds of rushes or bamboo are hung at each of the openings between the supports. If there is a violent rainfall, these are lowered; if not, they are left up. Some shaded electric lights now glow where torches used to be, but there is nothing so wide open, but still so seemingly private, as the Samoan fale. They glow like jewels in the evening as the families sit together before going to bed under their protective nettings. Should anyone have a little trouble getting to sleep, they can watch the stars any way they turn.

The shopping in both the Samoas is somewhat limited. In Apia, the prices tend to be cheaper than in Pago Pago, and the Samoans are wonderful craftsmen. What tapa cloth you'll see has probably been imported from Tonga, but the miniature canoes and ceremonial clubs, and the shell necklaces, woven mats, and coral earrings and bracelets are lovely.

If you needn't worry about shopping in the Samoas, you need worry even less in the Cook Islands. These are the most untouched and unspoiled islands in the South Pacific. On the largest map you can find, they are merely dots scattered over an enormous expanse of ocean. Yet they were found centuries ago by the daring explorers of the Pacific, sailing frail outrigger canoes. The islands are low-lying, barely visible beyond ten miles from the shores. The winds there can grow to hurricane force. Many of the islands are pure coral atolls which grow no flowers, yet the tradition of the lei flourishes, with seashells strung so that they look like tiny blossoms.

Rarotonga, the main island of the Cooks, literally explodes with flowers. There are so many of them, of so many colors and types, that people even hang leis around the necks of the dogs that trot amiably after everyone. As the passengers step ashore they are given leis—not like the ones we get in Hawaii, but long ones to the knees. My trouble is trying to see over them after all my friends there each give me one. We all come back to the ship so colorful and sweet smelling. This is the night on board I call Island Night; everyone dresses in Zulus and the men go barechested. We all wear our leis, and I get everyone up and teach them the hula and *tamure*. No one wears shoes, and some of the passengers go all out and dress in outlandish island costumes. They really let their hair down, and for a few hours we become simple and childlike and learn to play again.

Some of the women of Rarotonga rival its flowers for beauty. Like the Samoans, they are graceful, with cameo-like profiles, but unlike the Samoans, they are still very demure. This may be because Rarotonga has only recently become a tourist stopover of any consequence.

Back at Apia, in Western Samoa, there was a hotel connected with Aggie Grey's shop, and behind that a lovely pavilion with a ceiling of woven rushes and of tapa cloth and shells. The pavilion featured a dancing troupe of a dozen sweet, completely uninhibited girls. After watching their performance once, I asked them to come aboard ship to perform for the passengers and have luncheon. They danced superbly, ate heartily, then approached the officers of the ship. Apparently out of gratitude for the invitation to visit the great white vessel, and in the natural way they think of sex, they said, "You fellah come with me, baby, I show you good time." The poor shy captain blushed like crazy.

Rarotonga had no docking facilities, so the ship anchored in the harbor and the passengers were taken ashore by a barge towed out by a small boat. A jet strip is being planned for this green mountainous paradise where Robert Louis Stevenson spent the last few years of his life, as well as a modern hotel or two to supplement the meager accommodations available when I was there.

When all this has come to pass, I've no doubt the lovely dancing maidens of Rarotonga will learn to smear their bodies with grease so that the tourists can stick dollar bills to them, as they do in Apia.

Bora Bora, in French Polynesia, rises dramatically from the sea to provide the most spectacular approach of any of the islands of the South Pacific. It could have been the setting of the musical *South Pacific*, but the actual film location was nearby on the island of Moorea, near Tahiti.

Vaitape is a pretty village (there is a continuing competition for the most attractively decorated houses and gardens) and the two main hotels, the Bora and Noa (there should be a joke there someplace), are both beautifully run and can be of assistance in providing either snorkeling or scuba diving equipment. There is no better place in the world for drifting through the dissolving rainbows of tropical fish and coral formations. I must warn you, however, that you should buy special plastic footwear at the local market when you are swimming in these waters. Live coral can wound cruelly; it took a long time to recover from an incident when an unexpected wave threw me from my feet while I was leading a tour to one of the live reefs there. I can honestly say that snorkeling in Bora Bora is one of the most thrilling things that can happen to you. I could stay under and watch for hours. I wear my pareu on my back so it won't get sunburned because I can't tear myself away when I should.

Tahiti is a hundred miles or more east of Bora Bora. Because of its beauty, writers and artists have been praising the place for years.

Papeete, the most important town, is a more expensive place to shop than any of the other main ports in Polynesia. At Punaauia, a village nine miles from Papeete, is the only place where there is really excellent swimming on a white sand beach. The other beaches are largely of black volcanic sand.

The Tahitian men are handsome and some Tahitian women are utterly beautiful. They move with sinuous grace under their brief, colorful garments, and the clever male passenger will note the positioning of the flowers that ornament the women's hairdos. A blossom over the right ear means "otherwise occupied," over the left ear "available," and over both ears "make your best offer." They use up a lot of flowers in Tahiti, as befits a society that attaches no stigma to illegitimacy.

The wildest place in Papeete was Quinn's. An orchestra occupied a spot behind the bar, and the *tamure* made the Hawaiian hula seem like an advanced case of petrification. You have not seen anything until you've observed a Polynesian in drag. You probably would see one in Quinn's, along with members of the French Foreign Legion, tourists of all ages and nationalities, and sailors from all over the world. The restroom was coeducational and a must see!

A place not nearly so boisterous as Quinn's, but one regarded with great loyalty by the male members of our ship's crew, was the Golden Dragon in Suva, Fiji.

The Fijian girls are more subdued than the Tahitians, but not a whit less lovely, and to work in the Golden Dragon is a distinction in some segments of the culture there. Since Suva was the port of our turnaround each twenty-two days, we stayed overnight. After supplies were purchased and a general ship's cleanup attempted, the officers and crew alike whiled away pleasant hours in the large club.

At our last sailing of the season, after we had spent over six months on this run, the girls of the Golden Dragon came to the dock to bid the ship bon voyage until next year. Many of them were crying unashamedly; they had formed strong attachments to the crew, and this was probably the last they'd see of some of them. Everyone was out on deck waving good-bye.

A number of passengers were watching the girls; as the ship pulled out and the crack Fijian band played "Now Is the Hour," everyone cried and waved. At this point one English lady turned to an engineer. "Are those girls down there prostitutes?" she asked.

He frowned. "Well, not really," he told her. "Just sort of; you see, they don't charge anything."

chapter thirty-three

MAY DAY!!! MAY DAY!!!

"LADIES AND GENTLEMEN!" THE CAPTAIN'S VOICE SOUNDED over the loudspeaker. "We are taking a slight detour to answer an S.O.S." Passengers left their bingo cards, swimmers left the pool and even a gal having her hair done left the beauty shop, and everyone from the bars and cabins came out on deck to see who needed to send a distress call way out here in the middle of nowhere, deep in the Pacific. The sea wasn't very rough, but not very calm, either. We all strained our eyesight to the utmost for signs of life. Finally someone from the upper deck yelled, "There she lies, there she lies!"

Sure enough, floundering in the distance was a very small boat. As we sailed closer we could see there were people on board. Quite a few people, as a matter of fact.

What excitement! Our passengers now were all so involved! No need for the cruise director to keep activities going now, for most passengers were on deck.

The weather was warm so the rescued, water-drenched victims were still in pretty good health after being lost at sea for days. There were seven women, one little girl, and nine men, and none knew any English. The captain found space for them in a few spare cabins; the rest were put up in our ship's hospital. After they were examined and fed, the passengers were allowed to give them things to wear.

They were befriended immediately by the passengers and crew. The men were given all kinds of clothing. The women were not only clothed by the passengers but the next day they were even taken to the beauty shop. The goodness in people sometimes lies hidden until it has a chance to manifest itself, and this event was heartwarming, indeed.

Some kind passenger started a collection for the rescued. He kept a sign that showed how much was collected and with each additional donation he would change the amount. The passengers and crew would clap every time the "kitty" grew.

When it was time for the survivors to leave us, our captain arranged for large baskets of food for them to take, passengers gave them not only the "kitty" and bundles of clothing, but the women and little girl left wearing expensive jewelry that seemed to be the symbols of love we felt for them.

They were bewildered and overcome with this show of kindness. As they waved good-bye many had tears running down their cheeks. I still get a lump in my throat when I remember the love, generosity, and goodness shown by everyone on board.

chapter thirty-four

$\mathcal{B}$EER BOTTLES
AND BURIALS

Life at sea on a cruise ship is a life of partings. Like clockwork, there are the good-byes to passengers just as you become good friends, the occasional farewells to a shipmate who has been sacked or gone on to a better job; we all become so close that this can be very emotional. And finally, there is the wrenching farewell of death.

This doesn't happen very often, but once is too often, and when a thousand or more people are gathered together for periods of as long as a month, there is a possibility that it might occur.

Sailing in the South Sea Islands, I was in the middle of doing my evening show. It had been a long, hard day and I was tired and trying to hurry the show along. It was late and I was looking forward to a chance to go to my cabin, so I was a little taken aback when the captain appeared and indicated that he wished to speak to me. I quickly ended the show, then joined him off the dance floor.

A man who had been under the doctor's care after a heart attack that afternoon had just died. The doctor asked me to do what I could to comfort his wife and help her get to sleep. I was the only female working on this ship, so naturally I was elected to help her.

I remembered the woman, a really nice person in her mid-thirties. It was Sunday, and when I had conducted the nondenominational church service in the salon that morning, she had played the piano for me while I led the passengers in singing hymns. Her husband had attended. Though I'd heard that someone had been stricken during the day, I had no idea he was the person.

The captain took me to his own quarters, where the lady had been told of her husband's death. She was at a window, looking out at the cloud formations that spiraled up from the horizon, but she turned when we entered.

Her eyes were faintly red, though she was not crying. She said, "Oh, Jeraldine, I'm so glad we came to church service this morning. He was singing, you know," she told me.

I nodded and told her that the captain was putting a private cabin on the promenade deck at her disposal, and that I had stopped in the purser's office to get a sedative that would enable her to sleep. She was grateful for the attention, and thanked the captain for his thoughtfulness.

After the cabin steward let us into the stateroom and we were alone, she cried. The tears flowed unchecked as she sat, head lowered in a chair. After a while, I held her and said the softly comforting things like, "You know there is no death. We just leave our shell we call a body and go on to a different plane. Our mind or spirit or whatever you call it survives. Your husband's spirit is probably right here in this cabin with us now. He will always be near you." She quieted down with these words and suggested that it would probably be best if she took the sedative and went to bed—if I would be good enough to sit with her until she dropped off to sleep.

I volunteered to go to her cabin for her nightgown, which she said was hanging on the back of the closet door. She also asked if I would get a bar of facial soap from her cabin bath, since she was allergic to that provided by the ship.

It was by this time almost two in the morning; I had been working over eighteen hours and my nerves were on edge and I had to be up at the crack of dawn. There wasn't anyone awake on the ship, the lights of the public rooms were out, and the alleyways and companionways were only dimly illuminated.

The widow's former cabin was on the next to the lowest passenger deck, a four-deck descent through a dark creaking ship completely silent except for the muffled sound of the turbines even farther below. When I reached the cabin at the end of the dark alleyway I opened the door and entered, snapping on the lights, and screamed without being able to help myself.

I had assumed that the man had died in the surgery, since he was under the care of the doctor, and his body had been kept in the hospital. It obviously had not. The corpse lay on the bunk, a sheet covering its midriff, the bare feet hanging slightly over the end of the bunk, for he had been a big man.

I was so terrified that I leaped back into the alleyway and closed the door. The things that I had been saying so positively to the wife—that her husband should be thought of not as dead but now existing in the world of spirit—seemed useless to me as I tried to regain my composure. But I couldn't tell her now that I was afraid to get her things because his body was here—not after my speech to her.

I had to get the nightgown. Moreover, I had to get the soap, which meant brushing past the body on the bunk. I did it—and now that I think of it, I've no idea why we have this terror of cadavers, whether it is a mouse or a man. They really are only shells of something that once housed the soul.

I hope I didn't look too shaken when I returned to the stateroom. I tried to appear calm though my heart was pounding, and I gave her the sedative after she donned her nightgown and washed her tear-stained face. She dropped off into an exhausted sleep soon after. It took me a lot longer to fall asleep when I finally got to my cabin. What a long and strange day.

We were cruising at the time in the broad stretch of ocean occupied by the Cook Islands. There weren't any landing strips so there weren't any planes. These are tiny islands, widely scattered over an immense area, and they had no embalming facilities. Therefore, it had been decided sometime during the night that our deceased passenger would have to be buried at sea because our ship would be staying in the Islands for six months. There was no way to send the corpse home.

When I got back into action the following morning, a shroud of heavy canvas was being prepared for the body, and there was a big argument going on about how much lead weight would be required to carry the corpse to its resting place.

The chief engineer, the doctor, and I were all questioned as to our estimate of the man's bulk, and the consensus was that he must have weighed about 180 pounds. One of the sailors working on the canvas shroud told us with some relish that the final stitch is always taken through the corpse's nose to make sure he is really dead. The doctor lost his temper. He knew very well the man was dead, and there'd be no such goings-on.

We anchored in the harbor at Rarotonga in the mid-morning, and the captain arranged to talk to one of the important men in the village there. The captain asked for a minister to come out to the ship and say a proper benediction before the body was sent over the side.

The sweet people of Rarotonga wouldn't hear of it. Instead, they provided a casket and services were conducted in a lovely little church in Rarotonga. Burial took place in a beautiful cemetery ablaze with flowering shrubs and plants and overlooking the sapphire sea. A choir sang and the natives shed tears. The Rarotongans refused the captain's offer of a contribution for the time and the expense and didn't even charge the widow for the grave or casket.

There weren't any planes there, so the widow stayed on the ship for the rest of the cruise; there was no other way to get to our destination, Tahiti. Once there she flew back to her home. I noticed that the single man in the cabin across from hers went out of his way to care for her after her husband died. He also left when she did. I'm such a Cupid I do hope they saw each other again when they got to their homes and maybe are happily married to each other by now. They seemed perfect together, but then maybe that's just my romantic heart imagining things.

She will be glad to know that, on subsequent trips, we found the grave carefully tended with fresh blossoms, and that the empty beer bottles that had been set in the mound of sand on top are still in place. All graves are like this in Rarotonga. The natives told us these bottles serve to prevent evil spirits from entering and taking over the body of the deceased.

chapter thirty-five

MEN ON THE PROWL

LENNIE WAS A BIG, BLONDE GUY WITH HEAVY-LIDDED EYES and a deep, easy voice. He was a laconic man who said funny things in an offhand way. He would lounge behind the bar and look at the girls with a sleepy kind of smile. They'd come apart at the seams. Usually only the ship's officers who were inclined that way could pick and choose among the willing ladies on board. This was not true with Lennie as head booze dispenser. After a day afloat, he would be involved in more palace intrigues than those at Louis XVI's court.

"Scoring Lennie" bowled them over to the right and left, cruise after cruise. After one cruise, an older woman actually gave him a Ferrari automobile.

On another cruise Lennie's assistant bartender was a nice young bachelor. There were a number of bartenders, of course, but Earnest Eddie was unusual because he was entirely free to make any liaison he cared to, including marriage, but he couldn't score to save his neck. It was no secret; he complained about it to me as well as to everyone else on the staff. He was pretty nice looking, too, but he came on as Earnest Eddie. I suspect the girls he approached either were traveling with an Earnest Eddie or didn't dig his type. Personally, I like men who are selective and a little shy, I guess some girls go for the fellows with the quick come-on.

On this trip, Earnest Eddie finally made his connection. The girl was a person I had met on other cruise ships, a travel agent who was traveling on this cruise with a group she had put together. She and Eddie reached their agreement the first night at sea, found it a completely satisfactory one, and everything looked great for the formerly frustrated assistant bartender. He was happier than a kid with his first bicycle.

Unfortunately, Scoring Lennie had a thing about breasts, and Eddie's new girlfriend was more than amply endowed. Within two days, Lennie, who could have had his choice among all the free women aboard ship, had baited the hook, caught, and landed Earnest Eddie's girl. Earnest Eddie was left to thrash around in his cabin at night, and was just too darned nice to do anything else about it. He was no match for Scoring Lennie.

The crew was furious that Eddie's girl had been stolen. They evolved a scheme, and even enlisted the aid of one of the ship's medical staff to help carry it out—although if you breathe a word of this, we will deny it flatly.

The medical man called Lennie in for a very private consultation. He hemmed and hawed for a while, then asked if Scoring Lennie would submit to a urine test.

Scoring Lennie was properly surprised and asked why.

The medic hemmed and hawed some more and finally indicated that Lennie's assistant might have a venereal disease. Nothing had been done about it, because Eddie didn't directly handle food and because this had only recently been discovered. Tests were continuing. Now the medic got very delicate. It was definitely known that Earnest Eddie had enjoyed a relationship with a certain lady traveling aboard the ship, and it was suspected that Scoring Lennie had subsequently dallied with this female. Therefore....

Scoring Lennie promptly submitted a sample and all sadistically watched his worried face all that day and evening.

Scoring Lennie also gave up on the lady to her terrible bewilderment. Earnest Eddie, of course, had no idea what was going on, so he willingly accepted the return of the prodigal passenger to his cabin's doorstep.

The medic had it in for Scoring Lenny and kept needling him until the captain called a halt to the whole thing. He remembered a boy who had once been teased about having VD who had nearly committed suicide. Lennie was informed that the whole thing was a joke, but he was very careful about stealing a crew member's girlfriend from then on.

$\mathcal{S}$HOPPING IN ROMANTIC PORTS

HERE ARE SOME HIGHLIGHTS OF THE WONDERFUL SHOP-
ping opportunities available in cruise ports.

Alaska:	Jade, scrimshaw, parkas, hematite, pristine air
Australia:	Opals, beer, camaraderie
Azores:	Wine, lace, linen cutwork, romance, vacations
Baltic States:	Amber, antiquity
Catalina:	Sports clothes at Gulls & Buoys, sunburn
Colombia:	Cartagena—emeralds, straw hats, Nelson's Downfall
Denmark:	Langelinie Mermaid, Royal Copenhagen china, antiques

England:	Bone china, clothing, antiques, high tea at the Ritz Hotel
Fiji:	Pineapples, saris, sandals, friendliness
France:	Perfume, couturier fashions, wine, truffles, sex
Germany:	Clocks, cutlery, medical instruments, automobiles, cleanliness
Hawaii:	Coral, black pearls, MuMus, macadamia nuts, much Aloha
Hong Kong:	Custom-made shoes and clothing, jewelry, hurry scurry atmosphere
Ireland:	Crystal, Woolens, Lace, Beeleek China, Irish Whiskey, Friends
Italy:	Great food, wines, Florentine gold, arts, Antiquities
Japan:	Cameras, electronic items, copiers
Liechtenstein:	Craftmanship, numbered bank accounts
Mexico:	Silver and tin artifacts, papier maché artifacts, tequila, mariachis
New Zealand:	Woolens, kiwi fruit, peacefulness
Other South Seas Ports:	Grass Skirts, Durable Sandals, Rainbows
Philippines:	Embroidery, Barong Shirts, Mangos, Friendliness
Portugal:	Madeira work, woven bags, sandals, hats, gold carriages, sherry, port, liquors
Russia:	Black lacquer hand-painted boxes, dolls, samovars, Stoli vodka, L'Hermitage
Scotland:	Cashmere, woolens, especially tartans, Scotch whiskey, St. Andrew
Spain:	Castanets, dress shoes, wines, lace, flamenco
Sweden:	Crystal, Absolut vodka, massages

Switzerland: Cheese, chocolates, numbered bank accounts, organization

Tasmania: Great long-wearing sandals, great woven purses, baskets, nimble fingers

Venezuela: Caracas—emeralds, wigs, gold, the Funicular

U.S.A.:   Everything

A passenger's Cruise Diary might read:

Oh, happy am I to be sailing away
My cares are ashore and there to stay
While I am on this happy, fun-filled ship
I'm giving "ole devil blues" the slip.
As I embark on this pleasure-filled trip
Aboard this wonderful, beautiful ship.
I sail upon these thrilling seas
I'll seek to unveil Life's mysteries
Shall I uncover from the depths of my soul
What I have kept covered, Life's secret goal?
I feel this is the time for me to do
All the things I've wanted to.
I've learned Life is a result of attitude
So I'll put it to use at this latitude.
I am now free, in charge of my mind,
To seek new thoughts, leaving the negative behind.
On this cruise ship there are so many pleasures,
Exciting ports to shop and find treasures.
Oh, Diary, I look forward to each day
As our ship carries my troubles away.
New-found friends and delicious food
Do so much to build the romantic mood.
There are games and fun of every sort,
Different delights in each exotic port.
Will the roll of the ship, the music and dancing
Fill my craving heart with ecstatic romancing?
These are the things that I'll confide in you.
Oh, Cruise Diary,
Oh, Cruise Diary.
Will they come true?

up in the shampoo bowl. You gave me such a pitch, the shop is swarming with customers and I couldn't find time for breakfast!"

Good Heavens, I thought. I excused myself from the audience, telling them I would be right back. I told Tom to wait for me in my cabin and lie down. It was too late to give him a Dramamine tablet; once you start regurgitating, it won't stay down. So I dashed down to the unmanned hospital to look for liquid Dramamine to give Tom a shot. I had difficulty finding it since all the medications were labeled in Spanish. I came upon a vial that started with D and sounded like Dramamine. Then I searched for a needle. How much to use? I filled it to where I thought it should be and ran to my cabin. Poor Tom was urping in my wastebasket, mostly dry heaves by now.

I said, "Tom, dear, pull your pants down a bit so I can give you this Dramamine shot."

He pulled them down enough so that I could put the shot in the muscle high on his hip. "Now," I said, "just lie there for exactly ten minutes, then get back to your customers. I'll tell them you are on your way."

I finished my lecture as if the world was in perfect order. Tom promised me he would never go without breakfast again when we crossed Queen Charlotte Sound. He turned out to be a great hair stylist and I also had him help me when I was putting on the nightly shows. Later, I gave him a letter of recommendation and he became a first-rate cruise and tour director, one of the best in the business.

When you come to your cabin after dinner, the bed is always turned down and on top of your pillow is the breakfast menu and a chocolate mint. One of our beautiful blonde passengers had overindulged a bit. She didn't bother to turn on the lights, she just flopped on her bed fully clothed. In the morning she staggered into the bathroom, looked into the mirror, and screamed a mighty scream! Her hair and face were the splotchy brown of melted chocolate!

chapter thirty-seven

A Farewell Party

SNIPPETS OF CONVERSATION ON THE NEXT-TO-LAST DAY OF a cruise:

Room steward: "You know, none of us ever steals anything, but, Jeraldine, I so coveted this guy's shoes. I mean, I flipped for them. He's staying in the expensive Riviera suite, so I hid one, thinking that if he didn't find the one he would leave the other one, but do you know what he did? He said, "No sense packing this single shoe, is there?" and I agreed with him. "Well," he said, "this one isn't any use anymore," and he threw it out the porthole."

Room steward to waiter: "I indicated in a nice way that I expected a good tip. A real big mother, considering how I'd taken care of her. What do you think she said?"

"Haven't the foggiest, mate."

"She said, 'The way I've been accommodating, you cocko, I figure you owe me money!'"

"They're none of them grateful any more, Ronnie."

An entertainer told me the woman passenger he had been sleeping with said to him, "It's so wonderful, I hate to see it end. What will we do tomorrow after we land, darling?"

"I don't know about you, baby, but I'm getting the hell home to the wife and kids, I only have a few hours off and then we sail again."

I heard a man say to his wife, "Well, if we did that in San Juan, what the devil did we do in St. John?"

An elderly woman passenger said, "I bought this gorgeous unset star sapphire, Jeraldine. If I swallow it tonight, do you think I could get it past customs?"

"Eat a lot of cheese, dear, or you may leave it in the ocean."

I heard a young girl say to an older man, "If you're as rich as you are saying, why do I have to take a bus to Houston?"

Paul, the assistant cruise director, said to me after a Godzilla cruise, "You ever see a Humphrey Bogart picture where he was in the Merchant Marine?"

"Nope. And I thought I'd seen them all."

"It was a war picture and these guys were all in Liberty ships in convoys and getting the hell blown out of themselves by the U-boats and this one guy, Alan Hale, he says if he ever gets off this ship he's going to grab an oar, put it on his shoulder and start walking inland. The first guy that points at it and says, 'What's that?'—that's where he's setting down, to stay."

"I know what he meant. That Godzilla was the worst ever."

Then he added, "Jeraldine, let's put a lock on the Comment Form Box so Johnston, the company rep, can't get to them before the home office sees them. He will throw away any that are complimentary about us. You know that he wants to get that drunken broad of his on here."

I overheard two schoolteachers: "It would be so wonderful if the children could be sent on cruises like this, Grace. Think of what they would learn."

The other woman thought a moment and replied, "I think the sex education classes are quite liberal enough as they are, Hilda."

The last night at sea is the gala event of the entire cruise. The Captain's Farewell Dinner is the big feature, but there is also a special farewell show, awards made to certain passengers, and souvenirs from the company to the passengers aboard.

The last impression always is a very important one, so the officers are attentive and smiling, the cruise staff is in a whirl of activity making certain everything will go just exactly right, and the waiters and stewards are ready to jump out of their skins to attend to every desire. For these latter, it is also tip night, so they're all full of smiles and obsequious as all get out.

The farewell parties are always enormous fun, albeit a bit emotional at times, because by the end of a cruise everyone, no matter how initially inclined toward aloofness, has made a lot of friends. This is the final fling before the walk down the gangway when the inhibitions, which have been stowed in that invisible dockside bin all this while, can now reattach themselves.

The captain invites all the passengers to a farewell cocktail party an hour before dinner. By this time the cruise staff all have learned to love most of the passengers and hate to see them leave. I stand next to the captain in the farewell receiving line and try to tell him all the names of the passengers whose hands he shakes and says good-bye to. He then goes to the mike and proposes a toast of farewell. The celebrants are all gussied up—the only other occasion for dressing up is the Captain's Welcoming Dinner—and the champagne flows freely. There's something about ships and the bubbly—they seem to go together. The dining room is decorated with garlands and streamers, and balloons and paper hats are on each table. The chefs outdo themselves for the dinner and so does the company, because we give everyone more wine and champagne. Each delectable course has its own house-recommended wine. Naturally no one turns it down, so they really are in great spirits. The hilarity level rises steadily as dinner progresses.

At the end, the lights are turned off and the Baked Alaska is brought in. The corps of waiters stream in from the galley bearing the delectable flaming dessert raised high on silver platters as they march around the dining room. Baked Alaska is a shipboard favorite, and I have watched fascinated many times as the pastry chefs light the hundreds of them needed for the gala. They must be done expertly and served swiftly. When the Baked Alaska has been served and the brandy poured, I take over the microphone.

"Ladies and gentlemen, your attention, please." I say. "May I have your attention?"

When the hubbub has died down, which always takes time and further pleas for silence, I continue: "At this time I want you to meet a very important person, the man who has been both the angel and the devil to us all on this cruise. He is the one who has tempted your palate with all these luscious calories—the very talented Chef Gennaro!"

While this has been going on, if the real chef is busy then whichever man in the vast, gleaming stainless steel galley is free at the moment has been grabbed and had an extra-tall chef's hat popped on his head before he is propelled through the swinging doors into the dining salon. I take the chef's arm or that of his substitute and we proceed to the captain's table, smiling and bowing at the cheering throng. Women jump up from the tables, throw flowers, and plant moist kisses on his cheeks. The orchestra strikes up *Arrivaderci Roma*. The captain congratulates him warmly. The officers shake their heads and make bum jokes about their expanding midriffs, and the chef makes his way back to the galley to return to work.

Now comes the souvenir giving, the prizes, and the special show, then the dancing and the conga line that will often make its way through the entire ship, led by the orchestra, before returning to the dance floor, where everyone is squeezed together as tightly as possible and ordered to kiss one another. This squeezing together has a practical side: after the long dance through the ship, the drunks can't fall down.

After the farewell show is over, the party splits off into scores of smaller parties that continue to enjoy the dance music or they go to the casino or out on the deck for a romantic moon watch.

But something unusual can always be trusted to happen on a cruise ship, even on farewell night.

One particular evening, things had gone spectacularly well on the last night of a cruise that had itself been remarkable for the smoothness with which all services had been performed. There had not been a hitch in the engine room or with the plumbing. No one had belted anyone. The tours had all gone off beautifully and returned to the dock exactly on time. No one had been silly about drinking the water in port or over-exposing themselves to the sun. The bingo and horseplayers—even the bridge players—had not voiced even a single complaint.

The magic spell was broken following dinner, during the serving of the dessert. A waiter—the best of the whole lot, the handsomest, most courteous, and alert—accidentally dropped a whole gooey Baked Alaska right in the lap of a man who was elegantly dressed in a brocaded blue dinner coat and ruffled white dinner shirt. That poor man was a mess!

However, the waiter's blunder turned out to be very human and understandable. As he was about to serve that Baked Alaska, one of the quieter young lady passengers, a very prim and proper one, had slipped up behind him and whispered urgently:

"Carlo, I must have your home address. I have missed my period."

Now Jeraldine launches cruise ships, too!

chapter thirty-eight

It All Comes Together

I WOULD WRITE ABOUT MY ADVENTURES IN MY LETTERS home and sometimes there were terrible things—someone would die and we would have to keep the body in the meat locker. One of the officers would always say, "Doesn't the meat taste a bit gamey this evening?" I thought that no one would believe some of the things I was going through. I got very little sleep and all these passengers were coming to me with all their problems, or sometimes they just wanted small talk. I loved the passengers but I was always so in need of sleep.

I was sending more and more letters home. My spelling was so poor. My family knew I was a poor speller, so I wasn't self-conscious about it, but they still had to be able to understand what the word was—sometimes I would write the word three different ways—they could take their

275

choice and maybe make out what I was trying to spell. Those funny letters with that terrible spelling—I never realized that anyone would be reading them except my family.

One day someone said, "Why don't you send them to an agent?" When you are in the middle of the ocean, you can't do much wheeling and dealing on land, but I had a couple of hours off one day in our home port. (Because the ship would come in the morning after weeks or months at sea and sail again the same night, I never had a full day off.) Before we went down to the South Pacific for six months I took these letters to an agent, a lovely lady named Dorris Halsey. She sent me a cable while I was down in the South Pacific, saying that a publisher wanted to see me and that they wanted a couple of sample chapters first to see how I could make my letters into a book.

Well, a book. How do you go about that? The South Seas didn't have any libraries where our tours went, as far as I knew. I never saw any down there. There wasn't any time to ask the passengers or anyone about writing so I got a spiral top tablet out and just started writing with my pen—just the things that were happening and then I don't know why I did this but I tore off the first finished ten sheets and that's the first chapter, all raveled on top and stapled together. I guess the publishers thought it was different. Who would staple pieces of papers together? They said that when the ship came in they wanted to see me. So, when the ship came back to Los Angeles, the publishers of Pinnacle Books, Andrew Ettinger and David Zentner, happened to be in town that night from New York and said that they would give me a little bit of money in advance. Now I had to finish it, but I still had to do something in the meanwhile to earn a living. So more and more things were happening on my ships and I was getting plenty of material, working hard as a cruise director, but I had to keep on writing. The publishers said I had to use a little more dialogue. I thought, Hmmm, dialogue, how do you do that? What I did was put parentheses around the descriptions and make it into dialogue by adding "he said" or "she said," etc.

I found out how to write a television treatment which is very, very easy. But I wanted to write the treatment in such a way that I could get my book made into a TV Movie of the Week. I would need some ship line to let us use their ship on which to film, and what ship line would ever let my salty stories be told about their ships? A ship is like a city all by itself, the drama, some of the pettiness, some of the dangerous things, and some of the unbelievable things! This is always kept secret. I put all this aside, because for the television treatment the ship always has to be seaworthy, if you want the cruise line to allow filming. The captain always has to be sober too—in the script, that is.

To digress for a moment, that reminds me of the time when I was on this "Off Broadway" ship I told you about. Travel agents had promised the passengers we were going to spend Christmas Day on Christmas Island and have a picnic. When we got there, the life boats wouldn't come down. I don't think they had ever been used. With no life boats, we couldn't disembark the passengers! WOW, did I catch it from a Godzilla that day! Then our ship spent six months in the South Pacific making eleven-day cruises from Fiji to Tahiti. On the way back to the U.S.A. we stopped at Christmas Island again. The life boats had been fixed in the meantime. When the Coast Guard inspection was due on this same ship, a crew member was always sent to the hardware store to borrow a motor to replace the non-functioning motor on one of the life boats. After the inspection was over, the borrowed motor was returned to the store. Talk about running on a shoestring!

When we got to Christmas Island, the local people stopped whatever they were doing and came to greet us, because cruise ships seldom stopped there (maybe once every three years or so). They were so friendly! The passengers loved all the attention and enjoyed the hospitality. The natives wouldn't take money for anything. If a passenger admired some headdress or hand-woven basket or necklace or shells, it would be quickly handed to them as a gift. The locals were passing out their homemade booze to everyone. That night when we were back on the ship, passengers were wearing their beautiful flower leis and I had planned "Island Night." After dinner, they went up to the Grand Salon for show time, but the orchestra wasn't there, so I called down and found out they had been drinking the local *kava*—and were all passed out. This is terrible, I thought. The orchestra is not working! How on earth am I going to entertain these people without an orchestra?

I called the hotel manager to complain about the orchestra. I didn't like to complain about crew—you didn't want to get in bad with anyone on the ship because you might get pushed overboard. Never complain about anything. This time I went into the hotel manager's cabin and said, "Did you know that the orchestra is so bombed, they can't even come up and play tonight?"

He was lying on his bunk and said slurringly, "Is that so, Jerry?" Good heavens, he was drunk! I thought, Now this is the living end: the orchestra is drunk, the hotel manager is drunk, and I'm in charge of all these passengers up there. This is the limit. I have never gone to the captain with a complaint, but I'm going to have to go to him with a complaint now, because I'm so desperate.

I called up to the captain's quarters and the chief engineer answered and said, "Yes, Jerry."

I said, "You wouldn't believe it, Dave, but the orchestra is drunk, and the hotel manager is drunk. I want to tell the captain what is going on. I have the Grand Salon filled with passengers waiting for show time and I've no music!!"

He said, "Jerry, I can't wake him up, now. He just passed out."

Getting back to my television treatment—if you have an idea for a television show or a movie you must register it with the Writer's Guild. The Writer's Guild is in Beverly Hills and the cost is only twenty dollars. You can register it and then it is protected for you. You don't have to be a member. Thank God I registered my treatment on April 5th, 1974, #146910 at the Writer's Guild of America, West Inc. I am including a copy for you here.

For Motion Picture and Weekly Television Series Comedy Drama

"The Love Boats"

A book by Jeraldine Saunders, who was for the last six years the world's only woman cruise director on the luxury cruise ships.

In this recounting of her experiences, vivacious Jeraldine emerges as a Carole Lombard-Katherine Hepburn-Lucille Ball character who romps through the drama, the humor, the pathos, the funny in a tragic way that reality is, aboard the microcosm of life that plays out on the luxury cruises, a way of life that is becoming more popular for more persons than ever before in the history of cruise lines.

As a motion picture and as a weekly television series, this would appear to be a natural. Love and envy mix with hope and despair, the guest characters being etched by passengers who change with each cruise. The permanent cast is the cruise staff headed by Jeraldine. Adventures unfold through her viewpoint and give us a strong, exciting. running story, the thread of which is woven of the stuff of life itself, with all stops out after the ship is 12 miles at sea, where the laws of the land don't apply and anything goes and does—from boarding until disembarking. A slice of life that may, in actuality, be more concentrated in each episode than many people experience in a lifetime.

Permanent cast is the cruise staff: Jeraldine as cruise director, assistant cruise director (male), sports director, dance team. Appearing periodically will be the ship's captain, purser, officers, and the uninhibited Italian crew.

The job of attempting to keep passengers happy which involves all of the cruise staff is a series of great trials and tribulations for this tightly knit group which must live together, year in and year out, closer than brother and sister.

The passengers range from the high and the mighty to the low and the lonely, from captains of industry to the secretary who has saved her pennies for the one big fling aboard The Love Boats.

Publication Date: September 17, 1974
Available for Reading: Immediately

I didn't know a soul in the business. I didn't know any writers. I didn't know anyone who could help me—besides, I had to work on the ship all the time so I wasn't able to go out and push my idea for the TV movie.

I did find time to send my book's manuscript to all the newspapers and find the time to send out the treatment to all the studios hoping that I could sell an option on it. In an imaging class I had taken, they taught us that whatever you image, you can make happen. That theory is also taught in "Religious Science" and in "A Course In Miracles and Unity." It really is like praying—this imaging—so I imaged and prayed that I would find someone to buy an option on my book and that it would be made into a Movie of the Week. Well, Jerry Hulse, the travel writer at the *Los Angeles Times*, read *The Love Boats* manuscript that I had sent him and—God bless him—he gave it a fantastic critique that drew the attention of the big time producer, Douglas C. Cramer. Cramer bought the option and had Bud Baumes develop it.

I received a call from Doug Cramer after he had purchased the option. He explained to me that he was having trouble getting permission from the cruise line's management to film aboard a ship. There were only two cruise lines sailing out of Los Angeles in those pre-*Love Boat* days. He said that if we didn't get Princess Cruises to allow us to film on board there wasn't going to be any *Love Boat* TV movie at all.

Talk about watching one's dreams go down the tubes! I went into a panic. It was a Sunday. I knew the names of the people who owned Princess Cruises at that time, Mr. and Mrs. Stanley McDonald, and I knew they lived in Seattle.

Never having worked in an office, I didn't know that one isn't supposed to go over the head of a company executive. Actually, even if I did know, I guess I was in such a panic I would have done what I did anyway.

I asked telephone information for the home phone number of the owners and much to my surprise it was listed. The planet Mercury must have been direct; they answered the phone. I said, "I'm sorry to bother you at home but I feel your company is really passing up a fantastic chance for some great public relations by not allowing Douglas Cramer's production company to film my *Love Boat* story aboard your ship."

Well, the McDonalds didn't know anything about the movie offer. They knew of my book, *The Love Boats*, though, and they immediately had the foresight to see what the film could do for their company. "Jeraldine, we will call tomorrow morning and tell our company to give permission for *Love Boat* to be filmed on board."

I thanked them profusely, and after I hung up, I thanked God.

A couple of days later I received a note from Doug Cramer that to this day I have hanging in my study here at home to remind me of that happy day. It began: "Your magic is working, etc...." That was another very glorious day in my life.

When the first *Love Boat* was filmed I was on board as a lecturer and for a *Love Boat* book signing. The executive whose head I went over by calling the McDonalds was also on board, but he never introduced himself to me and on the last night of the cruise he made sure I wasn't invited to the cast party. The production company had to keep in good with him because they needed the ship for future filmings.

When I was a lecturer on this ship, I was always paid in cash on the last day of the cruise. On this cruise, however, the purser told me, "I'm sorry, Jerry, but the company's executive on board told us not to pay you today. I guess you will have to be paid by mail this time. I don't know why."

Suddenly, I felt like a helpless little girl, all by myself with no protection from this person in power.

I don't blame Princess Cruises for this happening; they didn't know about it until recently.

So, girls, be careful when you hurt a bully's ego.

That cruise company executive whose head I went over still has his nose out of joint (and has long since retired), but the decision to allow the production company to film on their ship has helped make Princess Cruises go from a very small company to one of the biggest and best lines in the cruise industry.

The Love Boat made millions of people, worldwide, wake up to cruising, and that has benefited Princess Cruises and all the other cruise lines. Now, I ask you, am I a bad girl?

After *The Love Boat* movie of the week, I imaged some more and prayed that it would be made into *Love Boat II*, and sure enough it was made into *Love Boat II*, and then I imaged some more for a *Love Boat III*. When Rockefeller was asked, "How much money does it take to make you happy?" he replied, "Just a little bit more." So I thought, If it only would go into a series, that would be really perfect! My prayers certainly came back threefold and more. This is when prolific producer Aaron Spelling hopped on board and joined Douglas S. Cramer, who was up to this time producing the television series by himself.

When Aaron Spelling joined forces with Doug Cramer, it made a powerful combination. Aaron did his magical things in recasting some of the regular characters and so after *Love Boat III* was filmed, it was picked up for the series on ABC. How good can life get?

We happily rolled over the "bounding main" for ten abundant years at the top of the Nielsen ratings. As I have said, the series is now in syndication in 115 countries and every time it is shown, I smile at my annuity in perpetuity. God bless the following people: the viewers, Douglas S. Cramer, Aaron Spelling, and thank you, my readers and God for my good fortune!

Another one of my new blessings is that I have sold the *Love Boat* feature film rights to Aaron Spelling for a film for the big screen theaters. The working title is *Love Boat: The Movie.*" I just can't believe after all these years of having jobs where I worked seven days a week that suddenly I get checks in the mail and I don't have to do a thing. I am so grateful. Now I have time to stay at home and enjoy domesticity. I have a sweet dear Libra husband; I write and we travel whenever we want to. I write about the topics that I lecture about on cruise ships such as motivation, the Four Seasons Color Concept, and nutrition.

My book, *Hypoglycemia: The Disease Your Doctor Won't Treat* with co-author Harvey M. Ross, M.D. has sold over one million copies and I have just updated and enlarged it in a nice, new quality paperback put out by Kensington Publishers, New York. It is considered the definitive work on hypoglycemia. Also, I lecture and write books on astrology, graphology, palmistry, face reading, and numerology. When lecturing on ships, I often remind passengers that there are no unnatural or supernatural phenomena, only very large gaps in our knowledge of what is natural, and we should strive to fill those gaps of ignorance.

I recently found a comment by St. Augustine that I'll quote: "Miracles do not happen in contradiction to nature, but only in contradiction to what is *known to us* of nature."

I loved working as a cruise director and I love my life now. "If you love what you do, you will never work a day in your life," my friend Ralph Portner says. Yes, life is exciting.

When the series first started I flew to New York with Lauren Tewes to do the "Good Morning America" Show on TV. I love the whole *Love Boat* cast as I am sure you do, too.

Recently I flew to New York to do the "Attitudes" show on Lifetime Network with Jill Whelan, who played the part of the captain's daughter, and I was talking with Bernie Kopell the other day. He and his wife Catrina are so happy with their new baby. (Bernie was the ship's doctor), and Lauren Tewes is very happy living in Seattle.

Jeraldine Saunders with Love Boat's *second McCoy, Patricia Klous.*

I see Gavin MacLeod, the captain, occasionally at charity affairs. He is a very nice, spiritual person. As for the ship's bartender, lovable Ted Lange, I have seen him in some plays recently and his acting is superb. I suppose you all know that Fred Grandy (Gopher) became a very successful congressman from Iowa.

It is now 1998 and as if I do not already have Paradise on Earth, the Universal Intelligence has blessed me with yet another huge chunk of luck. As I am writing this, Aaron Spelling is in the process of casting to bring back...yes...my hand shakes with joy as I write these words...yes indeed, the *Love Boat: The Next Wave* series will be back on your TV sets by the time this book comes out! I know that will make a lot of people happy. No car crashes, no torture, no violence—just comedy and romance, clean wholesome fun for the whole family. There isn't enough innocent amusement these days.

David Hartman interviews Love Boat's *first "Julie," Lauren Tewes, and Jeraldine Saunders on* Good Morning America.

*Aaron Spelling, Jeraldine Saunders, and actress Heather Hewett
at an awards luncheon in 1995.*

*It's great living on shore now! Jeraldine attends the ribbon-cutting ceremony
opening the Motion Picture Museum on Hollywood Boulevard. Among the
celebrities in the picture are Johnny Grant, Trudy Marshall, Don DeFore, Sybil
Brand, Vivian Blaine, Terry Moore, Jeraldine Saunders (with the headgear),
Caesar Romero, Newt Russell, and Fritz Field.*

One of the best-kept secrets in Hollywood is The Cinema Glamour Shop at 343 North La Brea Avenue in Hollywood. I am currently the president of the Motion Picture and TV Fund's auxiliary, The Screen Smart Set, the group that operates the shop. Motion picture and television stars donate their expensive clothes, artifacts, and furniture to the shop, the proceeds go to charities supported by the fund, and the donations are charitable deductions for income tax purposes. These items are sold at unbelievably low prices, so the next time you are in Hollywood, come by and purchase the belongings of the stars for a song. You will be assisted by famous stars, come away with a bargain, help a good cause, and have fun, too!

chapter thirty-nine

THE IMPORTANCE OF TIMING

THERE IS NEVER ANYTHING WRONG WITH ASTROLOGY, BUT there can be inadequacies with the astrologer. Astrology is a scientific art just as is medicine. Most doctors mean well but some are better diagnosticians than others. Consequently, one doctor may treat your symptoms a bit differently than the next. It is not an exact science but a scientific art. The same is true of astrologers. With the aid of computers the math is made easy so a horoscope will be drawn up accurately, but how it is interpreted is where the art comes into play. There are many places where you can order and receive a computerized horoscope. These are correct and useful so that you can be prepared for the aspects each day. Usually the interpolation from the computerized horoscope is accurate and very helpful, and it doesn't cost much. I would suggest calling Llewellyn Worldwide at 1-800-THE-MOON for this horoscope chart. To obtain a more individualized reading, find an astrologer to synthesize the transits and come up with an overall picture of your current influences.

Selecting an experienced astrologer is important. The 800 number above can give you the name of a good astrologer, or you may call the American Federation of Astrologers in Tempe, Arizona for a reference. The only people who don't accept astrology are those individuals who have not studied it. It is merely the study of time. An accurate horoscope is based on the month, day, hour, year, and place of the subject's birth.

The only thing that is permanent is change, because the planets and stars are always in motion and never remain in the same position in the skies.

As you learn about your unique horoscope you will realize that the Universal Intelligence has made us all different. Understanding our uniqueness leads to self-esteem and knowledge of our own specialness. I am so glad we live in a democracy because it allows us to express our uniqueness whereas communism doesn't.

The academic prejudice against astrology comes from ignorance of this particular subject.

Astronomers are usually the worst detractors. They keep measuring and measuring but never bring their learning down to the affairs of humanity.

Perhaps there is a reason for this. It is a four letter word: "fund." When funding for astrology becomes available, watch all the astronomers jump on the bandwagon. Suddenly, astrology will become respectable.

Knowing what influence the transiting planets have in each chart can help individuals understand when they are dejected or in trouble "that this too shall pass" because nothing remains the same. As I have said, the planets and stars are always in motion.

When J. P. Morgan was asked, "Do millionaires use astrology?" he replied, "No, but billionaires do."

In Carl Payne Tobey's introduction to the brilliant Grant Lewi's *Heaven Knows What* (Llewellyn Publications, 1967), Tobey writes that Lewi did not employ astrology as a causal phenomenon; to him as to some other astrologers, it was the "algebra of life." He was interested in the principles that were hidden behind life itself.

Tobey goes on to say there was no such word as "astronomy" at the time of Plato, yet copies of Plato that are sold to students at some universities today have been rewritten with the word "astronomy" substituted for "astrology" to give the impression that Plato's interest was in astronomy and not astrology. The word came into use only 500 years after the birth of Christ. Astrology dates back to 500 B.C. I recommend you read all of the introduction to this very great book for beginners.

Have you seen the Christmas Pageant at Dr. Robert Schuller's famed Crystal Cathedral in Garden Grove, California? If so, you have heard the three wise men referred to as "astrologers," as it should be.

In learning of the Universal Intelligence's great plan, astrology can be a road to your own freedom and security. There isn't any way one can learn about and understand astrology and still remain an atheist. With this study one comprehends God's beautiful order and the more one studies it, the more spiritual one becomes.

Reading has always been my hobby. I can't seem to find time for fiction but I love to read and study, especially anything that relates to nutrition, astrology, numerology, palmistry, physiognomy, and graphology. It came in handy while I was on the cruise ships as it does to this day. The Universal Intelligence has given us these great tools to be used. These signs of love can help guide us as we go through this university we call life. They help us have the ability to fulfill our soul's purpose in this lifetime.

I used to tell the passengers during my astrology lectures that we can close our eyes and cross a street, or we can utilize signals that indicate "go" or "stop." Astrology gives us those signals.

No two individuals can be born in the same spot at exactly the same time. Carl Gustav Jung said, "Every moment of time has the qualities of that particular moment in time." If you took a photograph of the heavens from your spot in time when you were born, it would be your horoscope, the hand of cards you were dealt at birth. As above, so below. Now you may say that smacks of fatalism. No, because how you play those cards is where the free will comes into play. Now, anyone can play a better game of life if they know which cards they are holding. Astrology is just the study of time. The importance of time is knowledge that is kept from the masses. Some people still think that astrology is just based on the month (the Zodiacal sun sign) as in the newspaper columns.

My book, *Love Signs: Find Your True Love Using: Astrology, Numbers, Handwriting, Palm Reading, Face Reading and Aura Reading.* (Llewellyn, Second Edition, 1998), contains a simple section where even a child can find their rising (ascendant) sign. It also is a fun book to help the layperson read his or her own or another's palm, analyze handwriting, and use physiognomy, the ancient Chinese art of analyzing character by facial features.

Our lives consist of various cycles. There is the cycle of each planet around the sun and there are numerical cycles. There are only nine numbers in the universe; the others are just combinations of these. Numbers were not invented, they were discovered and have always existed. They are a significant element of the ancient Kabbalah (mystical teachings based on Hebrew scripture) and they are fascinating!

After a lecture that I gave on board during a cruise, a very elderly lady came to me and asked if I would please give her a private "reading." She seemed so desperate that I took her to my cabin, when I had a few minutes before lunch, and I sat her on the bunk opposite mine. She could have been cast as the perfect white-haired, sweet-faced grandmother on TV. After looking up her birth planets in my ephemeris and telling her what kind of life she had had, she was amazed and said, "My! It is fascinating that you see all this so quickly just by looking up where the planets were on my birthday." After her reading I could sense that she was not completely satisfied.

Usually I tape my readings and the passengers were so pleased and full of compliments in the letters I received every time my ship returned to home port. But I had to find out what it was that this sweet little old lady with a cane was so eager about.

I decided to see which numerical cycle she was in currently. It was a number eight cycle, the power year. I asked if she was concerned about money. Usually a number eight year means intensified attraction, but because of her advanced age I was naturally omitting romance and assuming it could be a money concern. It was lunch time already and I needed food to avoid a hypoglycemia attack, so I took this shortcut. I knew number eight stands for intensity, either in emotional security, or money, or love, or pressure, or thinking big.

At her age I figured that money must have been the interest, but I was reminded that day of a lesson I have never forgotten, as she said to me, "I know you will laugh at me but I'll tell you what my real problem is."

I assured her I wouldn't think of doing that.

She began to speak, "I am desperately in love with Charles, my neighbor, and he is twenty-five years younger than I. Now you can understand my problem."

I replied, "Don't call it a problem, call it a situation—that is more positive. Now let's check his birthday with yours."

She knew his month, day, and year so I looked it up in my ephemeris and that match looked very, very good.

I told her more about this unusual, caring man. "You are not only going to enjoy the fulfillment of the healing power of love, your ability to love, but that younger man is being given an opportunity to gain wisdom, experience, and valuable lessons in life that he might not have found with someone younger than he. Your planets are so compatible I feel he could bring you much contentment and companionship."

She took my hand in hers and said, "You have just helped me fuel the flickering flame I have in my heart for him." She came back the next summer with Charles, her nice new husband, and they told me they were in seventh heaven. I enjoyed watching them in their happiness. That case is always a reminder to me that love, money, and health are the main interest with humans, with love running very high on the list no matter how young they are—even very, very young and very, very old. Isn't nature wonderful to make LOVE the most important interest to us?

I used astrology to select the correct timing for mailing my book chapters when we got in port and I also used it when I met a gentleman that I thought might be "Mr. Right." I would ask to see his driver's license for his birth date and I could check the spot where it said married or unmarried. I would then dash down to my cabin and look in my ephemeris to find out where the planets were when he was born, looking especially for Saturn. I started adding this information on the back of the cards in my file listing my hoped-for dates, if and when I ever got off the ship. I never used those cards, but that's another story.

Geraldine's book, Love Signs, *uses astrology, numerology, palmistry, and other techniques to help her readers find compatible partners*

chapter forty

I NEVER THOUGHT I WOULD KISS A SAILOR

Since I never had time off, my card file was becoming full of possible dates for when and if I ever got off the ships.

I had been working on one ship for a long time when I was transferred to the beautiful *Royal Viking Star*. I was to have a day off before boarding the *Star* on its maiden voyage.

I don't know how I did it, but because my agent Dorris Halsey called and said, "Your editor, Andrew Ettinger, is in town. Could I bring him over?"

I said, "Yes, I'll make dinner."

"Great" she said, "his uncle wants to come along because he found out you read palms."

I said, "Bring him along. That would be fine." So that night I managed to put together a really fun dinner party.

I had an apartment in this building that my family owned, and my mother had the apartment next to mine. I would just dash in and dump my purchases from each cruise and have a couple hours there and then run out again to catch the ship for our next cruise.

It was summer so I had my front door open with just the screen door in use. Dorris, Andrew, and his uncle, Arthur Andrews knocked on the door. Arthur told me later that he looked in through the screen door and saw me sitting on the floor (as is my habit), took one look at me and fell in love with me. He didn't know who I was because he didn't know if I was the hostess for this dinner party or perhaps one of the guests.

I love giving dinner parties and decorating the table with silver, crystal, fine china, flowers, and I always use different objects d'art. That's the Virgo in me. The evening went very well. I read Arthur's palm and saw that he had lots of admirable qualities, but I didn't really pay much attention to him. My mind was focused on preparing for my new ship the next day.

When my guests were leaving, I gave each of them the printed list of addresses of the port agents in each of the ports where my ship would be stopping for the rest of the season. I said, "Keep this list in case you want to write to me." Then as an afterthought I said, "Come on down tomorrow and see me sail, and I'll show you around my beautiful new ship."

The next day Arthur Andrews was there to see me off. I didn't pay much attention to him because there were a lot of other friends there to see me off too. Andrew Ettinger, my editor, wasn't there because he had to fly back to his New York office. (He soon left to become a Hollywood entrepreneur.)

We sailed on the first of our forty-eight-day cruises from Los Angeles's San Pedro Harbor, through the Panama Canal to the Caribbean and back to Los Angeles.

At the first port we came to (as usual it was about 7:00 A.M.), the steward slipped a letter from Arthur under my cabin door. Then every time our ship would arrive in the next port, there would be another friendly letter from Arthur. This happened at every port, so

I became like Pavlov's dog; every time the ship would get into port I would start looking under my cabin door to see if another letter would be there.

I thought, What is the gentleman doing writing me? He must think I'm his girlfriend or something. What's with this man? I had absolutely no interest in him at all.

Anyway, I was so busy working and we had gone through the Panama Canal, over to the Bahamas, and now we were on our way back, just about to arrive in Acapulco. I usually kept my car at the dock in Los Angeles while I was at sea. This time, however, when I boarded this lovely ship, I planned on staying for a year and I had so much luggage so I had someone drive me to the ship in their car. Now I started to wonder How am I going to get home for a few hours when our ship gets back to Los Angeles?

Then a bright idea came to me. I'll write this fella, who has been writing to me—I wonder if he'd pick me up when we get in? I knew that sometimes when you mail something from Acapulco it doesn't get to Los Angeles before the ship does but I thought I'd try. I wrote him a letter with my terrible spelling and said, "I don't know what kind of work you do (I didn't even know if he had a job), and I don't know if you can get off or not or even if you would be interested or not. My ship is due in San Pedro harbor at 8:00 A.M. and then I have to go through customs and it will be about 10:00 A.M. before I can get off. I need a lift to Glendale. I'm going to be working very late the night before we arrive. It's the farewell party and I'll probably be tired and I have a million things to do when I get to Glendale, so it won't be a very exciting trip, but if you don't have anything else to do and you can spare the time I certainly would appreciate your taking me home and back. Now if you can't make it or don't want to I certainly will understand."

Jupiter, Mercury, and Venus must have been in good aspect because when our ship pulled into San Pedro, I ran out on the deck to see if perhaps he was there. There was only one person standing on the dock waiting for our ship, and it was Arthur.

I disembarked with my empty luggage, which I didn't have room for in my cabin. As I came down the gangway there was Arthur and the first officer from another ship on which I used to work. I hadn't seen him for about a year and he had come down from Canada. He had a crush on me, I guess, but I didn't pay any attention to him even though he was very handsome and a gentleman. He was much too young.

I said, "Why, Malcolm, I didn't know you were going to be here! I wish I would have known. I asked Arthur here to take me home." I then introduced them to each other. Arthur's car was right there, so he asked Malcolm, "Would you please put her luggage in my trunk?"

When I got in the car with Arthur I asked him, "Would you mind going by the post office in Willmington? I want to mail some letters." Before we even went four or five blocks something came over me. It was really a very strange feeling, an intuitive thing, a very calm sensation that made me know that I belonged with this man. I didn't know a thing about him. I just sensed this feeling of comfort. Perhaps I was with him in another life or something like that, because I just felt good being next to this person. Not just good but with a complete feeling of belonging. I didn't tell him that, of course.

We stopped for lunch, and although I'd had a big breakfast on the ship, I was craving Mexican food. Arthur couldn't believe I could eat so much.

When we got to my apartment there was a note on my door. It was from Malcolm. He seemed crushed as he wrote, "I guess the only thing I'm good for is to carry your luggage." I felt so bad that I had hurt his feelings. Soon after that day his ship docked in Galveston, Texas. He was going ashore one night when he tried to fight off some thugs as they mugged him and he was shot and killed. I feel so very sad when I think of it.

But there I was back to Glendale. I left Arthur in my apartment talking to my mother while I dashed around doing all the things that had to be done.

He drove me back to my beautiful ship. I had to be at the gang-way at 5:00 P.M. to welcome the new passengers.

My ship then made three forty-eight-day cruises to the Caribbean and back. I would have from 10:30 A.M. free until I had to be back to greet the passengers at 5:00 P.M. Each time my ship got back to home port there would be Arthur waiting for me. This time our ship was headed for the Far East, and we would be board-ing passengers all day. The brass wanted me to be there all day and wouldn't let me go home for a few hours before leaving for a sixty-six-day Orient cruise.

Arthur was there to take me home. He was waiting for me as usual and when I stepped off the gangway he grabbed me and kissed me. He said, "I never thought I would be waiting on the dock to kiss a sailor."

I told him I couldn't go home today because I had to work. He came on board and he knew I was so eager to get home. My mother wasn't feeling well and I had been gone so long and now was leaving for such a long cruise. He could see I was not happy about this. He secretly was elated because he felt that now maybe I would get off the ship. He had asked me to before but I didn't know how I could earn a living on land. It was scary to think of giving up the ship. Of course, I had no idea the book I had written would be such a success.

I said good-bye to Arthur and I tried to smile as I greeted the new passengers. There was a passenger on board who had stayed on from the last cruise. He lived in San Francisco and we were on our way there to pick up more passengers before we sailed for the Ori-ent. He asked me if I would have lunch with him when we got to San Francisco. I said, "Well, let me think about it."

That night as we sailed I was very busy working, but in between activities I would dash to my cabin and say to myself, "How could I ever get off this ship? It is so scary to think about it, after all these years at sea. Besides my luggage is at home in my apartment. And I have all these clothes and stuff. Mother is not feeling well and this guy, Arthur, wants me to get off. I wonder if I should." A passenger had given me a bunch of zippered plastic travel bags on the last cruise, maybe I could get all my things in them. No, I shouldn't get off, I thought. I could never earn a living on land.

Each time I got a few minutes in my cabin I would sort of try to see if my things would fit into my plastic bags.

By the time my duties were over that night I had almost everything packed. Supposedly in my mind I was just experimenting to see if they would fit.

The next day this nice passenger asked me again if I would go to lunch with him. I said, "Well, I have to make a phone call first."

I was still uncertain about jumping ship, but I called Arthur. I said, "If I get off the ship could you pick me up at the L.A. airport?"

This was a Sunday and he said eagerly, "Well, I certainly could."

I had only seen him for a very few hours on the three home-port visits and here I was changing my whole life for someone I didn't even know! I said to him, "I'm putting all my things in thin plastic bags and I hope they don't tear open. I don't even know if I can get reservations on the plane but...."

Arthur said, "Well, I'll be there, you come on down."

I said to Mark, the passenger who wanted to take me to lunch, "Would you mind taking me to lunch at the airport?"

He said, "Oh, that's the only reason you're going to lunch with me—because you want a ride to the airport."

I replied, "Well, not exactly, I want to go to lunch with you, but would you mind carrying these bags and putting them in you car?" What a sweet man; he put all my stuff in his car and took me to the airport.

I told the people on the ship that my mother was sick and I had to leave. This was like mutiny, to jump ship. It was a big decision for me to make. Once you do that, it's like signing your death warrant—you'll never work on the cruise ships again.

It was certainly a good thing that I decided to fly home because "holy hell" broke loose. My mother had a stroke that very day and had already been taken to the hospital by the time Arthur drove me home from the airport. She was completely paralyzed from the stroke; although she did recover, she never got her balance back. She and my brother Bud were moving from our apartment building into a duplex. I guess the move was too much for them both. My brother ended up in a different hospital the same day. On top of all that, my brother had gone out "nightclubbing" the night before in my car and it had been stolen.

That week it was pouring rain. I was trying to visit both hospitals in my mother's car, which would stall each time I got to an intersection. I was trying to move the rest of their belongings to the duplex so we could rent their apartment. We also had two vacancies that needed to be cleaned so they could be rented and I was looking after my mother's dog and her bird and my other brother Jack's dog. Jack was living in Europe for a while so I had this menagerie to take care of. I hadn't unpacked my huge pile of plastic traveling bags yet. I was busy cleaning ovens and scraping the dirt with a razor blade from the bathtub of the empty apartments. A nurse had been living there for a year and I don't think she ever cleaned the bathtub in all the time she was there. I had to get these apartments rented or we would lose this lovely eight-unit building.

There was hardly time to breathe. I was so inundated with all these emergencies. I was also spending my precious time with the insurance people. They would give me very little for my stolen car until their man came over and I talked him into a settlement that seemed fair. I was running around like a mad woman, spreading myself thin trying to do all my things when the insurance company called me and said, "That man paid you too much, we are canceling the check."

I said, "But I have already written checks on it." They said that didn't matter because it said on the back of the check that they can change their mind within three days.

I was fighting with them off and on and trying to pack mother's things to move them when Arthur called and said, "May I take you out tonight?"

Because my mind was on a million things I just answered, "I don't have time for frivolity, but thanks anyway."

So he called the next day and said, "I know you are busy, but you have to eat. Can't I just take you to dinner?"

I said, "I don't have time to get dressed," and I hung up.

The next night he called and said, "Look, you have to eat and you don't have time to get dressed, how about my bringing dinner over to you?"

I said, "Well, I have to keep working. I mean it. It won't be any fun because I have to get these apartments cleaned."

He replied, "Can't I get you a cleaning woman?"

"No, thank you," I said quickly.

My mother had instilled in us three sisters that a "lady" never accepts anything from a boyfriend except candy or flowers, otherwise you were—the word was too nasty for her to repeat. In other words you were not a lady. I said, "If you want to bring that food over we'll eat and then I'll have to get back to work. If you want to sit and watch me work, it's all right with me, but I'm telling you I don't have time for frivolity."

He brought us dinner. We ate and I immediately said, "Now we have to go to the apartments and clean." He would sit on a crate and watch me clean the ovens, scrubbing the toilets, etc. What glamorous dates we had.

He must have thought to himself, as he watched my behind, scrubbing away, "Wow! What a hard worker she is." It must have impressed him more than if I had been running around in a black negligee and having him take me out to dinner! A really different approach to romance.

Every night for three weeks he came over. We would sometimes go visit my mother and my brother in their various hospitals and then we would go over to the duplex and feed the animals and then I would get back to my fixing up the apartments to rent. They were working (I guess you could call them) dates.

One night, after one of these working dates, just before he closed the door to leave he said, "Oh, by the way, look up in your ephemeris a good time to get married," and he closed the door and left.

I stood there stunned. Was that a proposal? He has never even told me he loves me. Of all the nerve!

Marriage was the farthest thing from my mind. I mean the farthest! In my study of palmistry I learned that when a person's top phalange of the thumb bends way back like mine does, it shows you are flexible. I found myself looking in my ephemeris (a book that shows where the planets are each day) just out of curiosity. Much to my chagrin, the aspects to my house of marriage were aligned so that it would be perfect if I got married the day after tomorrow at 12:00 noon, during the Venus hour. Otherwise I wouldn't have another good aspect for marriage for years to come.

Arthur's nephew Andy had asked him if he was taking me out. When Arthur told him, "No, I just watch her work," Andy said, "Take her to the theater to see a play."

Before he closed the door and told me to look up a good day in my ephemeris, Arthur had asked me if I would please go to the theater with him.

"Oh, yes," I replied. "*Streetcar Named Desire* is playing and I would love to see it. OK, I'll forget my work for one night and let's go."

He said, "If you get the tickets I'll pay for them."

Arthur called the next day about 11:00 A.M. "Did you get the theater tickets?" he asked.

"No, I haven't gotten them yet, but would you rather go to the theater tonight or fly to Las Vegas and get married?"

Amazed, he said, "I'd rather get married, of course!"

"Well," I replied, "we could try to catch a plane for Vegas tonight. That way we could have a regular date, maybe see a dinner show, and then get married tomorrow at noon."

The plane was to leave Burbank at 5:00 P.M. Arthur was so excited he said that he filed his lunch in the file cabinet and told his secretary he wouldn't be in until late tomorrow afternoon and to inform personnel that he would have another dependent. Then he drove to the Beverly Hills Hotel and bought me beautiful wedding and engagement rings. He stepped on the gas, packed some things from home, and as he drove to Glendale he was so eager to pick me up and make the flight, he said he prayed and the congested freeway opened up like the Red Sea and let him pass. He just tore through the crowd.

Now we had to condense this romance into one evening, our one real date. The hotel in Las Vegas sent champagne to our room when we checked in. We left our bags in the room and went down to dinner. Dinner went well. I thought to myself, He has nice manners. This was the first time I had seen him out in public.

We were about finished with dinner when he asked me to dance. Oh! I do love to dance. We danced and I thought to myself, Gee, he likes to dance. This was like the icing on the cake?

I didn't use astrology when I got married before. This time I had the astrological knowledge to select the right timing. At exactly 12:00 noon the next day we had a minister marry us. We waited for the Venus hour, which on that day happened to be at noon. I think the minister thought that was a little strange, but he went along with our, what seemed to him, unusual request.

I'm so glad we did because as I am writing this, I am, I guess, as happy as a human being can be. Next week Arthur and I will celebrate our twenty-fifth anniversary. We will celebrate it, guess where? On a cruise, of course, our favorite frivolity.

chapter forty-one

ℭome to the
Cabaret

AFTER ARTHUR AND I MARRIED I WENT BACK TO SEA ON A "Jeraldine Saunders Astrology Cruise," sailing for Mexico on board one of the friendliest and most posh ships in the cruise business. I had it selected because no other ship offered such stellar cuisine and service or so much fun generated by a most talented cruise staff. I had retired as a cruise director and had coordinated this cruise as a lecturer on one of my favorite subjects, astrology. This particular sailing had been chosen as the astrology cruise because the planetary aspects revealed this to be a most advantageous time period for passengers to have enjoyment, excitement, romance, fun in the sun, and after sundown, too—and excitement they did have, to say the least.

"Jeraldine Saunders, Jeraldine Saunders, please dial 105, please dial 105!" blurted the loudspeaker. I felt a chill, but it wasn't caused by the ship's air conditioning. I had noticed that strange things had been happening for the last few hours; and why was the cruise director paging me? It was Jim Brooks, my former boss years ago when I was his hostess on another ship. I dialed his number. "Don't ask questions," he snapped, and I could sense the tension in his voice. "Stay in the forward ballroom and entertain the first-sitting passengers. There will be a delay in our show tonight. Tell them it's because of technical difficulties. Think of some way to keep them busy so that none of them will leave the room. We are evacuating the second sitting from the dining room now and we are serving them drinks in the aft lounge." The click of his phone resounded in my ear. Then, silence.

The chill I had felt earlier was the result of a number of small variations in the ship's routine. Any one by itself was not meaningful, but now this urgent order! It was stranger still because I was being impressed into service, and I was not even a member of the cruise staff on this voyage. However, the years of training on the sea came to the fore, and without hesitation I found myself following orders, but wondering about the trouble we must be in.

It was then that I realized the apparent listing of the ship wasn't really listing at all but that we must be turning. Was it "Man Overboard" and a search for some hapless soul, or were we going back to Los Angeles? If so, why? And that Scandinavian talk over the loudspeakers wasn't just run of the mill orders, but the taut voice of the captain indicating that somewhere we had some major problem. Lord only knew what.

Fortunately, the happy passengers didn't notice our turning, and even though some were restless in that crowded forward ballroom waiting for the overdue show to begin, they joined readily in my little dance games while they waited for what I told them was "a technical difficulty" to be solved. In the midst of the gaiety and laughter, I was thinking, Here we are fiddling while Rome is burning. But my efforts were paying off. No passengers left and so none knew that the other half of their sailing companions, the second sitting diners, halfway through dinner, were being herded out of the dining room to the aft lounge for "free drinks." These passengers were told simply, right in the middle of their filet mignons, that the company had a surprise for them.

I kept smiling and would sneak quick glances out of the portholes to see what was happening. By now the list had lessened and we were slowing to a stop, allowing the big ocean swells to rock the ship, causing the passengers to reel as if they were drunk, laughing as they tried to dance. A crash from the bar was hardly noticed. I went over to see what had happened. Denise, the most avid bar patron, was stretched out on the deck with an upright glass in hand and her favorite bar stool beside her.

As I leaned over to see if she was okay, Denise opened one eye and said, "Jerry, that was a hell of a swell, but I never spilled a drop. Help me back to my stool." With the waiter helping, we managed to get Denise seated at the bar again.

As I turned to leave, she called, "If this keeps up, I want a damned seatbelt."

Just then, Ila Britton, the hostess on this cruise, came in. She had been with the passengers in the other lounge. I went over to Ila and asked, "What's up?"

"I don't know," she said. Ila is a darling lady, an excellent hostess and as beautiful as she is charming. She said, "Jim told me a few weeks ago that he went to a psychic and was told that our ship would be in danger sometime during the month of June, but that the passengers would be safe. Jerry, do you suppose that the psychic was right?"

I told Ila, "Jim went to the captain with that information from the psychic. The captain mentioned Jim's weird experience to me. I told him that some psychics are accurate but that a lot of them are phonies."

Just then, Jim interrupted Ila and me and snapped, "Thanks for keeping everyone calm. Let's start the show quick!" Without one word of explanation he dashed away. The show started with the magicians' ESP act, but if they had any real ESP they wouldn't have been so calm out there performing. Another hurried glance out of the porthole, and I saw that lifeboats were being lowered. I gulped. Whatever the situation was, it was serious, or these lifeboats wouldn't be at the ready.

All these years that I've been at sea, my worrywart mother has kept saying her rosaries for me, fearing the worst. Was what she had feared coming to pass? My jewels and other valuables were in my cabin. If only I could sneak away to get them. What if I did, and some passengers saw the lifeboats and started a panic? Would we all live through this, whatever it was? These thoughts flashed through my mind all the while I was outwardly calm and smiling.

"Jerry," Jim said to me as he reappeared, "we have to find something and find it fast! Do you have that heavy weight on a string you call a pendulum that works something like a Ouija board?"

"Jim," I replied, "I have something better. I have the 'Thought Dial' by Sydney Omarr. I lectured on it only this morning in astrology class. It has a chapter on finding lost articles." Jim, no mean astrologer himself, had studied many of Omarr's books.

"Get it, get it," he shouted. "How in the hell does it work?"

I didn't answer until I returned with the book. By this time Coby, the handsome sports director had joined Jim.

"This works," I said. "This theory is that the subconscious knows all the answers if we can get past the conscious mind. So you can trick the conscious mind and get by it by asking yourself for three numbers, then you add them all together. Now, quickly, give me three numbers, the first three that come to your mind." Jim gave me three numbers, which I totaled. Then I looked into the Thought Dial to read what the number symbolized. All I can remember is that the first words stated the article would be found. Jim breathed a sigh of relief. We then learned the direction in which to look for the lost article. With that, Jim motioned to Coby, and they both left instantly.

The next act was a sexy-looking singer in a slinky gown. She not only looked great, but had a voice to match. Again, since the passengers' attention was diverted to the singer, Joan Shields, they were not aware of the hurrying and scurrying of crew members that was beginning to be more than just a little obvious. Joan was about halfway through her song, "Cabaret," when the captain's voice became loud and clear over the music. Jim came running onto the dance floor and grabbed the mike from Joan's hand as he motioned the orchestra to silence. He placed one arm around our singer's waist and said, "Ladies and gentlemen, we had a radiophone call from our home office earlier. Please don't get excited. Everything is all right now. We were informed that someone had placed bombs on board this ship during the farewell parties prior to our departing from Los Angeles. The bombs have just been found and they have been put overboard. All is well. All is clear." Jim, one of the best cruise directors in the business, handled the whole ordeal as only a top director could.

The passengers gasped and a nervous jabbering started that was immediately overcome with a swell of relief and joy that cascaded and grew until surely we must have been heard back in Los Angeles. Jim continued, "It is now 8:57 P.M. We were advised that the bombs were set to go off at 9:00 P.M. Time was running out. So, if I seem nervous, you know why. The information on the time that the bombs were to go off and their general location was obtained from the man who planted them for ransom purposes. He was caught when he picked up the $75,000 ransom paid by the ship's owners. He told the FBI that one of the bombs was on the bridge and another under the kitchen somewhere. He wasn't familiar with ships and couldn't explain just where.

"We found them just in time. Guess somebody up there does like us," Jim said with a smile of relief on his handsome face.

Everyone started talking at once. Shawn Sullivan, one of our most extroverted passengers, shouted, "Hey, Jerry! Thought you said you picked this cruise astrologically. How come the bombs?" He finished his remark with a roar of laughter.

Now I was on the firing line. Yes, the planetary aspects were right for this cruise. Wasn't it a success already? How many other cruise passengers could go home with such a tale to tell? Would this cruise ever be forgotten? And now, wouldn't they be heroes as they returned home from this adventure with their tales verified by newspaper stories all over the world? You, too, probably read the newspaper accounts of the famous baseball player, Jerry Priddy, who turned out to be the bomber and received a stiff sentence of twenty years. He died in prison. So the planets were right; adventure and excitement we had, and no casualties.

Quickly I said, "Folks, please! Remember Joan?" The situation shifted to her. Being the real trouper she was, she beckoned to Jim and he gave her the mike. She smiled, as she signaled the orchestra to be ready and said, "Remember the line I was just starting when Jim took the mike from me? Well, it was…" The music started and she sang, "…No use permitting some Prophet of Doom to wipe every smile away; life is a Cabaret old chum; come to the Cabaret."

Never did a singer get such an ovation!

chapter forty-two

AFTER THE BALL IS OVER

WHENEVER I DISCOVER THAT ONE OR MORE PIECES OF ME has fallen off along the way, or that some person or event has taken another nip out of the old astral body, I rush back to sea to be healed. I sail now whenever I feel like it (no off-Broadway ship though), and only give lectures and take it easy the rest of the cruise, but I still have empathy for the cruise staff who are working almost around the clock, although these days they are given vacations and there is a huge staff to help the cruise director.

When the stately, elegant *Queen Elizabeth 2* (or as status-seeking world cruisers refer to it, "the Queen") sailed to Australia, I was the lecturer on board, and my husband, mother, and brother came with me. Being a passenger on a luxury cruise is the ultimate, and having my family with me, I was in seventh heaven! The love, joy, and laughter of ship-board life was weaving its spell.

There was a tall, handsome, very rich passenger on board who was sailing on the world cruise aboard this magnificent ship. He was a Sagittarian. Oh, how they love to travel. We met after one of my lectures in the afternoon and he told me his birthday. Also, being an open and frank Sag, he explained to me why he had taken this cruise, which would last over eighty days. Some passengers take only a segment of a world cruise, but he was going for the whole eighty days.

He said frankly, "Jeraldine, I took this world cruise to find a woman to be my mate. I have specific restrictions and qualifications for her. I'm looking for someone about your height. Are you 5' 7"?"

"Yes, I am 5'7"," I answered.

"And," he said, "she must have red hair like yours. In fact," he said, "you would just fit into my requirements. You're slim, too."

"I'm flattered," I remarked, "but I am very happily married; as a matter of fact my husband is traveling with me on this cruise."

"Well," he said, "would you both come with me when we arrive in Sydney? I would love to show you my favorite restaurant on the top floor of the Wentworth-Ryges Hotel."

I said, "Thanks so much for the invitation, but you see I am also traveling with my brother and my mother."

"Oh, well," he said, "bring them all along. They certainly will not find a better place to eat in all of Australia."

To make another story short, we all went with him to a most delightful and delicious repast. It really is an epicurean delight!

We left at that port to fly back to Los Angeles and he continued on around the globe on the cruise in his search of a 5'7" redhead. Oh, yes, she must be a Daughter of the American Republic-type, a Wasp, not a foreigner, and must have as much money as he so they could be independent. Sagitarrians love to be independent. He also didn't want to get married, he just wanted to live the rest of his life with this ideal of his.

We were back home for about a year when we received a letter from Mr. Sagittarius. He was back home enjoying married life, completely happy with his new bride. No, she wasn't 5'7", she is 5'4". No, she doesn't have red hair because, you see, she is a brunette South American Catholic, and doesn't speak English very fluently—and no, she doesn't have any money. She was his cabin maid on the ship!

If you have studied astrology, you would be laughing hysterically as I did when I read his letter. He acted exactly in sync with his Sagittarius zodiacal sign. They are drawn to foreigners. They are frank, that's why he told us his shopping list for the mate he was seeking. Any other sign would, if they had one, keep it secretly to themselves. Sagittarrians are surely the best travelers on cruise ships. God bless him and his foreign bride. They drop us a note often as they continue to this day their travels on cruise ships, and they seem so madly in love.

A few years later on another world cruise on the *QE 2*, we arrived in the port of Sydney, Australia, just as one of their other ships, the *Sagafjord,* pulled in. It was a spectacular arrival to that beautiful port. Everyone was on deck as we waved and the ships whistled to each other.

I think I'll go out on deck to watch our arrival in the Port of Sydney, Australia.

Valentine's Day aboard the QE 2.

This was merely the prelude to what turned out to be a hectic transfer of some of the entertainers, the dancers, one of the orchestras, and me as the lecturer from the *QE 2* to the *Sagafjord.* I was to go along with the others who were changing ships in this great port. We had all boarded the *QE 2* in Los Angeles for its annual world cruise. The night before the transfer was to take place, all the *Sagafjord* passengers were invited to come aboard our vast beautiful *QE 2* as our guests for a gala, swirling, fun-filled St. Valentine's Ball with the justly famous Joe Loss and his orchestra playing for our pleasure. I defy anyone to try to sit out a dance when this great orchestra and its signers perform. The ball was a gigantic, rhythmic success as the gentlemen in black ties danced the hours away with their ladies in lovely Valentine reds and pinks.

The "transfer morning" was all the more a logistics problem because everyone had either worked late, danced late, romanced late or packed late. Some had done all of the above. It was a very warm morning. The job of loading all the luggage, orchestra instruments, dancers' costumes, my lecture equipment, and getting us all into what at first appearance was a huge, empty bus, was a Herculean task similar to putting a size 12 foot into a size 4 shoe. By the time we had driven halfway to the waiting *Sagafjord,* the gang started to come to life, slowly, one by one.

"Hey, Jeraldine," the comic called, "how about letting me sit next to the window? My hangover is so bad that if a $1,000 bill were on the floor, I couldn't bend over to pick it up!"

One of the singers called out from the back of the bus, "Come on back here with me, Jim, and tell me about your dog act. I never knew you had one until I saw what you were dragging into your cabin last night."

The laughter, catcalls and noise lessened when Joe, the drummer, hollered, "Settle down, everybody, let me tell you about Jim and one of his sexual scams. Jim will do anything to get a little. Did he ever tell you guys how he got a lot? He meets this girl from Australia, when he was sailing out of Vancouver...."

"No, he never told us about that girl," several of us yelled back. Everyone except Jim was slumping into positions of comfort.

"Well," Joe said, "it seems this poor Australian girl came to Canada hoping to make it her home. However, it just didn't work out. She couldn't seem to make any new friends, so she became very lonely and was very anxious about getting a return trip home to Australia because she just couldn't seem to get enough money together for airfare. While hanging around the Vancouver docks she met our lover boy, Jim, here. He was a sailor then, before he got his act together. Anyway, this poor girl goes over to Jim and tells him all her troubles.

"So Jim, here, says, 'Heck, honey, I can solve all your problems. It's lucky you ran into me because the ship I work on is heading for Australia. I just might be able to smuggle you aboard to one of our store rooms without being caught.'

"'Gee!' she screamed, 'do you really think you could?'

"Jim said, 'If I'm caught, I'll get fired, it's a big risk I'm taking. I'll only do it if you pleasure me with your favors.' The poor girl was so eager to get to Australia that she agreed to his terms. Right?"

Jim said, "Yeah, but do you have to go into the gory details? My head is splitting and you're telling everyone about my personal life. It's making me sicker."

Jim got little sympathy as nearly everyone, including the sweating bus driver yelled, "Joe, this ain't no time to stop."

Joe said, "I'll shorten it up, don't want you should suffer too much."

"Come on," I said, "tell us, did he get that poor girl aboard OK?"

Joe replied, "Yeah, Jeraldine, he sure did and without anyone seeing them. Soon as the ship gets underway and he can get off deck duty, he starts extracting his tribute. However, he extracted it so frequently that she couldn't stand it any longer. She ups and goes to the captain and explains the situation. With tears in her eyes she says, 'I have tried to keep my part of the bargain, and I'm still willing but only on a reasonable basis.' The captain's mouth opened in shock as she continued, 'But this has reached a point where I am going to have to call a halt.' As he raised a helpless hand, she sobbed, 'Captain, I am worn out, completely, tell me, how many more days before we get to Australia?' With obvious surprise the Captain asked, 'Australia? This is the Vancouver ferry!'"

Our laughter was accompanied by the groans and growls of our overloaded bus. Jim, too, made noisy protestations and sounds of discomfort, but nary a sign or sound of sympathy did he get.

When the hilarity quieted somewhat, complaints began about the enveloping heat and the mess still ahead of us in unloading the bus, getting our precious gear safely aboard the *Sagafjord* and then the chore of unpacking. A single voice started singing, "Old McDonald had a farm..." another joined in, and another. Quickly, the grumbles, whines and sighs were drowned in a flood of song as camaraderie and the joy of life crept back into our bones again, overcoming our supposed tribulations.

Now that I've retired as a cruise director, whenever I get a longing to feel the pulse of the sea and to visit friendly old ports again, I call a cruise line whose ships are going where I wish to go again and I am hired on as a lecturer. Usually, I give only one lecture called "The Love Boats." It's about how and why the "Love Boats" came about. Some ships have me give another lecture called "Vim and Vigor" about nutrition. The rest of the cruise my dear husband Arthur and I enjoy as passengers. For this cruise, I had made the mistake of sending the agent for the line a list of possible topics on which I could lecture. I thought they would choose one or two in addition to those mentioned above.

Cruising as a lecturer is a lot less hectic.
My husband, Arthur Andrews, loves it.

Here is the list of other topics I also lecture on:

FUN WITH BIRTHDAYS—A Key to Better Understanding of Yourself and Others and to Learn of Your Current Cycle

PHYSIOGNOMY—The Ancient Chinese Art of Analyzing the Character Through Features of the Face

PALMISTRY—Your Character and Your Potential as Shown in the Lines of the Palm

GRAPHOLOGY—Analyze Your Own and Others' Handwriting and Discover Its Hidden Meanings

NUMEROLOGY—Learn About the Numbers in Your Life, Which Numerical Cycle You Are in Each Year

MOTIVATIONAL—Dynamic Principles Put to Work for You

CHARM—This Lecture Is Based on My Experience as a High Fashion Model. Here are Unique Hints in Poise, Walking, Sitting and How to Look Your Best By Knowing How to Pose for Any Camera

And my favorite:

ILLUMINESCENCE—Learn of Your Very Own Color Harmonic Tone. Illuminesence is the Taylore B. Sinclaire revelation dissecting personalities using the tools of psychology, philosophy, spirituality, art, and science to understand each color tone's nuances that help promote confidence, communications and performance. Learn of your tone's attributes, nonverbal communications, shapes, angles, texture, colors, and designs.

Learn which harmonic tone you are. This knowledge reveals secrets that beautify you, your home, your life, and results in attracting admiration and love!

It was a long cruise and much to my surprise as I read the ship's daily bulletins, I learned that every day at sea I was scheduled to give a lecture on a different topic. The only one I didn't give was the graphology lecture because the *QE 2* had already engaged a graphologist for the cruise. But, anyway, it was a far cry from the hectic schedules of my cruise director days and I not only enjoy the cruise but they are generous with their honorariums.

Our bus pulled onto the dock and we saw our beautiful five-star *Sagafjord* waiting for us. As we all walked up the steep gangway, the cruise director greeted us warmly. We were to be on this ship until Hong Kong so I thought I had better keep silent about all my lectures and I might just get away with giving only my two regular lectures. The gods did not so ordain.

"Hi," he said, "are you Jeraldine Saunders?"

"Yes," I replied, "and this is my husband, Arthur Andrews."

"Welcome aboard, Love Boat Lady, I'm your cruise director, Bob Le Blanc, and I understand that you gave ten lectures on the *QE 2*. I would like to ask you a favor. You see, we don't have a graphologist on board. Would you mind adding a graphology lecture to your schedule?" he asked pleadingly.

"Ohhh, that would be just fine," I said, hiding my chagrin. Here we go again.

My first evening on board the classic *Sagafjord*, as I entered the Polaris Lounge, the beautiful pianist commenced playing the music from *The Love Boat* theme.

After playing a few bars, she saw me give her a wide smile of acknowledgment. She then paused and introduced me to the pre-dinner crowd who were enjoying their cocktails. As the applause quieted, to my utter surprise and delight, pretty, talented Sue Maskaleris began singing her own rendition of *The Love Boat* theme that she had prepared in anticipation of my arrival on the ship. What a thrill I had when I heard these lyrics to *The Love Boat* theme.

> *Jerry's here*
> *Well, she ought to be*
> *'Cause she wrote the book on loving nautically.*
> *Those notes signed, "Love, Jeraldine"*
> *Now have come to life*
> *Upon your TV screen.*
> *THE LOVE BOATS takes her all over the world today.*
> *THE LOVE BOATS,*
> *Making new friendships along the way.*
> *Any ship that's afloat*
> *Is a LOVE BOAT if Jerry's there.*
> *And that's where*
> *You'll have an affair*
> *With your champagne glass*
> *A Baked Alaska, the ocean air.*
> *It's Love*
> *It's Love*
> *It's Looooove.*

☽ REACH FOR THE MOON

Llewellyn publishes hundreds of books on your favorite subjects! To get these exciting books, including the ones on the following pages, check your local bookstore or order them directly from Llewellyn.

ORDER BY PHONE

- Call toll-free within the U.S. and Canada, 1-800-THE MOON
- In Minnesota, call (651) 291-1970
- We accept VISA, MasterCard, and American Express

ORDER BY MAIL

- Send the full price of your order (MN residents add 7% sales tax) in U.S. funds, plus postage & handling to:

  Llewellyn Worldwide
  P.O. Box 64383, Dept. K 607–6
  St. Paul, MN 55164–0383, U.S.A.

POSTAGE & HANDLING

(For the U.S., Canada, and Mexico)

- $4.00 for orders $15.00 and under
- $5.00 for orders over $15.00
- No charge for orders over $100.00

We ship UPS in the continental United States. We ship standard mail to P.O. boxes. Orders shipped to Alaska, Hawaii, The Virgin Islands, and Puerto Rico are sent first-class mail. Orders shipped to Canada and Mexico are sent surface mail.

International orders: Airmail—add freight equal to price of each book to the total price of order, plus $5.00 for each non-book item (audio tapes, etc.).

Surface mail—Add $1.00 per item.

Allow 2 weeks for delivery on all orders.
Postage and handling rates subject to change.

DISCOUNTS

We offer a 20% discount to group leaders or agents. You must order a minimum of 5 copies of the same book to get our special quantity price.

FREE CATALOG

Get a free copy of our color catalog, *New Worlds of Mind and Spirit*. Subscribe for just $10.00 in the United States and Canada ($30.00 overseas, airmail). Many bookstores carry *New Worlds*—ask for it!

Visit our web site at www.llewellyn.com for more information.

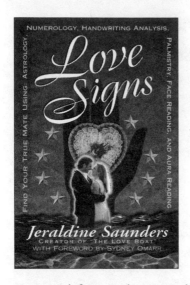

INSTANT HANDWRITING ANALYSIS
A Key to Personal Success

Ruth Gardner

For those who wish to increase self-awareness and begin to change some unfavorable aspect of their personality, graphology is a key to success. It can help open our inner selves and explore options for behavior change. With practice, one can make graphology an objective method for giving feedback to the self. And it is an unbeatable channel for monitoring your personal progress.

Author Ruth Gardner makes the process quick and easy, illustrating how letters are broken down vertically into three distinctive zones that help you explore your higher philosophies, daily activities and primal drives. She also explains how the size, slant, connecting strokes, spacing, and amounts of pressure all say something about the writer. Also included are sections on doodles and social graphology.

Instant Handwriting Analysis provides information for anyone interested in pursuing graphology as a hobby or career. It lists many resources for continuing study, including national graphology organizations and several correspondence schools.

0–87542–251–9, 176 pp., 7 x 10, illus., softcover $15.95

INSTANT PALM READER
A Roadmap to Life

Linda Domin

Etched upon your palm is an aerial view of all the scenes you will travel in the course of your lifetime. Your characteristics, skills and abilities are imprinted in your mind and transferred as images onto your hand. Now, with this simple, flip-through pictorial guide, you can assemble your own personal palm reading, like a professional, almost instantly.

The *Instant Palm Reader* shows you how your hands contain the picture of the real you—physically, emotionally and mentally. More than 500 easy-to-read diagrams will provide you with candid, uplifting revelations about yourself: personality, childhood, career, finances, family, love life, talents and destiny.

With the sensitive information artfully contained within each interpretation, you will also be able to uncover your hidden feelings and unconscious needs as you learn the secrets of this 3,000-year-old science.

1–56718–232–1, 6 x 9, 288 pp., 500 illus., softcover $14.95

LOVE NUMBERS
How to Use Numerology to Make Love Count

Margaret Arnold

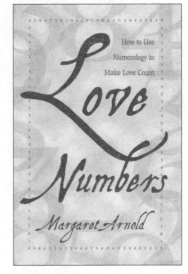

Why do some relationships work and others fail? Why do you immediately like some people while others leave you feeling cold? Why do you click with someone, even when it appears by worldly standards that you shouldn't?

The answer to these questions lies in the interrelationships of energy patterns called vibrations, which make up our bodies and personalities. One way to understand and analyze these patterns is through the science of numerology.

With a knowledge of numerical vibrations you can know ahead of time how your own and another person's personalities will interact. If you're a "4," for example, you want dependability, order and structure—and you will want to avoid "5s," which crave change and lots of freedom. You'd be better off with an "8" because you can both be very hard workers. This book gives you all the simple formulas you need to determine the numerology for anyone.

1–56718–040–X, 304 pp., 5 ³⁄₁₆ x 8, softcover   **$9.95**

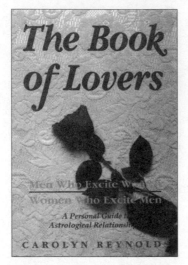

THE BOOK OF LOVERS
Men Who Excite Women, Women Who Excite Men

Carolyn Reynolds

What are you looking for in a lover or potential mate? If it's money, set your sights on a Pisces/Taurus. Is exercise and health food your passion? Then a Virgo/Cancer will share it with you.

Where do you find these people? They're all here, in *The Book of Lovers.* Astrologer Carolyn Reynolds introduces a new and accurate way to determine romantic compatibility through the use of Sun and Moon sign combinations. And best of all, you don't have to know a single thing about astrology to use this book!

Here you will find descriptions of every man and woman born between the years 1900 and 2000. To see whether that certain someone could be "the one," simply locate his or her birth data in the chart and flip to the relevant pages to read about your person's strengths and weaknesses, sex appeal, personality and most importantly, how they will treat you!

0–87542–289–0, 464 pp., 6 x 9, softcover   **$14.95**